AF449966

Restore the Truth of History:
Mao Zedong and His Comrades-in-Arms

Li Shenming & Li Jie

translated by Xu Xiaofan

CANUT INTERNATIONAL PUBLISHERS

Istanbul - Berlin - London - Santiago

Academic Research on Contemporary China Book Series
Restore the Truth of History: Mao Zedong and His Comrades-in-Arms
Authored by Li Shenming, Li Jie
Translated by Xu Xiaofan
The English version is published with financial support of
the Innovation Program of the Chinese Academy of Social Sciences
Chinese Title: 还历史的本原
Copyright © China Social Sciences Press, Beijing, 2014

Canut International Publishers
Canut Intl. Turkey, Batı Mh. No.29., 34890, Pendik, Istanbul, Turkey
Canut Intl. Germany, Heerstr. 266, D-47053, Duisburg, Germany
Canut Intl. United Kingdom, 12a Guernsay Road, London E11 4BJ, England
Copyright © Canut International Publishers, 2020

ISBN: 978-605-9914-72-7

www.canutbooks.com

About the Authors

Li Shenming, born in October 1949 in Wenxian, Henan Province, postgraduate degree, research fellow, doctoral supervisor, major general military rank, former vice-president of the Chinese Academy of Social Sciences and deputy secretary of the Party group. Representative of the 16th and 17th National Congress of the Communist Party of China, Standing Committee of the 10th, 11th and 12th National People's Congress, vice-chairman of the 12th National People's Congress Internal Affairs and Judicial Committee. Director of the World Socialism Research Center attached to the Chinese Academy of Social Sciences.

His representative works include: *Live in Peace and Think about Danger - Historical Lessons from the Collapse of the CPSU, China's Great Party Building in the Context of Globalization, Li Shenming's Selected Works;* editor-in-chief of *World Socialism Tracking Research Report - and Listen to the "Trough and New Tides" (Series), Global Political and Security Report (Yellow Paper Series)* and *Frontiers of Deng Xiaoping Theory Research (Series)*.

Li Jie, born in February 1955 in Beijing, postgraduate degree, research fellow, doctoral supervisor, former vice-president and member of the Party Committee of the Chinese Academy of Social Sciences, former deputy director of the Party Literature Research Center of the CPC Central Committee, Representative of the 16th and 17th National Congress of the Communist Party of China, former president of the journal *Qiushi,* president of the Chinese History Society.

He has long been engaged in the study of the history of the Communist Party of China and the study of the life of Mao Zedong Thought. He is the author of *Mao Zedong and New China's Internal Affairs and Diplomacy, Li Jie's Selected Works, A Quiet Thinking over China's History, Mao Zedong's Historical Contribution to New China,* etc.

Preface

On December 2013 at the anniversary of 120th birthday of Mao Zedong. General Secretary Xi Jinping addressed at the commemoration forum and pointed out: "Comrade Mao Zedong is a great Marxist, proletarian revolutionist, strategist and theorist, great pioneer of Marxism with Chinese characteristics, great patriot and national hero of China since modern times, at the core of first-generation CPC central collective leadership and the great man who led Chinese people to thoroughly change their destiny and the national condition." He specially stressed: "The analysis on historical figures should be conducted under the historical conditions of times and society in which they were born with comprehensive knowledge of historical conditions, historical process and scientific command on historical laws, should not neglect the relation between historical necessity and historical contingency. The successes in historical prosperity should not be attributed to individuals; neither the setbacks in adverse situations of the historical course should be blamed on individuals simply. We cannot use today's conditions and level of development and understanding to judge our predecessors, nor can we expect the predecessors to have done things that only the successors can do." Revolutionary leaders are not gods, but human beings. Although they master high theoretical level, abundant struggle experience and extraordinary leadership talents, it does not mean that their knowledge and actions are not restrained by the conditions of times. We cannot not worship them like god due to their greatness, whose fault and mistakes cannot be raised and corrected; we should not completely repudiate them and erase their historical achievements just because they made mistakes and be lost in the quagmire of nihilism." The above statements indicate the right direction to further deepen the research of history of the CPC, research of national history and research of Mao Zedong Thought and consciously resist the impact of historical nihilism.

In recent years, historical nihilism trend has raised many false views in the researches of the CPC history, national history and Mao Zedong Thought. They hold a part as the whole, deliberately distort the truth, or confuse right and wrong in order to justify complete repudiation. The articles included in this book are written by researchers on the CPC history and national history to clarify various false views with historical truth, stand point and methods of historical materialism. They not only give necessary counterattack to historical nihilism but also explain and answer the important questions regarding the CPC history and national history. To present such aim, the book is named as "restore the truth of history".

The articles included in this book are divided into two parts. In the first part, the articles are collected for the book, some of which are newly written by the authors and some of which have been published with good reaction. In the second part, the articles have been published in the columns like "commentary series of academic thoughts" and "commentary series of history" in the journal *Social Sciences in China* with distinct views and statements and simple explanations. Sincere thanks are extended hereby to the authors and editors of the articles included in this book . We also extend our gratitude to the leaders of the journal *Social Sciences in China* for allowing us to include relevant articles into this collection.

We will carry on this meaningful work and we welcome criticism and suggestion of the readers.

Contents

1

In Defence of Mao Zedong's *On Contradiction*
—*Response to the Article "Is On Contradiction the Original Work of Mao Zedong?"*

Xu Quanxing

On Practice and *On Contradiction* (hereinafter referred to as "Two Theories") are the combined product of Marxist philosophy and China's concrete reality, as well as two shining pearls in the development history of Marxist philosophy. "Two Theories" are the most important philosophical works of Mao Zedong, which lay a theoretical foundation for the Chinese Communist Party's ideological line of seeking truth from facts. In recent months, there has been a debate on whether *On Contradiction* is a plagiarism, someone even has overturned history, made a big splash on *On Contradiction* and denied that Mao Zedong was the original creator of *On Contradiction*. In this debate, some debaters have referred to the relevant papers written by me. To this end, it is necessary for me to write this article to clarify the chaos on this issue made by some people so as to restore the historical truth.

I. It is an already-solved problem whether *On Contradiction* was a product of plagiarism

In the article *My Course of Thinking in the "Cultural Revolution"* (Yan-Huang Historical Review, 9th Issue in 2011), Mr. Liu Zehua put forward that *On Contradiction* was suspected of plagiarism and there were similarities with Yang Xiufeng's *Outlines of Social Studies*. When this conclusion was drawn, several media organs including the *People's Daily Online* and

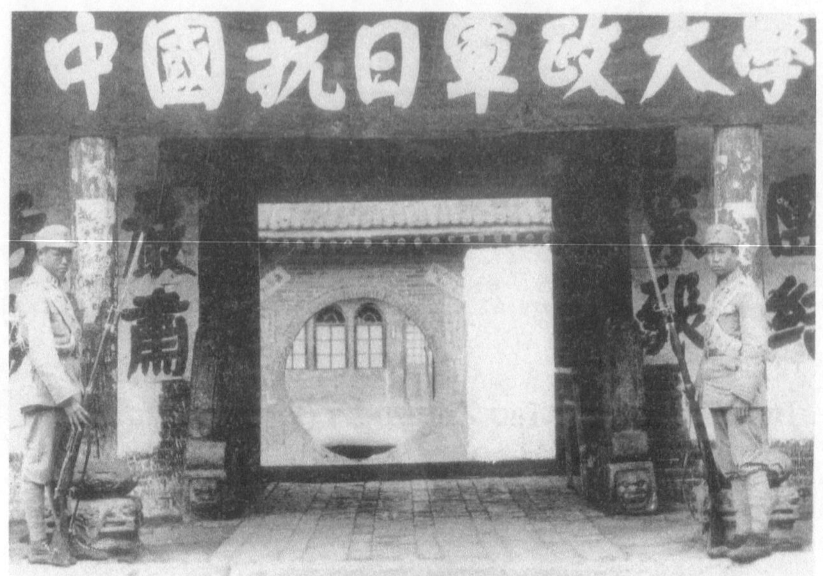

In July 1937, Mao Zedong wrote On Practice, and soon afterwards wrote On Contradiction in August 1937. Once Mao Zedong used the viewpoints included in these two philosophical papers for his speech at Anti-Japanese Military and Political College in Yan'an. The photo above is the gate of Anti-Japanese Military and Political College.

Phoenix Net reproduced it in succession, meanwhile it caused confusion among some people, saying that this was nothing but "recklessly creating and spreading rumours in order to confuse the public." In response to Liu's Article, Mr. Chen Dingxue published the article *Is On Contradiction the Original Creation of Mao Zedong?* (Yan-Huang Historical Review, 2011(12), hereinafter referred to as "Chen's Article"), further thinking that: "most of the main viewpoints of *On Contradiction* are the rewriting of the philosophical works by Soviet Union researchers besides Li Da's *Outlines of Social Studies*. The original text of *On Contradiction* might also be drafted by Chen Boda, included some additions by Ai Siqi, and finalized by Mao Zedong at last. Therefore the query to *On Contradiction* by Liu Zehua and others is not recklessly creating and spreading rumours to confuse the public, but based on facts." In order to advocate and demonstrate this judgement, there are 14 citations in "Chen's Article", including four citations quoted from my texts. The viewpoints and argument methods in "Chen's Article" have surprised me greatly.

Whether in the development history of Marxist philosophy, or in the development history of Chinese philosophy, the "Two Theories" have an important historical position. Because of this, the "Two Theories" have always been concerned by both domestic and foreign researchers.

In the 1950s, the "Two Theories" were highly evaluated by Marxist philosophers of the Soviet Union and other countries. The editorial department of the *Pravda* attached to the Central Committee of the Communist Party of the CPSU published several articles which were dedicated to the publication of *On Practice* in the Soviet Union, and praised that "the author has comprehensively surveyed the epistemology of dialectical materialism as well as demonstrated and developed every principle of it."[1] The "Two Theories" were included into a series of philosophy textbooks in the Soviet Union. About *On Contradiction*, the text books included such evaluations: "Comrade Mao Zedong's *On Contradiction*, this outstanding, profound, valuable work, is a great contribution to the dialectics theory of Marxism."[2] There are 12 citations in the *Materialism and Dialectical Method* which were directly quoted from *On Practice* a comprehensive book edited by the famous British Marxist philosophers, and 9 citations which were directly quoted from *On Contradiction*, which mentioned the following: *On Contradiction* "has made the most comprehensive discussion on the concept of contradiction particularity among contemporary Marxist works"[3]. Many praising comments were made on the "Two Theories" by Marxist philosophers of the Soviet Union and other countries, which are quite numerous to mention.[4]

In the 1960s, due to the worsening of the relations between China and Soviet Union as well as between their two parties, the Soviet philosophical circles have made a big change in the evaluation of Mao Zedong's philosophy, and published a large number of articles and works which criticized Maoism. After the "Period of 1966-1976" ended, I have translated abundant critical works written by the Soviet and Eastern European philosophers (which were printed as manuscripts for internal communication) and these translations included more than 60 million characters, some of the books I have translated mentioned that the "Two Theories" plagiarized 1930s works which were published in the Soviet Union, but did not mention which books were plagiarized. At that time although the "plagiarism" was not claimed by the Chinese theoretical circles, in order to answer the Soviet blame, it had become necessary to make the issue clear. At that time, I was teaching in the Philosophy Department of Peking University, in order to clarify this issue,

---

1 Soviet *Pravda* editorial department, On Mao Zedong's Book *On Practice*, *People's Daily*, December 30, 1950.

2 Institute of Philosophy attached to Soviet Academy of Sciences, *Principles of Marxist Philosophy*, Vol. 1, People's Publishing House, 1959, p. 297.

3 M. Cornforth, *Materialism and Dialectical Method*, Joint Publishing, 1956, p. 115.

4 Xu Quanxing, Chen Baohua, Feng Guorui, *Foreign Selected Works of Study on Mao Zedong Thought*, published by CPC Central Party School Scientific Research Office, 1987.

I have not only examined all the Chinese versions (including all Chinese translations and books written by our own people) of Marxist Philosophy works which were collected in Peking University Library, which were allowed for borrowing, especially those works written before Mao Zedong's "Two Theories", but also visited the former Beijing Library to examine the Journal of University of Anti-Japanese War which firstly published the *Dialectical Materialism (Lecture Outline)*; besides visited the Library of the Compilation and Translation Bureau attached to the CPC Central Committee to study and examine the relevant versions of the *Dialectical Materialism (Lecture Outline)*. Through nearly two years of academic research, I have had great harvest: first, gained a basic understanding of what Chinese and foreign philosophy works had been referred by Mao Zedong in addition I have studied the translated Marxism-Leninism works when comrade Mao Zedong taught philosophy at the Anti-Japanese Military and Political College and when he wrote the "Two Theories", gained a more complete understanding on the relations between the "Two Theories" and Soviet philosophy of the 1930s (mainly three works: *Dialectical Materialism Course*, published under the general editorship of A. Aizenberg, N. Shirokov et al., which was translated by Li Da and Lei Zhongjian, published in 1932; *The Outline of New Philosophy*, edited by Soviet researcher M.B. Mitin and Ral'tsevich et al, translated by Ai Siqi, Zheng Yili, published in 1936; *Dialectical Materialism and Historical Materialism* Volume I, written by leading Soviet philosopher Mitin et al., translated by Shen Zhiyuan, published in 1936), Li Da's *Outlines of Social Studies* (1937), Ai Siqi's *Philosophy for the Masses* (1936) and so on; secondly, I have gained a substantial understanding on the writing, publishing and revising situations of the "Two Theories"; thirdly, gained the general conception idea on the dissemination and development of Marxist philosophy in China in the 1920s and 1930s as well as the evolution of the Marxist philosophy and its teaching system in the Soviet Union after the October Revolution.

According to my own academic research, I wrote a text of nearly 60,000 characters with the title of *Study of On Contradiction* (completed in December 1980, and printed by the philosophy department of Peking University in the spring of 1981, for internal communication), later I wrote and published *The Relationship between On Practice, On Contradiction and Soviet Philosophy in the 1930s* (1981), *Writing and Editing of On Practice and On Contradiction* (1982), *On Practice, On Contradiction and Outlines of Social Studies* (1984), *Re-debate on "Two Theories" and Outlines of Social Studies* (1985) and other papers. In the summer of 1982, I was invited to give a lecture on Comrade Mao Zedong's Contribution to

Materialist Dialectics at the seminar titled as *Mao Zedong's Philosophical Thoughts* which was convened in Xi'an. In August 1987, I made a speech on the topic of the relationship between "Two Theories" and Soviet philosophy in the 1930s at the Fourth National Session of Mao Zedong's Philosophy Thought Academic Seminar. The above-mentioned papers were collected into the book *In Defense of Mao Zedong* (Contemporary China Publishing House, published in 1996). These papers have clarified the relations between the "Two Theories" and the Soviet philosophy in the 1930s and Li Da's *Outlines of Social Studies* and evaluated the theoretical value and historical position of the "Two Theories" in a realistic way.

After the publication of my paper, although our academic circles still have different viewpoints on the study of the "Two Theories", the "plagiarism theory" was never advocated in these works of mine. *The Annotations of Mao Zedong's Philosophy* (edited by the Party Literature Research Center of the CPC Central Committee, published in 1988) has affirmed my research on the "Two Theories". Unfortunately, the editors of this book could not find the annotated copy of *The Outline of New Philosophy* therefore it was not included in this book. I am convinced that any ordinary reader who respects historical facts, not to mention an honest historian, will never utter such groundless words such as "there are similarities between Mao Zedong's *On Contradiction* and Yang Xiufeng's *Outlines of Social Studies*, or *On Contradiction* was suspected of plagiarism". Professors Liu Zehua, Mr. Chen Dingxue haven't made an in-depth academic investigation on the issue, but have initiated a discussion on an already-solved problem to "argue something", what's the intention of this? Everyone may know.

II. Comprehensively and correctly evaluate the relationship between *On Contradiction* and the Soviet philosophical works in the 1930s

From the founding of New China to the early 1980s, most of our theorists did not understand which books Mao Zedong referred to when he taught philosophy at the Anti-Japanese Military and Political College, and only few people had read the three Soviet philosophical works of the 1930s, thus they didn't understand the relationship between the "Two Theories" and the Soviet Philosophy in 1930s[5]. In the late 1970s and early 1980s, many re-

---

5   Li Da, Ai Siqi, Chen Boda, Hu Sheng and other veteran philosophers are quite aware of the relationship between the "Two Theories" and the Soviet philosophy in the 1930s, and thus they have wrote articles and works about learning the "Two Theories", which have mainly emphasized that the "Two Theories" are the products of combining Marxist Philosophy with the Chinese revolution, and emphasizes the application of the "Two Theories" in Party

searchers only considered their relationship with Marxist-Leninist classics when evaluating the theoretical contribution made by the "Two Theories", for example they have argued that the particularity of a contradiction, principal contradiction, principal aspect of a contradiction and other concepts in the *On Contradiction* were brand new concepts put forward by Mao Zedong for the first time. This was argument on the one hand. On the other hand, some scholars from the Soviet Union and other foreign countries have only evaluated the "Two Theories" as learned from the Soviet philosophy of the 1930s, thus ignored or belittled the theoretical contributions made by the "Two Theories", and even argued that they were products of plagiarism. In my opinion, we should realistically and properly evaluate Mao Zedong's contribution to the development of Marxist philosophy. One of the most important aspect is to correctly understand the relationship between the "Two Theories" and the Soviet philosophy textbooks in the 1930s. In response to these two mistaken tendencies, I wrote *A Question That Should Be Paid Attention to When Evaluating Mao Zedong's Philosophical Thought* in July 1980, which was mimeographed internally, and was presented at the "May 4th" Symposium held by the Philosophy Department of Peking University in 1981, then was published in the internal journal with the title of *Theoretical Discussion of Wen Weipo's Ideas* (5th Issue, 1981), this title was changed as *The Relationship between On Practice, On Contradiction and Soviet Philosophy in the 1930s* by the editor of the journal.

This article is divided into two parts, the first part talks about the issue of "Two Theories" learning from the Soviet philosophy of the 1930s, and argued that the "Two Theories" were the two sections of *Dialectical Materialism (Lecture Outline)* when Mao Zedong taught in the Anti-Japanese Military University. I have to point out that most of the contents in Mao Zedong's lecture outline, except for the *On Practice* and *On Contradiction*, are either the compilation of the relevant original excerpts taken from the above-mentioned three textbooks or included the rewriting of the relevant content in the above-mentioned three textbooks. *On Practice* and *On Contradiction* have also adopted many new ideas and materials from the above three philosophy textbooks, but Comrade Mao Zedong combined have combined them with the practice of the Chinese revolution and has made a great theoretical creation and mental exertion. In fact, *On*

---

works, besides they have evaluated the theoretical contribution of the "Two Theories" in a practical and realistic way. Ai Siqi once said, the "Two Theories" "have fully utilized the positive results of the Soviet philosophic circles gained in their struggle against the ideas of the Deborin School". See Ai Siqi's *Understanding and Application of Dialectics Seen from On Contradiction* (June 1952), Vol.2 of *Collected Works of Ai Siqi*, People's Publishing House, 1983.

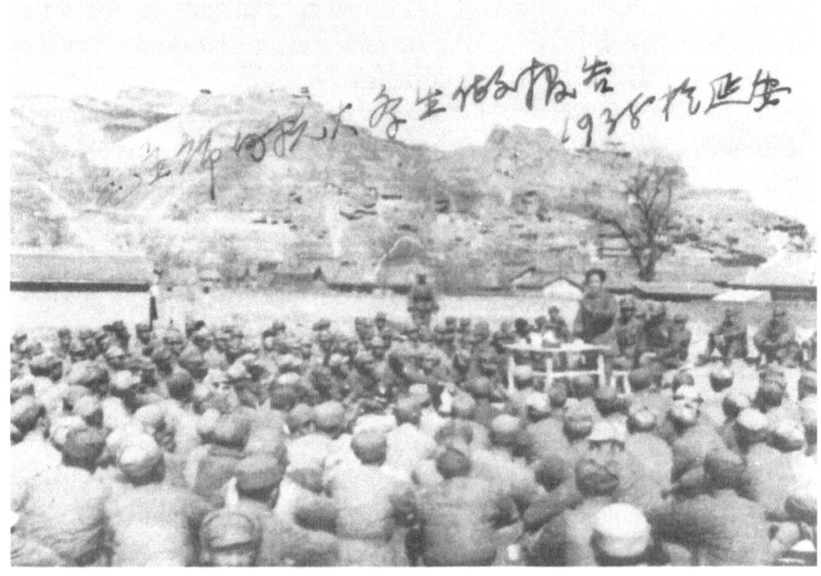

In 1938, Mao Zedong made a speech in the Anti-Japanese Military University.

Practice and *On Contradiction* were not outlines of lectures, but included detailed notes for lectures."[6] I have discussed the issues of "main contradiction" and "main aspect of a contradiction" as examples to explain the inheritance and development link, utilized by Mao Zedong in regard to three aspects of Marxism-Leninism works, Soviet philosophy textbooks and *On Contradiction*. My article was planned to be included into a book titled as *Marxist Philosophy Historical Essays* edited by Prof. Huang Nansen at the initial stage of publishing, but later it was deleted due to an objection raised by the publishing house during the process of editing. The reason might be that the article has specifically mentioned the "Two Theories" and *Lecture Outline of Mao Zedong* learning from the Soviet philosophy.

The second part of this article has discussed about the creative contributions made by the *On Practice* and *On Contradiction* and rejected the claim of *Plagiarism*. The article has argued that the "Two Theories" were definitely not a simple repetition or copying of the Soviet textbooks, instead a product of movement of social contradictions in the Chinese society and a crystallization of the revolutionary experience of China. The article has discussed the internal relations between the "Two Theories" and the Chinese revolution, and explained that the "Two Theories" have

---

6   Xu Quanxing, *Defence for Mao Zedong*, Contemporary China Publishing House, 1996, p. 176.

presented the summarization of philosophical thoughts in the articles such as *On Correcting the Mistaken Ideas in the Party, Oppose Book Worship, The Tasks of the CPC during the Anti-Japanese War, Strategic Problems of Chinese Revolutionary War* and other works. By comparing *On Contradiction* with Li Da's *Outlines of Social Studies*, this article has explained that people who was not personally involved in and didn't lead the Chinese revolution or those who didn't directly struggle against the opportunist lines of Chen Duxiu and Wang Ming would not create such outstanding philosophical works. This article, looking the aspects of structural systems and concrete contents of the *On Practice* and *On Contradiction*, has affirmed their theoretical creation characteristics in regard to Marxist epistemology and in regard to the doctrine of unity of opposites.

In my opinion, this article's discussion on the relationship between the "Two Theories" and the Soviet philosophy of the 1930s is comprehensive and accurate, and its evaluation on theoretical contribution of the "Two Theories" is realistic and proper.

If we look into the first part of Chen Wen's article *On Contradiction and Soviet Philosophical Works*, it is a pity that the first paragraph of this part falsely paraphrases some words of mine in my article of *On Practice, On Contradiction* and *Outlines of Social Studies* and it collates my critical viewpoints upon my viewpoints of advocate. Chen Wen wrote: "The predecessor of *On Contradiction* is the *Dialectical Materialism (Lecture Outline)*, and this outline is in fact Mao Zedong's lecture at the Anti-Japanese Military and Political College in Yan'an in July-August 1937. ...most of the contents of Mao Zedong's lecture include the compilation of the relevant original excerpts from the above-mentioned three textbooks or the re-writing of the relevant contents adopted from the above-mentioned three textbooks."

There are two places in this short passage which tampers with the original: firstly, *On Contradiction* is only a work following the *Dialectical Materialism (Lecture Outline)*, while Chen Wen has made the two texts having equivalent value; secondly, he has closed over and didn't refer to the key words emphasized in my article, which are very important passages for showing the article author's real intention, such as "except for *On Practice* and *On Contradiction* in the *Lecture Outline*, and *On Practice* and *On Contradiction* have also learned many new ideas and quotes from the above three philosophy textbooks, but Comrade Mao Zedong combined Marxist philosophy with the practice of the Chinese revolution and made a great theoretical creation and exertion"[7], the result of such a selective

---

7   Xu Quanxing, *On Practice, On Contradiction* and *Outlines of Social Studies*, see *In Defense of Mao Zedong*, Contemporary China Publishing House, 1996, p. 176.

paraphrased references given in "Chen's Article", is bound to give the reader the impression that paper author Xu Quanxing (me) thinks that *On Contradiction* is simply "re-writing of the Soviet philosophy textbooks". In order to "prove" his own point of view, "Chen's Article" does not hesitate to use the technique of distorting and tampering with the citations and impose the viewpoints opposed by the author on the author himself, which an unhealthy attitude in academic research and debate.

III. *On Contradiction* and *Outlines of Social Studies* don't have any textual relationship

The second part of "Chen's Article" deals with the links between *On Contradiction* and *Outlines of Social Studies*. The conclusion of this part in "Chen's Article" says: "In fact, with respect to the issue of similar contents in the both texts of *On Contradiction* and *Outlines of Social Studies*, there has been discussion in the academic theoretical circle for a long time. Some scholars have pointed out that Mao Zedong's *On Practice* and *On Contradiction* is plagiarized from Li Da's *Outlines of Social Studies*; some people even say that any argument in *On Practice* and *On Contradiction* is adopted from the *Outlines of Social Studies*. And "Chen's Article" points out that the source of this citation is from my article *On Practice, On Contradiction and Outlines of Social Studies*. Such comments put in this way in "Chen's Article" are to tell the readers that they are Xu Quanxing's views. In fact, "Chen's Article" just quotes the point of view which was criticized in my article. Such way of citations in "Chen's Article" have turned the viewpoint criticized by me into the viewpoint advocated by me, and this cannot but lead me to question Mr. Chen Dingxue's academic morality again.

"Chen's Article" has argued that *Outlines of Social Studies* was published as early as 1935 (note: in fact it was only a letterpress printing lecture note of School of Law and Business in National Peiping University), and "that for Mao Zedong it was entirely possible for him to read or give quotes from it. Secondly, in August 1937, *On Contradiction* was not yet created, at that time it was still the first section of Chapter III in *Dialectic Materialism (Lecture Outline)–A Unified Explanation on the Law of Contradiction*, later this section was rewritten as *On Contradiction*, and it was possible that it could give references to *Outlines of Social Studies* in the process of rewriting". This paragraph by Chen is also worthy of debate. The viewpoint that *On Contradiction* was not yet created in August 1937" in "Chen's Article" contradicts historical facts. In fact, it was already created when Mao Zedong gave a lecture based on the basic viewpoint

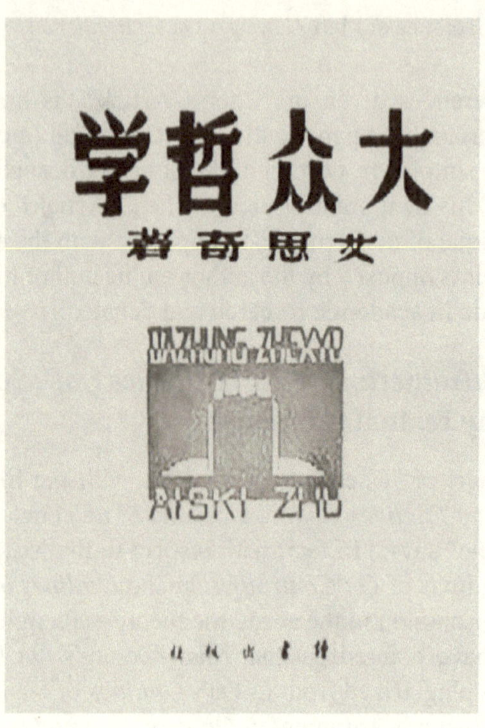

Ai Siqi's book of Philosophy for the Masses (June 1936)

of *On Contradiction* at the Anti-Japanese Military and Political College, and after this event the mimeographed copy was printed. Although *On Practice* and *On Contradiction* are two inherent sections of *Dialectic Materialism* (*Lecture Outline*), as mentioned above, they are not an outline, but a finalizing of the lecture notes and have made a theoretical creation by combining *Marxist Philosophy* with China's revolutionary experience and also combined them with the Chinese philosophy. Mao Zedong himself has particularly valued the two sections from the very beginning and distinguished them from other parts in the *Dialectic Materialism* (*Lecture Outline*). The "Two Theories" were mimeographed separately in Yan'an at that time. According to the memory of Comrade Wu Liping (namely Wu Liangping), Chairman Mao has personally signed and gave the mimeographed copy of the "Two Theories" to him, to Ai Siqi who just arrived in Yan'an and to other comrades. Wu Lipinghas been treasuring this mimeographed copy till now.[8] This mimeographed copy was exhibited during the National Academic Seminar for Commemorating the 40th Anniversary of

8   Wu Liping, *A Loyal and Honest Revolutionary Philosopher*, see *A Philosopher's Road – In Memory of Comrade Ai Siqi*, Yunnan People's Publishing House, 1985, pp. 119-120.

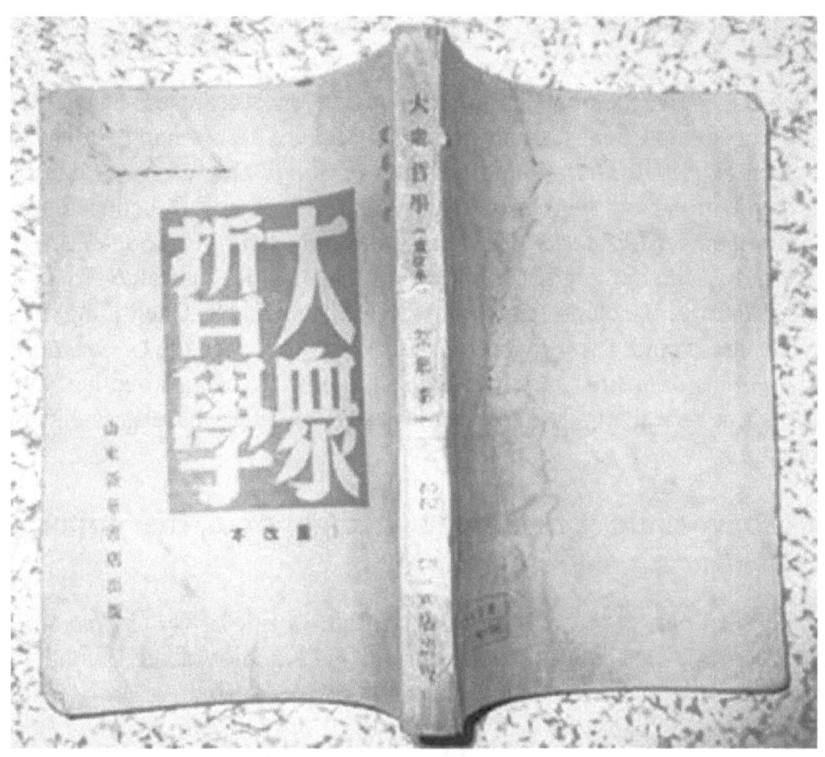

Philosophy for the Masses written by Ai Siqi,
second edition after its revision in 1947

Publication of *On Practice* and *On Contradiction* in Beijing in September 1977, and I was fortunate enough to be able to see it. "Chen's Article" puts forward that from the perspective of time, Mao Zedong might have read the letterpress printing lecture note of *Outlines of Social Studies* (1935) which was printed by the School of Law and Business in National Peiping University, and Mao Zedong might refer to *Outlines of Social Studies* when reviewing *On Contradiction* before it was compiled into Selected Works of Mao Zedong. These two points raised in "Chen's Article" are not new problems, but the old problems which were raised by some scholars after the publication of *Collected Works of Li Da* in the early 1980s. Everything is possible, but possibility is one thing, while the fact is another thing, possibility is not equal to the facts. I give a negative answer to these two questions in my article *Re-debate on "Two Theories" and the Outlines of Social Studies*. The article pointed out: "I investigated the modifications made on the "Two Theories" when being collected into the *Selected Works of Mao Zedong* in 1980, and did not find out any of the modifications which was impacted by the Syllabus, or any direct literal connection with the

Syllabus."[9] After the publication of my article, no researchers have objected to this idea. "Chen's Article" insists that there are so many similarities between *On Contradiction* and *Outlines of Social Studies*, but it does not list any "similarity" with even twenty or thirty words. Whether there is any similarity between *On Contradiction* and *Outlines of Social Studies* belongs to a matter of fact, rather than the question of value. Facts are facts. I dare to conclude that Professor Liu Zehua, Mr. Chen Dingxue or anyone else cannot find any literal "similarity" between *On Contradiction* and *Outlines of Social Studies*, because there is no such a so-called "similarity". The so-called "so many similarities" is a purely baseless subjective fabrication.

IV. How could Chen Boda change from the editor of *On Contradiction* to its author?

The third part of "Chen's Article" contains a title of *On Contradiction* and *Chen Boda*. "Chen's Article" wrote: "The author of the second volume version which was collected into the *Selected Works of Mao Zedong* is Chen Boda". It also wrote: "The first draft of *On Contradiction* (Please notice, it is not the first draft of the first section of Chapter III in *Dialectic Materialism (Lecture Outline)–A Unified Explanation on the Law of Contradiction* may be written by Chen Boda.

Here we should first ask to Mr. Chen: have you seen the first draft of *On Contradiction* which "may be written by Chen Boda" claimed by you? I have only known the first draft of the first section of Chapter III in *Dialectic Materialism (Lecture Outline)–A Unified Explanation on the Law of Contradiction*, but have never heard of such kind of draft as claimed in "Chen's Article". Chen Boda had not arrived in Yan'an when Mao Zedong taught philosophy at the Anti-Japanese Military and Political College and when Mao Zedong wrote the "Two Theories", therefore the real first draft of *On Contradiction* claimed in "Chen's Article" cannot exist.

I have been engaged in the study of Mao Zedong's philosophy for more than 30 years, It is the first time that I have heard the idea that *On Contradictory* is written by Chen Boda, or "the first draft of *On Contradiction* may be from the hands of Chen Boda". What are the viewpoints in "Chen's Article" based on? "Chen's Article" continued to say that "many articles and speeches of Mao Zedong were drafted by Chen Boda according to the sayings of Mao Zedong's bodyguard Li Jiaji (note: should

---

9   Xu Quanxing, *Re-debate on "Two Theories" and Outlines of Social Studies*, see *In Defense of Mao Zedong*, Contemporary China Publishing House, 1996, p. 214.

be called as "Jia Ye"), 'Some of these articles were given a thought and drafted by the secretary, then finalized by Chairman Mao and some were given a thought or an idea by Chairman Mao, drafted by the secretary, then modified and finalized by Chairman Mao; some were drafted by Chairman Mao, then asked the secretary for opinions and finalized by joint research. At that time in our minds, Chen Boda was talented, Chairman Mao trusted him very much, and he was really involved in drafting a lot of important documents and articles." Is this saying really reliable? The bodyguard of Mao Zedong even could see that "many articles and speeches of Mao Zedong were drafted by Chen Boda, "This is simply unheard of strange talk, and so I doubt this saying. In view of the way used in "Chen's Article" when citing passages from my article, I wanted to check how Mr. Li Jiaye's speech. So, I accessed to Mr. Li Jiaye's interview from the Internet: published under the title *Chen Boda Who I Have Known*. After reading it I have indeed found that Chen Wen has distorted Mr. Mr. Li Jiaye's speech.

Originally Mao Zedong's Bodyguard Li Jiaye's speech in *Chen Boda Who I Have Known* was a interview record by Mr. Yang Qingwang (a journalist from the magazine called Hundred Year Tide) to Mr. Li Jiaye who had once been a bodyguard of Mao Zedong for 13 years, and the magazine Hundred Year Tide authorized the CPC News Network to publish this interview exclusively. On the basis of his long-term contacts, Mr. Li talked about his views on Chen Boda himself, and believed that Chen was quite talented and was trusted by Chairman Mao as his secretary. One example was given to the effect that on the eve of the People's Liberation Army's cross-river campaign, Chairman Mao delivered the March Order (to the Whole Country) personally-drafted by himself to Chen Boda to ask for Chen Boda's advice. Mr. Li wrote: "From this incident, I feel that Chairman Mao trusted Chen Boda very much, such an important directive was asked for his advice. This matter also reminds me of the early years of the founding of New China, as far as I know, many editorials and important articles were finalized in such way...". The above words in the quotation marks quoted in "Chen's Article" were omitted. Obviously, we can see that "Chen's Article" falsified "many editorials and important articles were finalized in such way" into "many articles and speeches of Mao Zedong were drafted by Chen Boda". Chen Boda, as a secretary of Mao Zedong, indeed did gain the trust of Mao Zedong, participated in drafting a lot of important documents and articles, and also sorted out a lot of Mao Zedong's speeches. However, starting from this, it is untenable to infer that "many articles and speeches of Mao Zedong were drafted by Chen Boda". Thus further, we cannot conclude that "the first draft of *On Contradiction* might be created by Chen Boda" which is even more absurd.

I once compared *On Contradiction* collected into the *Selected Works of Mao Zedong* with the first draft of August 1937, and made a comment on the finalizing work and gave a description on the main "supplements, deletions and modifications."[10] Compared with *On Practice*, *On Contradiction* was modified greatly, the section which discussed logical critique was deleted, and some new content was added, but its basic idea and structure still contained the ones included in the first draft. When *On Contradiction* was collected into the *Selected Works of Mao Zedong*, the first draft was only revised and made more accurate, rich and was thus completed, besides the wording was polished and made more concise and fine. Chen Boda and Tian Jiaying participated in the review and editing of *On Contradiction*, but can we say that the modifier and the editor was the author of *On Contradiction*? No serious author or editor would agree with this statement. The originator and writer of *On Contradiction* is only one person, Mao Zedong. If Chen Boda was alive, he would not accept the title as the "author of *On Contradiction*. However, in some people's eyes, Chen Boda passed away long ago, it is natural to listen to Mr. Chen Dingxue's hypothesis. But do you not know that Chen Boda had made some words before his death, on this issue.

The famous biographer Mr. Ye Yonglie has written a book *Chen Boda Biography* of 580,000 characters. Ye Yonglie at the beginning of the Preface wrote: "In order to write this book, I have made many special trips to Beijing (note: Ye Yonglie was a Shanghai native) to interview Chen Boda himself, and also interviewed Chen Boda's relatives, secretaries, and other relevant personnel" Ye Yonglie wrote his *Chen Boda Biography* on "the basis of studying and mastering a lot of first-hand information". Ye Yonglie established a friendship with Chen Boda in the process of his interview and got Chen's trust. He said he would value have liked to ask Chen Boda to review the whole manuscript, but Chen Boda could not read such a long biography, but said to Ye Yonglie, "I believe you can write truthfully and I believe you can write well."[11] Thus, it can be seen that *Chen Boda Biography* is credible.

It was an important work in Chen Boda's life to participate in editing *Selected Works of Mao Zedong*, As a biography, it could not fail to write this aspect. For this purpose, Ye Yonglie specifically listed the content of work when Chen Boda "edited the *Selected Works of Mao Zedong*". "According to what Chen Boda said, the Introduction for the Publishing of the Book before the book text included in the Volume I of *Selected Works of Mao Zedong* was drafted by him." Ye Yonglie recorded the whole text of

---

10 Xu Quanxing, *Writing and Editing of On Practice and On Contradiction*, see *In Defense of Mao Zedong*, Contemporary China Publishing House, 1996, pp. 186-199.
11 Ye Yonglie, *Chen Boda Biography*, People's Daily Press, 1999.

the Introduction, including such words "each article in the Selected Works has been reviewed by the author, and the author has made literal amendment in some places, there are individual articles which encountered some additions and amendments in regard to the content". After completing the transcription of the Introduction, Ye Yonglie wrote: *Publication Committee for Selected Works of Mao Zedong of CPC Central Committee* affixed in the end of the text was temporarily drafted by him when writing this article, originally called as *Editing Committee for Selected Works of Mao Zedong of CPC Central Committee*, and Liu Shaoqi, was the head of it. Chen Boda thought that the use of the word "editing" should be avoided because he thought "how could Mao Zedong's articles be 'edited' by others? It may even cause trouble." However the Publication Committee was nominally only responsible for the publication, although in fact did the editing work. What kinds of job did Mao Zedong do in the process of editing the *Selected Works of Mao Zedong*? And what kinds of jobs did the editor do? Chen Boda recalled his memories on this issue. Ye Yonglie wrote: "according to Chen Boda's memory, Mao Zedong himself made a careful elaboration on the *Selected Works of Mao Zedong* before publication, and he was careful to listen to other people's opinions. Some differences between the articles collected into the *Selected Works of Mao Zedong* and the original texts published originally were changed by Mao Zedong himself when it was published. According to Mao Zedong's opinion, Chen Boda made some literal technical changes."[12] Chen Boda might not expect that someone using his name would use his editing work for the *Selected Works of Mao Zedong* to blemish and smudge Mao Zedong, but the above words that he left back will undoubtedly give a heavy blow and a strong reply to the rumormongers. Gentlemen like Chen Dingxue, be awakened please! If Old Master Chen Boda who had even avoided the use of thee word of "editing" knew this in the paradise, he would say to Mr. Chen: "Junior Dingxue, although we have the same surname, we are not on the same path, the title as the author of *On Contradiction* I cannot bear, because it is unworthy of the name." Gentlemen like Chen Dingxu, isn't it like this?

How was *On Contradiction* revised or modified concretely before being collected into the *Selected Works of Mao Zedong*, how many kinds of modified copies, we have no such material in our hand until now. it can be seen in the book of Mr. Pang Xianzhi which recalled Tian Jiaying, the book said: during March to April of 1951, Mao Zedong once wrote three letters (the first letter was written to both Chen Boda and Tian Jiaying, the other two letters were only written to Tian Jiaying) which were addressed

---

12　Ye Yonglie, *Biography of Chen Boda*, People's Daily Press, 1999, pp. 270-274.

to Chen Boda and Tian Jiaying who were in Beijing (later they both went to Shijiazhuang to work with Mao Zedong) when Mao Zedong was reviewing *On Contradiction* in Shijiazhuang. The first sentence in his first letter was "modification *On Contradiction* has been made, please re-arrange two proof copies, one to be delivered to Chen Boda, another to me." In the second letter he said "the parts where proofread and modified, should be delivered to me together with the original proof copy."[13] The above three letters showed that Mao Zedong had indeed modified its own writings personally, Chen Boda and Tian Jiaying who participated in the modifying and editing had mainly made some "literal technical changes".

I do not intend to deny that Mao Zedong together with his secretaries, Chen Boda and Tian Jiaying would have discussed on how *On Contradiction* should be modified, also I do not intend to deny that some of their views would have been adopted by Mao Zedong, also I do not intend to deny what they both have done in the process of editing furthermore, but in my opinion if someone claims editors as "authors" and denies that *On Contradiction* is Mao Zedong's original work, he is not ignorant but has ulterior motives.

V. Mao Zedong's *On Contradiction* was prior to Ai Siqi's *Outline for Study*

The fourth part of "Chen's Article" is titled as *On Contradiction and Ai Siqi*. "Chen's Article" puts forward that "after arriving in Yan'an, Ai Siqi raised many views of amendment, most of which were included in the article written by Mao Zedong. Overseas scholars, through literature comparison and other research, have argued that there are 'numerous similarities' among *On Practice* and *On Contradiction*, and Ai Siqi's writings. For example, they have argued that the fourth part of *On Contradiction* with title of 'principal contradiction and principal aspect of a contradiction' is also almost similar to the ideas presented in the several works of Ai Siqi." In view of the annotation, this passage is based on the research made by two foreign scholars: one of them is Mr. Takeuchi Minoru, a Japanese well-known expert who researches Mao Zedong. In the view of Mr. Chen and most people, he is authoritative enough, and his views could convince people enough, but in my opinion, this viewpoint by Mr. Takeuchi Minoru is not only untenable, but also reverses the history. However, this is an error which has been corrected already.

---

13   Dong Bian et al., *Mao Zedong and His Secretary Tian Jiaying*, Central Literature Publishing House, 1989, pp. 91-94.

Ai Siqi was famous for his *Philosophy for the Masses* in his Shanghai period. At the time of studying philosophy after arriving in Yan'an, Mao Zedong not only read Marxism-Leninism books, Soviet philosophy textbooks, history of Western philosophy and other books, but also read the Marxist writings by Chinese authors. He had studied and read the *Philosophy for the Masses* before he taught philosophy at the Anti-Japanese Military and Political College and wrote the "Two Theories", and he praised it as "a real popular and valuable" work and recommended it as a textbook to the cadres in Yan'an[14]. In September 1937, Mao Zedong also carefully studied and read Ai Siqi's Philosophy and Life and made several excerpts. In October 1937, Ai Siqi as a young philosopher came from Shanghai to Yan'an and was warmly welcomed by Mao Zedong. After Ai Siqi arrived in Yan'an, he established a close relationship with Mao Zedong and exchanged ideas with him from time to time. Once Mao mentioned about a passage included in the page 19 of *Philosophy and Life*, to Ai, and said to him: "this book is a more profound book among your other works, I've learned a lot from your book" in his letter to Ai Siqi.[15]

Mao Zedong in his youth time was modest and eager to learn and was as able to "collect hundreds of sayings into a single school". When I did the academic research about Mao Zedong's reading of philosophical books, I found that Mao Zedong's *On Practice* did not only fully utilized the achievements of Soviet philosophy in the 1930s but also absorbed the ideas presented in the *Philosophy for the Masses* of Ai Siqi. In 1984, I had pointed out that the expressions about the universality and absoluteness at the end part of *On Practice* did not originate from Ai Siqi's *Outlines of Social Studies*, but from his *Philosophy for the Masses*[16]. This was the first time among Chinese publications which argued that there are literal relations between *On Practice* and *Philosophy for the Masses* (*Philosophy for the Masses*). In 1986, in order to commemorate the 20th anniversary of the death of Ai Siqi, I wrote the *Philosophy for the Masses* and *On Practice* to comprehensively discuss the superior aspects of *Philosophy for the Masses* (*Philosophy for the Masses*) in regard to the epistemological aspect and the absorptions made by Mao Zedong in *On Practice* from *Philosophy for the Masses*. My speech at the seminar and the relevant paper received the attention and affirmation of the participants. Compared with *Outlines of Social Studies*, the "law about the identity of contradiction" was written more general and didn't contain theoretical characteristics, anymore. Therefore, *On*

---

14 *Mao Zedong's Selected Letters*, People's Publishing House, 1983, p. 80.
15 *Mao Zedong's Philosophical Annotations Series*, Central Party Literature Press, 1988, p. 204.
16 Xu Quanxing, *Writing and Editing of On Practice and On Contradiction*, see *In Defense of Mao Zedong*, Contemporary China Publishing House, 1996, p. 203.

Contradiction has learned very little from *Outlines of Social Studies*, or even we can't talk about any kind of literal relations with *On Contradiction*. So I do not write about the relationship between it and *On Contradiction* in the above article.

My above article has also pointed out that Ai Siqi's *Philosophy for the Masses*, which was revised in 1947, greatly drew on Mao Zedong's thought such as the idea of seeking truth from facts, integrating theory with practice, investigating and studying, the mass line, and on regard to the two conditions for leaping from perceptual knowledge to rational knowledge discussed in the *On Practice*. I wrote: "The rewritten *Philosophy for the Masses* disseminates Mao Zedong Thought to a certain extent. This is another kind of relation between *Philosophy for the Masses* and *On Practice*"[17] It needs to be added and pointed out that the law of unity of opposite's part in the re-edited version of *Philosophy for the Masses* has fully absorbed the elaborations on the particularity of contradiction, principal contradiction and principal aspect of a contradiction in *On Practice*. Therefore, in case we use this version of *Philosophy for the Masses* when comparing it with Mao Zedong's works, Undoubtedly, we can find many similarities (to say "numerous similarities" is an extreme exaggeration), but this demonstrates that *Philosophy for the Masses* has learned from Mao Zedong's works, rather than the opposite.

"Chen's Article" said that the fourth part of *On Contradiction*, discussing "the principal contradiction and principal aspect of a contradiction" was "also almost similar" to Ai Siqi's *Outline for Study*, and gave reference to the textual analysis of Mao and Ai Siqi's works in the book titled as Mo Takuto which is written by Mr. Takeuchi Minoru. Can this basis be solid enough? Of course not.

Mr. Takeuchi Minoru is really a well-known expert who researches Mao Zedong and edited *Collected Works of Mao Zedong* and its *Supplementary Volumes* and *Special Volumes*, which include total 20 volumes, his works include *Mao Zedong Biography* (1965), *Mao Zedong's Career – Charisma Source of Mobilizing Eight Hundred Million People* (1972), *Mao Zedong* (1989), *Mao Zedong's Reading Life* (1999) and so on. He has spoken highly of Mao Zedong, and said that Mao Zedong was "a historical figure who has rewritten the Chinese history", and a great man in China's history which can be compared to be a unity of Confucius and Qin Shi Huang. But limited by historical conditions, even the most famous people will inevitably

---

17 Xu Quanxing, *Philosophy for the Masses and On Practice*, see *In Defense of Mao Zedong*, Contemporary China Publishing House, 1996, pp. 224-230.

have the limitations of knowledge, make mistakes in some problems, as well as come up with tragic fates.

During the "Cultural Revolution", Mr. Takeuchi Minoru made a particularly detailed research on the "Two Theories" in the *Archetype of Mao Zedong's On Contradiction* (Journal of Thought, 1969/4). Later, some other Japanese scholars continued the work and published the *True Colours of Mao Zedong's Philosophy* (as internal data with letterpress printing arranged by Reference Room of Philosophy Department of Xiangtan University in April 1982, but it did not indicate the author, original writing time and source) Japan researchers' "starting point and logic" for the research can be described as follows: *Dialectical Materialism (Lecture Outline)* with the signature of Mao Zedong was formed around 1940; Ai Siqi's *Outline for Study* (1939) was drafted for the purpose of writing the *Dialectical Materialism (Lecture Outline)*. "In the process of writing the *Lecture Outline*, Ai Siqi's *Research Outline* may have played a full role", "it has directly used a large section of Ai Siqi's *Outline for Study*", and "the main arguments in the *On Contradiction* can be seen as written in the former (Ai Siqi's *Outline for Study*) without any omission." The conclusion of the Japanese scholars is that "the completion of these philosophical papers (the "Two Theories") is the collective work of the Chinese Marxist theoretical circles at that time, which should basically be regarded as their common wealth, rather than being Mao Zedong's personal works." Long ago, I have pointed out that the above-mentioned view and inference was completely contradicted the historical facts and was a reversal of history in my article titled *Writing and Editing of On Practice and On Contradiction* written in 1982[18]. Because the historical fact is that *Mao Zedong's Lecture Outline* was prior to Ai Siqi's *Outline for Study*.

There are also some foreign scholars who hold similar views with Mr. Takeuchi. This error is either due to lack of the relevant data which could be collected and due to misunderstanding, or due to prejudice or ignorance. In fact, the *Lecture Outline* was mimeographed with the signature of Mao Zedong in September 1937, was serially published with the signature of Mao Zedong in the Journal of University of Anti-Japanese War published in Guangzhou in 1938, and was also published in Yan'an Eighth Route Army Military and Political Periodical Office (this edition was not signed, but Chinese researchers have never doubted that this is the outline work used by Mao Zedong for teaching philosophy at the Anti-Japanese Military and Political College in 1937, *Mao Zedong's Philosophical Thought* (Excerpt)

18　Xu Quanxing, *Writing and Editing of On Practice and On Contradiction*, see *In Defense of Mao Zedong*, Contemporary China Publishing House, 1996, pp. 187-189.

compiled by Philosophy Department of Peking University in the 1960s had quoted abundantly from the *Lecture Outline*). The historical facts and logic can be described as follows: Mao Zedong has compiled and written the *Lecture Outline* on the basis of his philosophy lectures at the Anti-Japanese Military and Political College in 1937. In order to solve the textbook problem needed for Yan'an cadres, Ai Siqi has selected and edited his *Philosophical Selections* in 1939. The book by Ai Siqi was based on the three Soviet philosophical works mentioned above and also was based on Li Da's *Outlines of Social Studies*. Additionally there were two appendices, one was Stalin's *Dialectical Materialism and Historical Materialism*, and another was Ai Siqi's own *Outline for Study*. The *Research Outline* edited by Ai Siqi was did not only learn from philosophical works of the Soviet Union and other foreign philosophical works and Li Da's *Outlines of Social Studies*, but has also learned from *Mao Zedong's Dialectical Materialism* (*Lecture Outline*) (especially the "Two Theories" therein), so there are literal similarities and relevance in the both texts, especially in the parts on epistemology and law of unity of opposites. This kind of reference and learning is quite normal. A variety of versions of *Philosophical Selections* was published in China and the *Selected Works of Ai Siqi* which is mentioned in the note of "Chen's Article" actually is an error which confused it with the *Philosophical Selections* published by Reading Bookstore in 1947. All people who have a little background knowledge in the academic circle will know that a book called *Selected Works of Ai Siqi* was never published in China. If Mr. Chen had made a comparison between the *Research Outline* included in Ai Siqi's *Philosophical Selections* and the first draft of the *On Contradiction* in Mao Zedong's *Lecture Outline*, it would not be difficult for him to find that Ai Siqi has learned from the first draft of Mao Zedong's *On Contradiction*, rather than the opposite.

How did Mr. Takeuchi Minoru make the textual analysis on Mao and Ai's works in his book Mo Takuto (Japanese short name of the book)? I haven't found the original book of Mo Takuto, so there is no way to know the answer of this question. But one thing is certain, if there is such a textual analysis, then he must reverse the time of creation in regard to *On Contradiction* and *Outline for Study*. I have found Volume IV (the 2002 version) titled as *Three Types of Mao Zedong Biography* which is included in the *Collected Works of Mr. Takeuchi Minoru*, in which there isn't any "textual analysis on the two persons (Mao and Ai)" as mentioned in "Chen's Article". The compiler (publishing company) of *Collected Works of Takeuchi Minoru* said in its *Compilation and Publication Notes* that the *Collected Works Mr. Takeuchi Minoru* was compiled and published "with the consent and cooperation of the author Takeuchi Minoru".

As known, respecting historical facts and correcting a mistake a real scholar's scientific attitude. When commenting on the foreign scholars' researches on "the contribution of Ai Siqi to the development of Marxism in China", Mr. Li Jinshan, a famous expert in the study of Ai Siqi, once pointed out that Takeuchi Minoru finally recognized that *Dialectical Materialism (Lecture Outline)*", which included the "Two Theories" was the work of Mao Zedong in 1937, which includes the same idea but presented in different ways compared with the view of Stuart Schramm, which is also a famous expert on study of Mao Zedong. Mr. Li Jinshan also pointed out: "when recalling what had happened in this period of history (note: refers to the issue of reversing the time order of *Lecture Outline* and *Outline for Study*), Joshua A. Foge (namely Joshua A. Fogel in the 13th Annotation of Prof. "Chen's Article") has argued that they (note: refers to Mr. Takeuchi Minoru, et.al) have ignored the true nature of "Two Theories" on which Ai Siqi had a very profound understanding. Joshua A. Fogel has cited Wu Liping's words: 'Comrade Siqi says that Chairman Mao's philosophy is summed up from the experience of revolutionary struggle, which is also practical, theoretical and easy to be understood, besides it is our role model.'"[19] This shows that Takeuchi Minoru, Joshua A. Fogel and other foreign scholars have corrected their original mistaken views in the face of the facts.

In conclusion, the solid historical fact is that Mao Zedong's *On Contradiction* is prior to Ai Siqi's *Research Outline*. Today some people still insist that Mao Zedong's discussion on "principal contradiction and principal aspect of a contradiction" has learned from the text of Ai Siqi, which not only shows the ignorance of the debaters but also exposes their ulterior motives.

"Chen's Article" has proposed that Ai Siqi "has put forward a lot of modification opinions and suggestions to *On Practice* and *On Contradiction*, and most of them were incorporated into the text written by Mao Zedong". "Chen's Article" did not cite what specific "modification opinions" were proposed by Ai Siqi, or even did not cite which opinion of Ai Siqi was adopted by Mao. This general statement in "Chen's Article" is difficult to figure out. First, the first draft of the "Two Theories" didn't encounter any modification before the founding of New China. Some philosophers of our country recalled that in the spring of 1939, Mao Zedong organized a six-people philosophy

---

19   Li Jinshan, *Public Philosopher. Analects in Memory of the Centenary of Ai Siqi's Birth*), Communist Party History Press, 2011, pp. 386-387.

conferences in his own house, including Ai Siqi and Chen Boda and others, once a week to solicit their opinions and discuss philosophical issues, mainly about the "Two Theories". Mao Zedong was good at listening to and absorbing the views of the masses, and considered all the views in the process of his revising of the final draft. But this is only a memory of a witness, but there is no any modified text as evidence and concrete opinions put forward in this memory of the witness doesn't accord with the facts, i.e. the existing first draft. From the perspective of text logical research, memories that do not match the historical materials (whether a person or a few people) can't prove the point[20]. Second, Ai Siqi did not participate in the modification and editing activities of the "Two Theories". Third, nobody has mentioned about any written evidence that Ai Siqi himself proposed modification suggestions for the "Two Theories", while in this regard; there are several letters as evidence for the modification suggestions proposed by Li Da[21]. It can naturally be further studied whether Mao Zedong absorbed some of Ai Siqi's philosophical thoughts when revising *On Contradiction*, but it is difficult to agree that Ai Siqi had "proposed many modification opinions or suggestions" to Mao and that they were accepted by Mao Zedong, because so far there is no written evidence in this respect.

In recent years, some researchers have put forward some ideas as following: the "Two Theories" have benefited from Ai Siqi's methodology of thinking, and "Mao's methodology of thinking has derived from Ai Siqi's but is higher than Ai's. I have made a detailed response to these views in the article *Discussion between Ai Siqi's Philosophy in the Yan'an Period and Maoist Philosophy* and have demonstrated that these views are not consistent with historical reality and cannot hold water, which show there is lack of understanding on the modern history of Chinese philosophy.[22]

VI. Research methods in "Chen's Article" are problematic

Philosophical thought has its own continuity and succession, any real philosophy in history "has been handed down to it by its predecessors and it takes the specific ideological materials arising from it as a prerequisite"[23]. Li Da's *Outlines of Social Studies* has largely learnt from Soviet philosophical

---

20   Xu Quanxing, A Number of Historical Facts to Be Examined and Corrected in the Research of the Two Theories, *Journal of Hunan University of Science and Technology* (Social Science Edition), 2010(2).

21   *Mao Zedong's Selected Letters*, People's Publishing House, 1983, pp. 407-455.

22   Xu Quanxing, *Evaluation on Mao Zedong in History*, Xiangtan University Press, 2010, pp. 206-217.

23   *Selected Works of Marx and Engels*, Vol. 4, People's Publishing House, 1995, p. 703.

thought of the 1930s, but this does not diminish its great social role, and it does not prevent its historical position of being China's first Marxist philosophy textbook. It is not surprising that Mao Zedong naturally had to learn from it and inherited the ideological materials of his predecessors and his contemporaries when he taught philosophy at the Anti-Japanese Military and Political College and wrote his "Two Theories". As explained in the second part of this article, it is necessary and a significant work to clarify the theoretical sources of the "Two Theories". However, if we only limit ourselves to solve this issue, it will be insufficient. Because philosophy is the product of the times, and the times determines how the previous ideological materials will inherited and developed. "Each *philosophy* is the *spirit* of *its own time* comprehended in thought"[24]. This is our fundamental viewpoint and method when studying and evaluating any philosophy. My colleagues who are in the same teaching and research section with me were engaged in making comparison of literal materials among the "Two Theories", Soviet philosophy of the 1930s and *Outlines of Social Studies* long ago, which were printed and distributed at the National Seminar for *Mao Zedong's Philosophical Thought* in October 1981. In view of this information and the status of the theoretical circles at that time, Comrade Gong Yuzhi pointed out in his speech in this seminar: "when we study the "Two Theories", we certainly need to understand its connection with the works of Marxist philosophical circles at that time, but more importantly, we need to understand its connection with the demands of historical conditions, i.e. the summarization of the experiences of the Chinese revolution and understand its connection with the other works written by Comrade Mao Zedong for the purpose of summarizing the experiences of the Chinese revolution. If we ignore the latter connection, we will completely fail to grasp the essence of the "Two Theories"."[25] In my opinion, "Chen's Article" puts aside the close relation among the *On Contradiction*, its times and the practice of Chinese revolution, and the research method which seeks to evaluate the relationship between it and other works only from words and phrases is quite one-sided and unscientific.

It is absolutely not an accidental consequence that "Two Theories" have appeared in China. It is a reflection of the sharp, complex and tortuous movement of the social contradictions in China in the 20th century. Mao Zedong could write the "Two Theories", which is certainly the product of his painstaking study of philosophy, good at inheriting and absorbing the essence of Marxist-Leninist philosophy, moreover it is closely related to

---

24   *Selected Works of Marx and Engels*, Vol. 1, People's Publishing House, 2001, p. 222.
25   The Standing Group of the Preparatory Group of the Research Group Mao Zedong Thought in China, *Selected Articles of the National Symposium on Mao Zedong Thought*, Guangxi People's Publishing House, 1982, p. 59.

his deep understanding of ancient Chinese philosophy, as well as his abundant readings on ancient history and philosophy (Edgar Snow, who has interviewed Mao in 1936, considered Mao to be "an accomplished scholar of the literature of old China," and a philosopher who possessed his own "philosophical system"[26]), but more importantly he had unique advantage of abundant practical experience in leading the Chinese revolution, especially in command of the Chinese revolutionary war and the struggle with the mistaken ideas within the Party. Here if we only mention about the particularity of the contradiction, the main contradiction and the main aspects of a contradiction as an example to illustrate.

In the comparison between the "Two Theories" and the Soviet philosophy of the 1930s, although the Soviet philosophy of the 1930s has discussed the same concepts of dialectics such as the particularity of the contradiction, main contradiction and the main aspects of a contradiction, though the latter has given some preliminary explanations on these concepts, it has failed to define these concepts comprehensively, and could not fully expound on the particularity of contradiction. Li Da's *Outlines of Social Studies* (1937) and Ai Siqi's *Philosophy for the Masses* (1936), *Methodology of Thought* (November 1936), *Modern Philosophy Reader* (March 1937) and other works have failed to learn from the products of Soviet philosophy when discussing the law of unity between opposites, and even these three philosophical concepts were not mentioned in these works. On the basis of absorbing the essence of Soviet philosophy and combining Marxist philosophy by the practice of Chinese society and Chinese revolution, *On Contradiction* has not only defined these three concepts clearly, but also expounded how to analyze the particularity of contradiction, expounded on the essence of the main contradictions, the mutual transformation between the main contradiction and the secondary contradiction, and the mutual transformation of the aspects of main contradictions and the secondary contradictions, thus enriched and developed the Marxist dialectics theory, and accomplished the historical task of "explaining and developing" the law of unity between opposites which has developed new ideas discussed by Lenin in his *Philosophical Notes*. Why Li Da and Ai Siqi were so different from Mao Zedong in the theory of contradiction? Was their philosophical book knowledge less than Mao Zedong? No. In fact, in this respect, as experts of philosophical studies, Li Da and Ai Siqi are better than Mao Zedong. The fundamental reason for this difference is that they lacked the position of Mao Zedong as the leader of the Chinese revolution, the difficult experiences of this revolution which included twists and turns and rich practical experience, so they could not feel as Mao Zedong

---

26   Edgar Snow, *Red Star over China*, Joint Publishing, 1979, pp. 65-68.

and be aware of the extreme importance of these issues, which forced Mao Zedong to combine Marxist philosophy with the rich experience of Chinese revolution and enrich and develop the doctrine of contradiction. The "Two Theories" are the philosophical summary of the experiences and lessons of the Chinese revolution. They are not philosophies in the den, which cannot be copied from other books. Chen Wen has dedicated himself to find the links between the *On Contradiction* and other works among the words, but has failed to understand them which are a reflection of the philosophical summarization of the contradictions in the Chinese society, and the objective relations with the theory of dialectics and the experience of Chinese revolution as a result, he couldn't fundamentally grasp the basic spirit and theoretical value of the "Two Theories".

In short, *On Contradiction* was the combination between the Marxist philosophy and the practice of Chinese revolution and the ancient Chinese dialectics, which has enriched and developed the theory of Marxist dialectics. It was not copied from any books. Mao Zedong is its only author, originator.

The author Xu Quanxing is professor in CPC Central Party School and director of Academic Committee of the Mao Zedong Thought Research Center in Xiangtan University

2

The Relationship between the Party and the Intellectuals in Yan'an

Gong Yun

The relationship between the CPC and the intellectuals, especially the relationship with the intellectuals belonging to literature and art circles during the Yan'an period, has become a hot topic in recent years. Especially in the 70th anniversary of Mao Zedong's speech at Yan'an Literature and Art Symposium in 2012, some scholars have used the so-called "Wang Shiwei problem" to distort the relationship between the CPC and the intellectuals in the Yan'an period, especially the relationship between the CPC and the literary and art intellectuals. This article attempts to review and analyze the large amount of available historical data, to describe the relationship between the CPC and the intellectuals during the Yan'an period of the Party in order to restore the true features of history.

During the Yan'an period of the Party, the work of the CPC in respect to intellectuals has gone through three stages. On April 22, 1943, the Xinhua News Agency published a broadcasted article which presented an introduction on the work experiences of cultural workers in Yan'an, which summed up the post-war work of cultural workers in Yan'an, which mainly commented on the works of literary and art workers. This article had divided the cultural work of Yan'an period into three stages:

The first stage is from the beginning of the Anti-Japanese War to the first Congress of Literary Association of Shaanxi-Gansu-Ningxia Border Region (January 1940). During this period, there have been many intellectuals came to Yan'an and the front, visited and left according to their needs. Since at that time the rear areas environment controlled by the KMT was

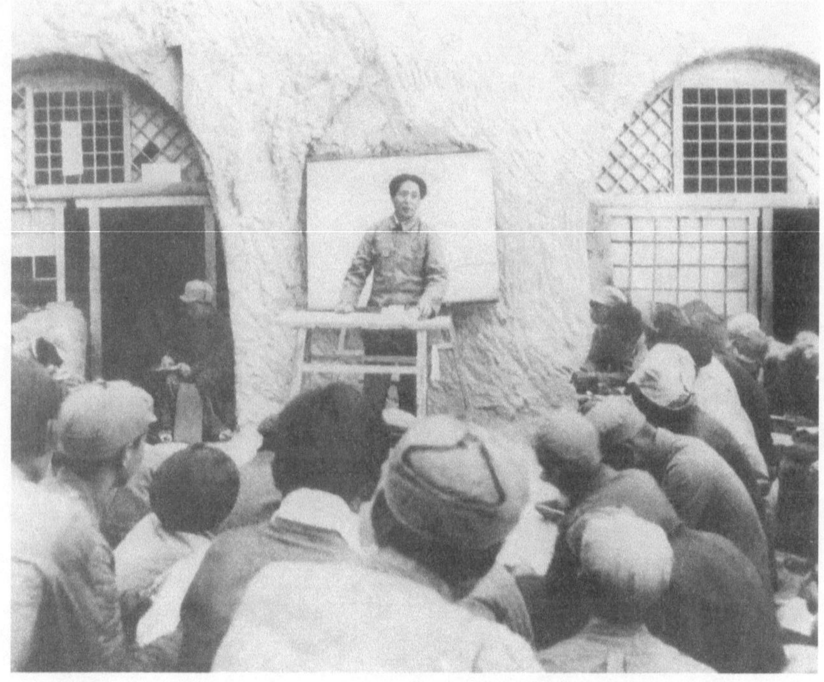

April 28, 1938, Mao Zedong lectured in Lu Xun
Art Institute on the topic of "How To Be Artists"

still relatively good, it was relatively easy to visit the front, some of the intellectuals stayed in Yan'an, some of them lived for a period time and could still go back to the rear areas controlled by the KMT. Since the Party was fully engaged in the war and other relevant work, except providing hospitality for the intellectuals and helping them go to the front, the general attention to the work in respect to intellectuals was not complex enough.

The second stage is from the Convention of Culture Association of the Border Region to the Literary and Art Conference that took place in May 1942. During this period, Mao Zedong put forward the concept of New Democratic culture as the general goal of unity and progress of the intellectuals. But when Mao Zedong had proposed this policy, many comrades dealing with the cultural work didn't have a deep understanding of it, and the relevant Commission has not fully studied the concept to put it into reality. Mao stressed the characteristics of cultural people and adopted a liberal attitude towards them. Combined with the rapid negative changes in the situation in the rear areas, it had become difficult to go to the front, therefore a large number of cultural people had to stay in Yan'an, and they don't work and live in an unrealistic way. Due to the dark and oppressive domestic political environment, due to the increasing difficulties in the material conditions, the vague concepts about the Chinese revolution among some of the cultural people, and the counterrevolutionary sabotage efforts secretly carried out by some slander, the cultural people in Yan'an exposed a lot of serious problems.

The third stage started after the Seminar in 1942. In this stage, Mao Zedong's ideas and conclusions were largely discussed among the cultural workers, and they were expected to make ideological transformation of themselves, i.e. remolding. Meanwhile, concrete steps were set to mobilize them to participate physical work with the laboring masses...[1]

The relationship between the CPC and the intellectuals in the Yan'an period can be divided into the following three aspects:

I. Vigorous recruitment of intellectuals into the ranks of the revolution

Intellectuals have played a very important role in China's revolution and construction. The CPC always attached great importance to the special role of intellectuals in the Chinese democratic revolution, especially during the War of Resistance against Japan.

After the outbreak of the January 29th Movement (1935), Mao Zedong praised intellectuals as the "pioneer of the national liberation struggle" at the cadres meeting in Gushan town. With the launching of the War of Resistance against the Japanese Aggression, Chinese Communist Party paid more attention to the role of intellectuals.

On May 1939, in the speech for the commemoration of the 20th anniversary of the May Fourth Movement, Mao Zedong pointed out: the Chinese youth "has played a vanguard role, to defend the nation in addition to the die-hard caputilationists, all people admit that.[2]

In May of the same year, the CPC Central Committee issued the Instructions on the Propaganda Work. It stressed: "Considering the significance of Chinese cultural movement (including literary and arts) in the Chinese revolution, the Propaganda Department must always pay attention to the leadership of cultural movement, and actively participate in various aspects of the cultural movement... When necessary, they can recruit a part of the cultural workers into the Party ranks as comrades organize culture working committee above the Party committees, and propaganda department of the provincial level Party committees."[3]

---

1 See *Anti-Japanese Democratic Base in the Shaanxi-Gansu-Ningxia Border Area*, Vol. 2, 1990, published by the CPC History Press, pp. 449-450.
2 *Selected Works of Mao Zedong*, Vol. 2, People's Publishing House, 1991, p. 565.
3 *Selected Documents of the CPC Central Committee*, Vol. 12, CPC Central Party School Press, 1991, p. 21.

In June of the same year, Mao Zedong pointed out in his report and conclusion at the meeting of senior cadres in Yan'an: "We must protect the revolutionary intellectuals from the mistakes of the past, there is no victory without revolutionary intellectuals, the Kuomintang and CPC were pursing for the young people, the army should recruit a large number of revolutionary intellectuals. We must persuade the cadres with workers and peasant origin to respect the revolutionary intellectuals and welcome them; the workers and peasants will not improve themselves without the help of revolutionary intellectuals, without the help of the intellectuals, CPC will not be able to govern the country or the Party or the army. During the campaigns, we should actively recruit revolutionary intellectuals."[4]

On 25 June 1939, the General Political Department issued the *Instruction on Recruiting of Intellectuals and the Cultivation of New Cadres*, which said: "due to the lack of veterans, we must increase the participation of revolutionary intellectuals in the military work, and this task has become one of the most important tasks in current cadre policies."

Instruction further required: "Recruit a large number of pure revolutionary intellectuals to participate in the labor, orderly pay attention to their thoughts about our movement, and timely guide them a healthy path; fully understand and play their strengths in all aspects and gradually improve their organizational concepts of discipline and firmness, with an open mind to accept the glorious tradition of the army.".... "We must educate all the veteran cadres that they pay great attention and understand the new revolutionary intellectuals, boldly recruit and patiently lead them to undertake responsibilities, and avoid any discrimination and prejudice toward them. On the other hand, we must call on new revolutionary intellectuals so that they learn in practice, learn from the veteran cadres, workers and peasants, put forward a slogan that the workers and peasants looking down on the revolutionaries is not a real revolutionary attitude, in order to develop their proletarian outlook on life, thus eliminate the gap between new and old and lead and educate the new forces in a gradual approach".[5]

On December 1, 1939, Mao Zedong stressed in the resolution called *On the Substantial Recruitment of Intellectuals into the Party Ranks* which was adopted by the Central Committee of the CPC:

In the long and ruthless war of national liberation, in the great struggle to build a new China, the Communist Party must be good at winning intellectuals, for only in this way will it be able to organize great strength for

---

4   *Selected Works of Mao Zedong,* Vol. 2, People's Publishing House, 1993, p. 233.

5   *Selected Documents of the Central Committee of the Communist Party of China,* Vol. 12, CPC Central Party School Press, 1991, pp. 134-135.

the War of Resistance, organize the millions of peasants, develop the revolutionary cultural movement and expand the revolutionary united front. Without the participation of the intellectuals, victory in the revolution is impossible.

Our Party and our army have made considerable efforts to recruit intellectuals during the last three years, and many revolutionary intellectuals have been absorbed into the Party, the army, the organs of government, the cultural movement and the mass movement, thus broadening the united front, this is a major achievement. But many of the army cadres are not yet alive to the importance of the intellectuals, they still regard them with some apprehension and are even inclined to discriminate against them or shut them out. Many of our training institutes are still hesitant about enrolling young students in large numbers. Many of our local Party branches are still reluctant to let intellectuals join. All this is due to failure to understand the importance of the intellectuals for the revolutionary cause, the difference between intellectuals in colonial and semi-colonial countries and those in capitalist countries and the difference between intellectuals who serve the landlords and the bourgeoisie and those who serve the working class and the peasantry, as well as the seriousness of the situation in which the bourgeois political parties are desperately contending with us for the intellectuals and in which the Japanese imperialists are also trying in every possible way to buy over Chinese intellectuals or corrupt their minds; in particular, it is due to the failure to understand the favorable factor that our Party and our army have already developed a hard core of well-tested cadres and are thus capable of leading the intellectuals.

From now on attention should therefore be paid to the following: (1) All Party organizations in the war areas and all army units led by the Party should recruit large numbers of intellectuals into our army, training institutes and organs of government. We should use various ways and means to recruit all intellectuals who are willing to fight Japan and who are fairly loyal, hard-working and able to endure hardship; we should give them political education and help them to temper themselves in war and work and to serve the army, the government and the masses; and, taking each case on its merits, we should admit into the Party those who measure up to the requirements of Party membership. As for those who do not qualify or do not wish to join the Party, we should have good working relations with them and give them guidance in their work with us. (2) In applying the policy of recruiting intellectuals in large numbers, we must undoubtedly take great care to prevent the infiltration of those elements sent in by the enemy and the bourgeois political parties and to keep out other disloyal elements.

We must be very strict about keeping out such elements. Those who have already sneaked into our Party, army or government organs must be firmly but discriminatingly combed out on the basis of conclusive evidence. But we must not on that account suspect reasonably loyal intellectuals, and we must be strictly on guard against the false accusation of innocent people by counter-revolutionaries. (3) We should assign appropriate work to all intellectuals who are reasonably loyal and useful, and we should earnestly give them political education and guidance so that in the long course of the struggle they gradually overcome their weaknesses, revolutionize their outlook, identify themselves with the masses, and merge with the older Party members and cadres and the worker and peasant members of the Party. (4) For some cadres who oppose intellectuals participating in the labor, especially those cadres in the leading posts should be persuaded about the issue, so that they understand the need to absorb intellectuals participating in the work. At the same time, we should work effectively to encourage worker and peasant cadres to study hard and raise their cultural level. Thus worker and peasant cadres will at the same time become intellectuals, while the intellectuals will at the same time become workers and peasants. (5) In the main the principles stated above are also applicable in the Kuomintang areas and in the Japanese occupied areas, except that, on admitting intellectuals into the Party, more attention must be paid to their degree of loyalty, so as to ensure still tighter Party organization in those areas. We should maintain suitable contact with the huge numbers of non-Party intellectuals who sympathize with us and organize them in the great struggle for resistance to Japan and for democracy, and in the cultural movement and the work of the united front.

All our Party comrades must understand that a correct policy towards the intellectuals is an important prerequisite for victory in the revolution. There must be no repetition of the incorrect attitude towards intellectuals which Party organizations in many localities and army units adopted during the Agrarian Revolution; the proletariat cannot produce intellectuals of its own without the help of the existing intellectuals. The Central Committee hopes that the Party committees at all levels and all Party comrades will give this matter their serious attention.[6]

On December 6, 1939, the Central Military Commission promulgated the Directive on Recruiting Intellectuals and Educating the Workers and Peasants in the Army, in order to carry out the Central Committee's decision on recruiting intellectuals, the resolution demanded: Completely correct all kind of negative tendencies of rejection and refusal of intellectuals

---

6   *Selected Works of Mao Zedong*, Vol. 2, People's Publishing House, 1991, pp. 618-620.

to join our army. "Every effort should be made to recruit intellectuals and semi-intellectuals join our army." "To educate and lead intellectuals who have already participated our army, correct their weaknesses in good faith so that they can become the intellectuals of the proletariat, the new cadres with intellectual background should be promoted in due course. Improve the conditions of workers, office employees and teachers, orderly and in long term." "For political suspects, the best way is to test them in the actual struggle, if no problem they should be trusted and scrubbed when there are problems, but do not treat the inherent weaknesses of the intellectuals (such as lack of organization) as a basis for political suspicions."

"Old and new forces have the possibility to exchange intellectuals with old workers. The peasant cadres should become intellectuals, no matter how long the revolutionary history of peasants' cadres, if they are unwilling to make progress and try to improve their knowledge, and if they have no development prospects, will cause them to become outdated and degenerate. Military and non-military schools should try their best to recruit intellectuals and semi-intellectuals, deepen their political education and sum up our experiences in the education of intellectuals and disseminate them to various units."[7]

In 1939 December, Mao Zedong in his text titled as *The Chinese Revolution and the Chinese Communist Party*, once again stressed: "In China, it was among the intellectuals and young students that Marxist-Leninist ideology was first widely disseminated and accepted. The revolutionary forces cannot be successfully organized, and revolutionary work cannot be successfully conducted without the participation of revolutionary intellectuals…the mass of revolutionary intellectuals in China can play a vanguard role or serve as a link with the masses…"[8]

On October 10, 1940, the Central Propaganda Department and the Central Committee for Cultural Affairs jointly issued Instructions on Cultural Workers and Cultural Organizations in the Anti-Japanese Base Areas and pointed out: "In order to develop cultural movements in the anti-Japanese base areas, and in order to correctly handle our relations with intellectuals we must try to incur and recruit a large number of intellectuals into our ranks in the base areas. We should not only enable them to reassure themselves in their work, achieve their own progress, but also make the most of their progress at a place where they can display their genius."[9]

---

7   *Selected Works of the CPC Central Committee Document*, Vol. 12, CPC Central Party School Press, 1991, pp. 213-214.

8   *Selected Works of Mao Zedong*, Vol. 2, People's Publishing House, 1991, p. 641.

9   *Selected Works of Central Committee of Communist Party of China*, Vol. 12, CPC Central Party School Press, 1991, pp. 496-499.

In December 1940, Mao Zedong drafted the Party instruction letter on policy for the Party Central Committee which included the following:

"Bourgeois-liberal educators, men of letters, journalists, scholars and technical experts should be allowed to come to our base areas and co-operate with us in running schools and newspapers and doing other work. We should accept into our schools all intellectuals and students who show enthusiasm for resisting Japan, give them short-term training, and then assign them to work in the army, the government, or mass organizations; we should boldly draw them in, give them work and promote them. We should not be over-cautious or too afraid of reactionaries sneaking in. Unavoidably, some such elements will creep in, but there will be time to comb them out in the course of study and work."[10]

During the rectification period in 1942, Mao Zedong once again stressed the importance of welcoming and recruiting intellectuals: "Adopt the welcome attitude toward the intellectuals, understand their importance, we cannot achieve success without these people. In the Eighteenth Congress of the CPSU, Stalin treated this question as a theoretical issue. Any class should recruit such a group of intellectuals to do favorable things, the landlord class, the bourgeoisie and the proletariats are the same, they all make use of their intellectuals."[11]

After the outbreak of the Anti-Japanese War, the CPC held high the banner of anti-Japanese national united front, carried out democratic politics, and formulated policies to vigorously largely recruit intellectuals. The Shaanxi-Gansu-Ningxia Border Region became the "holy place" to guide China's war of resistance and attracted tens of thousands of the patriotic intellectuals full of enthusiasm and dedication for the pursuit of revolutionary truth have greatly moved to Yan'an. The famous poet Ke Zhongping wrote a poem in 1939 which truly reflected why a large number of young people greatly moved to Yan'an: "Youth, Chinese youth, eat millet and wear hemp waved shoes in Yan'an. Why do you love Yan'an? The youth answer: we have no fear of wearing out of our feet, and no fear of "nine demons and eighteen monsters". But we are afraid that we can't have the Yan'an millet, can't go to the front line, can't learn from the lectures of Yan'an, and can't become the most revolutionary youth. There are tendons left the flesh is cut off. There are hearts left even bones are broken. As long as we can breathe, we want to go to Yan'an even by crawling."[12]

---

10   *Selected Works of Mao Zedong, Vol. 2, People's Publishing House*, 1991, pp. 768-769.
11   Ibid, p. 432.
12   Quoted from CPC Yan'an Municipal Committee United Front Department, *United Front Study in the Yan'an Period*, Chinese Press, 2010, p. 314.

Well-known musician Xian Xinghai, in his diary recorded his arrival of Yan'an as follows:

"The first time that I heard the name of Yan'an was in "August 13" after the KMT-CPC cooperation was established. But I didn't pay much attention. When I arrived in Wuhan, I often saw the enrollment ads which suggested joining the "Shaanxi public", besides calling to meet young people from Yan'an. At that time, I was greatly impressed with their hard work, vitality, enthusiasm and the fame of Yan'an. Just when I wanted know more about Yan'an, "Lu Xun Art Institute "of Yan'an sent a letter to me which was signed by all the teachers and students of, they wanted me join them in Yan'an. I asked them for some acquaintance, for example I asked them whether they could give me the freedom of mind and creative working environment, their answer was affirmative. I asked if I could visit and leave when I wished, they replied I should be free to do that. When I was thinking about the acceptance of the invitation, "Lu Xun Art Institute" delivered me another two telegrams, finally, I set off northbound with full of temptation, I calculated that I would leave Yan'an if the conditions didn't suit me. It was the winter of 1938."[13]

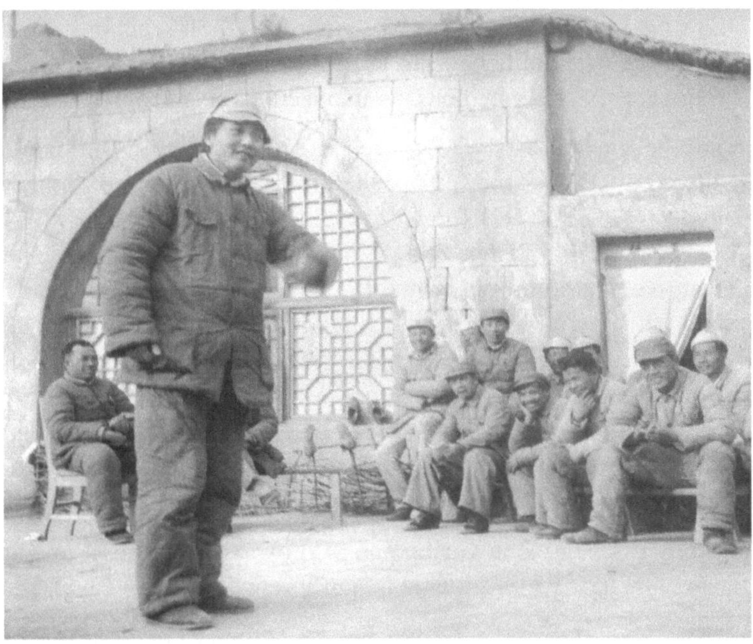

Mao Zedong lecturing senior technical cadres' quarterly meeting held in Yan'an

13   *Yan'an Literature Series* edited by Zhong Jingzhi, Jin Ziguang; *Literature and Art History Volume,* 1987, Hunan Literature and Art Publishing House, pp. 42-43.

Graduated from Wuhan University, the main designer of Yan'an Central Auditorium and the Yang Jialing CPC Central Committee Office, Yang recalls as follows: "At that time a large number of intellectuals from all across the country flood into the border area, especially after the Twelve Incident, until the Marco Polo Bridge Incident. The Kuomintang did not pay any attention to the situation at that time, so there was no serious obstacles to travel to the Border Region, as in the case of the 1938's summer and the 1938's autumn. Consequently, every day about 80 people arrived in Yan'an. In the spring of 1938, after I had received the invitation letter from Mr. Dong working in the Wuhan Office and Chen Kai I started from Guilin, Guangxi, through Wuhan, and finally arrived in Yan'an."[14] According to the statistics of the Eighth Route Army's Xi'an Office, in 1938, from May to August, 2,288 young intellectuals were sent to Yan'an for education.[15] Some source wrote that more than 10,000 youths were allowed to go to Yan'an arranged by the Office of the Eighth Route Army in Xi'an.[16] At the end of December 1943, at the working meeting of the Secretariat of the CPC Central Committee, Ren Bishi said: "After the war began there are more than forty thousand intellectuals who have arrived in Yan'an , in terms of the educational level, more than 70% were junior high school (19% High school 21%, junior high school 31%), junior high school about 30%[17]. In the spring of 1944, Mao Zedong said: "There are six or seven thousand intellectuals in Yan'an."[18]

Among the intellectuals who arrived in Yan'an, there were many literary intellectuals. Before the Yan'an literature and Art symposium which was held in 1942, such well-known names had visited Yan'an: Ding Ling, Ai Qing, Zhou Yang, Li Chu, Zhou Libo, Guo Xiaochuan, Xian Xinghai, Cheng Fangwu, Xiao Jun, Liu Baiyu, He Qifang, Yan Wenjing, Wang, Wei, Yang Shuo, Zhou Erfu, He Luting, He Jingzhi, Hua Junwu, Gao Changhong, Wang Zhaowen, Gu Yuan, Jiang Feng, Yan Han, and others. Mao Dun, Lao She also had been in Yan'an, as visitors. Mao Dun had decided to remain and take root in Yan'an, his son and daughter were with him, his son Shen worked in the northern Shaanxi Public Works and Northwest Art Troupe, his daughter Shen Xia studied in the Women's College.

Well-known scholar Zhu Guangqian also expressed his will to come to Yan'an. In January 1939, Zhu Guangqian wrote a letter to Zhou Yang in

---

14   *Historical Materials of Yan'an Academy of Natural Sciences*, CPC Historical Materials Press, Beijing Institute of Technology Press, 1986, p. 384.

15   Zeng Lu Ping, *Yan'an University History*, People's Publishing House, 2008, p. 25.

16   Quoted from CPC Yan'an Municipal Committee United Front Department, *United Front Study in the Yan'an Period*, Chinese Press, 2010, p. 315.

17   *Hu Qiaomu Memories of Mao Zedong*, People's Publishing House, 1994, p. 257.

18   Ibid., p. 251.

Yan'an, saying, "Your December 29 letter will be transferred to Chengdu from here on the 15th of this month, and if it arrives a month earlier, I may not be at Jiading at the moment instead stayed with you together." "I have met several Yan'an friends, and read several books which describe the cause of Yan'an, and mention that there is still a ray of life there. Consequently since the last fall, I intended to come, so I wrote to the Zhilin, Fang and expressed my wish."[19]

The CPC Central Committee paid a high degree of attention and warm welcome towards the intellectuals who were engaged in literature and art during their presence in Yan'an. In October 1936, Ding Ling arrived in Yan'an at a late night time, the CPC Central Committee held a welcome party for her. Mao Zedong, Zhou Enlai, Luo Fu (Zhang Wentian), Bo Gu (Qin Bangxian) personally attended this party and after the party Mao Zedong also wrote a poem for Ding Ling titled with the name plate "Lin Jiangxian":

One who is similar to a fiber pen
Three thousand Maose soldiers
The map opens to Shandong
Miss Wen yesterday
Military commander today.[20]

When the famous poet Ai Qing arrived in Yan'an he also received a warm welcome. "The CPC Central Committee certainly knew about his approximate arrival day to Yan'an, due to the telegram sent by Premier Zhou, the General Secretary Zhang Wentian, the minister of Propaganda Department Kai Feng, and the minister of the Organization Department, Ke Qingshi, arranged a welcome meeting for him."[21]

---

19   Quoted from *Yan'an Literature and Art History Series*, edited by Zhong Jingzhi, Jin Ziguang, 1987, Hunan Literature and Art Publishing House, pp. 45-46.

20   Linjiang Xian: The name of the nameplate was originally the name of the Tang Dynasty teaching workshop. The song is often used for daffodils. There are two forms of this word plate, and here is one of seven words for each head sentence. The other is six words.

21   August 16, 1982 records of the interview with Ai Qing, quoted from Li Jiefei, Yang Jie, *Interpreting Yan'an Literature, Intellectuals and Culture*, Contemporary China Press, 2010, p. 34.

II. The policy of uniting with and respecting intellectuals

During the Yan'an period, the CPC had followed the policy of uniting and respecting towards the intellectuals who had come from afar and had treated the work with equal care and political care.

In January 1939, during the first session of the Shaanxi-Gansu-Ningxia Border Region Government meeting, the approval was given Border "to set up Natural Science Research Institute, so as to develop scientific research of industrialization, civil engineering, biology, zoology, chemistry and geology."[22]

On October 10, 1940, the Central Propaganda Department and the Central Committee for Cultural Affairs jointly issued the Directive on Cultural Personalities and Cultural Organizations in the Anti-Japanese Base Areas. This directive fully reflects the Chinese Communist Party's policies of uniting with and respecting the intellectuals. The Instruction has demanded a high degree of attention to intellectuals, and has pointed out: "We ought to realize the importance of cultural personalities and rectify the backward mentality of some comrades in the Party to belittle, loathe, and mistrust [them]... We should realize that a cultural personality with considerable social position, prestige, and skill in some art and its product often has very great influence internally and externally." "We ought to use every means to guarantee the spiritual, material, and other necessary conditions for their literary production.... life so that they can give full play to express their talents. It is necessary to know the writing is the hobbies of intellectuals, their work is the greatest contribution to the cause of revolution." "The leading organs of the Party, in addition to giving them the task and general direction for their writings, we should avoid interference in their work. We should ensure that they are free to write in practice, and that it is certainly undesirable to stipulate specific topics for the artists and impose them time limits for their creations.

We Should Correctly Evaluate the Works of the intellectuals. "For the works of intellectuals, we should take a serious, critical, but a flexible and tolerant attitude, it is not allowed to use the power of political slogans and narrow formula to torture the author, in particular, we should not take a ridiculing attitude toward the authors. We should correctly evaluate their work, lead their efforts in the right direction, and encourage them to write by ignoring their temporary failures.

---

22   *Lin Bo Collections*, Huayi Publishing House, 1996, p. 128.

Respect the Living Habits and Life Style of Intellectuals. "Estimate the varied living habits of the cultural personalities, especially that of the new and non-Party cultural personalities, more encouragement, inducement and help should be given to them so as to promote their progress, so that they can be close to the public, reality, and the Communist Party, respect for the revolutionary order, be subject to revolutionary discipline, the Communists should be ready to work with cultural people who have different habits. It is not appropriate to have highly demands for the living habits of the cultural personalities."

Support the Intellectual's Cultural Groups. "Different kinds of cultural personalities (such as novelists, dramatists, musicians, philosophers, etc.), can organize various types of cultural groups, such as literary studies, drama associations, music associations, new philosophy research. These groups may also join forces to form joint groups such as the National Salvation Association for the Culture, but they should estimate the different nature of these groups with other groups of people and define their specific tasks. Generally, the tasks include the research, publishing, promotion of various cultural works. We should absorb and cultivate all kinds of cultural talents, to guide the public aspects of cultural activities; contact between cultural personalities and protect their personal interests, organize them around the newspapers and magazines. We should publish and send their works or translations to the National Publishing House, and should arrange

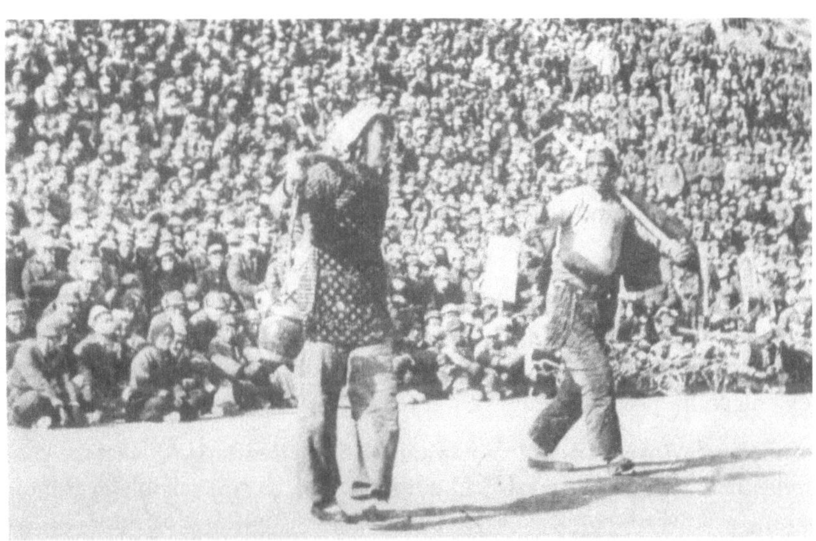

Literary and art workers in Yan'an performing a dance for the reclamation of brotherhood and sisterhood for the masses

regular contact with the cultural groups outside and behind, rectify the mistaken situation in which cultural organizations are treated in the same way as other mass organizations, and inappropriate phenomenon of carrying out ordinary mass work among them." "The above-mentioned various cultural groups generally consist of the culture and the culture-loving intellectuals. The vital point here is the good quality instead of quantity. They do not have to establish the top-down, systematic, universal organization. Only in the cultural center of the concentrated people, you can build their own club. There is no need to have a strict organization towards these organization and a lot of meetings to ensure that cultural people have full freedom of study and writing time."

"These cultural organizations should endeavor to guide the cultural movements of schools, institutions, units, and mass organizations to help them organize cultural groups such as singing groups, troupes and literary groups, and provide them with instructors and research materials. If it is necessary, encourage them to convene in certain representative meetings or symposiums. But in the organizational system, these people's cultural small groups do not belong to the various cultural groups and still belong to the schools, institutions, the various cultural and educational propaganda departments of the various units and various public organizations, in order to avoid the cultural organizations being busy with the routine organizational work, and affect the completion of the basic tasks of the cultural personalities."

Help Intellectuals to Publish Their Works. "The greatest demand among the cultural personalities and the greatest encouragement for the intellectuals is the publication of their works, so we should pay our full effort to publish their work, such as in the form of publications, opera performances, public lectures, exhibitions, etc. Meanwhile, the publishing of their works is the most important way to promote cultural movement."

Be Concerned About the Material Life of Intellectuals. "In places where there is a greater concentration of cultural centers, there should be places such as cultural clubs for the gathering and entertainment of the cultural personalities, and suitable places for the creation of writers, so that they can calm down and engage in their creative efforts."

Cultivate More Cadres from among the Intellectuals. "Select the young intellectuals who are interested in cultural work to run schools or establish training classes for cultural cadres to cultivate the cultural work of new cadres. It is also very important to select the genius of art in the organs and give them long-term training. It is necessary to encourage intellectuals to take up certain classes of teaching." "Cultivating a small number of cadres who are capable of organizing themselves in the cultural movement, from a culturally or non-Party cultural cadre with considerable prestige and status. Although they are cultural personalities, they should focus on organizational work, not writing. Without these organized cultural workers or cadres, it will be very difficult to give full play to the enthusiasm among cultural personalities and will be very difficult to unite with them. Nowadays, there is a special shortage of such cadres in various cultural movements."[23]

On May 1, 1941, Article 14 of the Outline of the Shaanxi-Gansu-Ningxia Border Region Area Policy approved by the Political Bureau of the Central Committee of the CPC clearly stipulated: "Encourage free study, respect intellectuals, and promote scientific knowledge and literary and artistic movements."[24]

At the same time, the Central Committee of the CPC issued the Decision on Party Members' Participation in Economic and Technical Work, which called for "explaining to the whole Party that various economic and technical works is an indispensable part of the revolutionary work and constitutes a concrete revolutionary work." "All Party members serving in the economic and technical sectors must learn from non-Party and Party specialists." "The Party must strengthen its leadership upon the Party members and non-Party members in the work to be made in the economic and technical sectors take care of their political progress and assist them in all aspects."[25]

In June 10, 1941, *Yan'an Liberation Daily* published an editorial titled as "Welcome the Personnel of Science and Art Talents" , pointed out: "We need to carry out more extensive and more in-depth enlightenment work and look forward to the science and art talents with more willingness to lead the work."

In June 12, 1941, *Yan'an Liberation Daily* published an article titled as stressed again Promote natural science, called for "popularizing the most basic scientific knowledge among the people," "We believe that it is the effectiveness of our efforts which can lead us to the success of this popularization work."

"In the same year, the second session of the Natural Science Research Council in Shaanxi-Gansu-Ningxia Border Region has stressed the

---

23 *Selected Works of Central Committee of Communist Party of China*, Book 12, CPC Central Party School Press, 1991, pp. 496-499.

24 Wu Heng, *Anti Japanese War Period of the History of the Development of Science and Technology in the History of the Data*, Vol. 1, China Academic Press, 1983, p. 69.

25 Ibid., pp. 32-33.

publication of popular science books and called for the promotion of universal scientific knowledge."[26]

On September 17, 1942, the General Political Department of the Eighth Route Army issued directive on the problems of treatment and leadership towards the intellectual cadres, the directive proposed embracing the intellectuals to join our ranks, transformation of their petty bourgeois ideology, and assigning their work, in a proper manner.

During the Yan'an period, the CPC adopted a policy of unity and preferential treatment towards intellectuals, which included the following contents:

First, high degree of political concern towards intellectuals.

The Chinese Communist Party highly affirmed the aims of resistance against Japan and salvation of the country when mobilizing the broad masses of intellectuals in Yan'an and in Shaanxi-Gansu-Ningxia Border Region, with the pursuits of progress and revolution. Mao Zedong and other leaders of the Central Committee of the CPC and the leaders of the Party, government, and the Army of the Shaanxi-Gansu-Ningxia Border Region often took time to visit the representative figures of intellectuals in Yan'an and solicited their opinions and suggestions and encouraged them to work for the construction of the border areas, and encouraged them to contribute to the cause of Chinese revolution. In the practical work, considering the specific talents of the intellectuals they have arranged training classes in various types of cadres' schools, so that the majority of intellectuals could receive the education of Marxism-Leninism and revolutionary theories. All kinds of Party, Government and Army units were encouraged to actively absorb intellectuals with technical expertise as the technical backbone, to actively help them join the ranks of the Communist Party of China. The Party committee of the Shaanxi-Gansu-Ningxia Border Region have stipulated specifically that: "whether in the Army, Government, the salvation groups, the cultural movements, all those personalities who have no Party affiliation and who really struggle for the nation, should be politically pure, should be able to bear hardships and stand hard with communist consciousness, and that "for those intellectuals who are willing to fight for the revolutionary cause of the proletariat, we should absorb them into the Party in large numbers.[27] Party organizations at all levels should actively absorb

26   *Yan'an Natural Science Historical Materials*, Communist Party of China Historical Materials Press, Beijing Institute of Technology Press, 1986, p. 40.
27   Quoted from CPC Yan'an Municipal Committee United Front Department, *United Front Study in the Yan'an Period*, Chinese Press, 2010, p. 316.

intellectuals who have the conditions for joining the Party as party members. Thus 5562 students of Anti-Japanese University of fourth period were enrolled, 530 Party members among 4655 intellectuals initially, and this number increased to 3340 students after graduation, which accounted for the 70% of the total number of intellectuals.[28] The Shaanxi-Gansu-Ningxia Border Region has also encouraged the intellectuals in fully using their democratic rights. In 1941 October, the Deans were elected and employed by the Natural Science Research Institute of the Second Border Region (Shaan-Gan-Ning Border Region), among them were Zhao Yifeng (the director of Border Region Government Construction Bureau of Industry), Lu Zhijun (the Dean of the International Peace Hospital), Dwarkanath Kotnis (the Indian Medical Team to Assist China), Weng Yuan (the director of the Eighth Route Army Pharmaceutical Factory), He Mu (as the pulmonary specialist of the Central Hospital), Dr. Jin Maoyue (the director of Gynecology Department of Central Hospital).[29]

The CPC unceasingly overcame its mistakes when implementing its policy of uniting with intellectuals. In its early history the CPC has made mistakes on the issue of intellectuals. On May 28, 1942, Mao Zedong pointed out in his report to the meeting of the Central Study Group that during the ten years of the first civil war, "at that time, we were isolated from the majority of intellectuals both in the base areas and the central cities, in this period we have made mistakes in the issue of intellectuals, and believed that the intellectuals do not seem to be much of use, if without these mistakes, the situation might be better."[30]

After the outbreak of the Anti-Japanese War, a small number of cadres within the Party still continued to ignore the issue of intellectuals; many cadres coming from the workers and peasants origin looked down on intellectuals, they showed unwillingness to work with intellectuals. Mao Zedong, on behalf of the CPC Central Committee, issued a number of documents, and demanded that the whole Party should attach great importance to intellectuals and should learn and adapt themselves to work with intellectuals. Mao Zedong called the Party cadres at all levels to understand and accommodate the weakness of intellectuals. In his report to the Central Study Group, he pointed out: "In the recent period, some articles and certain literary works have problems, only some of them are good and some comrades have shown dissatisfaction with some matters and have made several comments on them. We are all right to ask these questions and

---

28   Ibid., p. 316.
29   Ibid., p. 317.
30   *Selected Works of Mao Zedong*, Vol. 2, People's Publishing House, 1993, p. 424.

prove that our comrades are worthy of being a political soldier. Although our level of education is low, our political sense of smell is very sensitive, thus we can feel if the atmosphere is not good. While there are all these kinds of problems, many problems in our works, we continue to say that there is no big problem. Why do we say so? Because those comrades are basically revolutionary, they are from rural areas or base areas. There are many people among them who have spent quite a long time in our revolutionary work. As for some articles published at certain times, or comments at a certain time, which is not a big deal since that those problems belong to partial nature, I think these problems can be solved easily, we should not see them as a serious problem .What we should pay attention to is comrade Wang Shimei, his thought is more systematic, it seems there is something bad which is deeper than we see in various other works, others are minor problems which can be solved easily.[31] "This is a transitional period. I think it will take 50 years in China. This is a very complicated process. In our efforts to unite with bourgeois and petty-bourgeois artists and in our efforts to unite them with workers and peasants, some difficulties will be inevitable. Our policy should be to carefully guide them consciously so that they can change their habits of reluctance to work with workers and peasants. Towards those few people who are reluctant to work with us we should adopt a tolerant mind towards them since this is an ideological problem, these people should not be labeled. We cannot adopt a rough attitude toward them. Our general policy is winning the support of writers, artists and help them to unite with the majority of workers and peasants, so that they can distinguish low-level things (works), so that they can fancy mean literary and art works."[32]

In order to unite with the broad masses of intellectuals, Mao Zedong proposed: "We ask our comrades, comrades working in the army, government, education, democracy, Party affairs, to adopt a welcome attitude toward literary and art workers, whether they are low-level or high-level, the correct attitude towards them is very important, we should take a tolerant attitude toward their shortcomings, on the contrary in the sectors of literature and art, they should take same attitude toward the shortcomings of peasants and soldiers. It is inevitable to take the right attitude in the future. Some intellectuals, writers and artists are unwilling to make friends with us, our problems are not only related to intellectuals, writers and artists, some departments also have shortcomings and problems. Since the central of the decision on intellectuals has been published, there are

---

31   Ibid., pp. 426-427.
32   Ibid., pp. 430-431.

some problems which still remain unresolved. Therefore, it is necessary to follow the same principles as the Three Rules of Disciplines and the Eight Points for Attention are emphasized every day, so that the comrades in the military, government, Party affairs, economy and education can take a welcome attitude toward the intellectuals and understand their significance for our cause. Without these people we cannot succeed." "Before the stage of their full knowledge, we still should use other intellectuals. Therefore, so we take it easy, gradually carry out propaganda and education, just a few articles or several speeches cannot make a Rome. In this respect we must work step by step, Rome was not built in a day."[33]

Secondly, boldly use the intellectuals at work.

The Communist Party of China, in accordance with the actual situation in the Border Region, has boldly made use of all kinds of intellectuals and gave full play to their various skills.

July 13, 1942, the Shaanxi-Gansu-Ningxia Border Region Government in accordance with the instructions of the CPC Central Committee, proposed the nomination of director, director of the hospital for the military strategist, engineers, technicians, doctors and other types of personnel based on the their skills rather than their political consciousness thus placed full confidence in them. The instruction said: "For the majority of literary and artistic intellectuals, we should give full play to their literary talent, so that they can organize all kinds of literary and artistic groups, literary magazines, establish the various educational research institutions, and can publish their works freely." Due to benign policies adopted by the CPC, in Yan'an, a secluded town, a variety of institutions, associations, other kind of cultural organizations have sprung up like mushrooms, Yan'an became a city of culture. From 1936 to 1942, the major cultural units in Yan'an included: the Chinese Literature and Art Association, the Shaanxi-Gansu-Ningxia Border Region Cultural Salvation Association (referred to as "Bian Wen Ji"), the Shaanxi- Gansu-Ningxia Border Region Music Salvation Association (later in 1939 its name was changed its name to "the All-China Literary and Art Circle Anti-Japanese Association Yan'an branch"), the Shaanxi-Gansu-Ningxia Border Region Artists Association, the People's Anti-Japanese Dramatic Society of the Border Region (referred to as "Border Region Drama Society"), China Association of Music Composers, Yan'an Culture Music Department, War Songs Society, Anti-Japanese Literature and Art Group, Mountain Literature Society, Literary Group, Public Reading Society, Literary Monthly, Yan'an Poetry Association, Lu

---

33   Ibid., pp. 431-432.

Xun Research Institute, Central Academy of Literature and Art , Fiction Research Society, the Northwest Field Service Corps, Progressive People's Entertainment association, Experimental Theater Group under Yan'an's Lu Xun Academy of Art, Northwest Literary and Artistic Group.

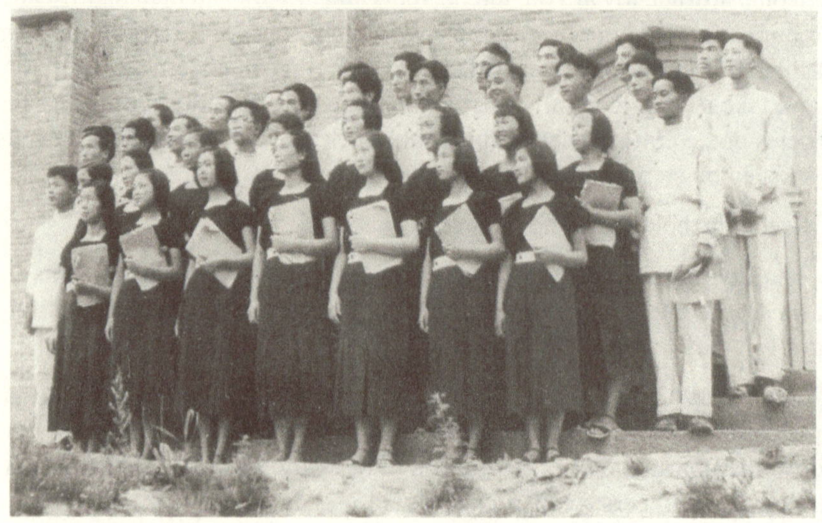

Yan'an's Lu Xun Art College Choir in a performance

In the music, art, film fields, we should note the Yan'an Choir, Yan'an's Association of Music Composers, the Chinese Folk Music Research Association, the Central Philharmonic Orchestra, Lu Xun Art Workshop, the People's Art Research, Publishing Research Group, Anti-Japanese Film Club, the Eighth Route Army Headquarters Film Mission, and Yan'an Film Studio and so on.

The institutions in the field of literature and art include, the Lu Xun Art College (referred to as "Lu Yi" in short), the Yan'an Military Art College (referred to as "Institute"), week art academy, Shaanxi-Gansu-Ningxia Border Region Cadres Art School.

The major cultural and artistic publications the Yan'an period were the *Literary Front, Chinese Culture, Popular Literature, Reader Monthly*, the Journal *Gu Yu, Poetry Monthly*.

It was under the correct policies of the CPC towards the intellectuals that intellectuals, especially the literary and art intellectuals, enjoyed a prestigious status in Yan'an. As the *Liberation Daily* editorial "Welcome the Personnel of Science and Art Talents" wrote: "Only in the border of the anti-Japanese democratic base areas, especially in Yan'an, they have seen the most favorable places for their freedom of mind and boldness." "In Yan'an, all sorts of cultural activities flourish despite that all the difficulties and limitations of objective conditions. Science and art gained their own respect. The freedom of creation of thought is fully guaranteed under the common principle of resistance to Japan. The imagination of art and the design of science can be played in a freeway. "The shortcomings of the Border Region (that is also inevitable in any new society), also need to be reflected from the artistic side. We paid great attention on the 'self-criticism', and especially cherished the true 'artist's courage'."[34]

Thirdly, the preferential treatment in regard to the livelihood conditions of the intellectuals[35.]

During the 1930s and 1940s, Yan'an headquarters and the Shaanxi-Gansu-Ningxia Border Region government were located in remote mountainous areas of China, and the level of economic development was quite low. Especially during the intensive war years, especially during the most difficult period of 1941-1942, under the double military encirclement and economic blockade of Japanese imperialists and the Kuomintang, the Army and people in the Shaanxi-Gansu-Ningxia Border Region had almost no clothes to wear, no food to eat. It was under these conditions that the Chinese Communist Party has done everything possible to ensure the daily livelihood of the intellectuals in the Region so that they could work and create with peace of mind. In order to ensure the preferential livelihood conditions of intellectuals, the Border Region Government, adopted the policy of livelihood as priority and revolutionary cause as supplementary. In the Anti-Japanese War period, the Border Region Government allocated almost the two-thirds of its financial funds to ensure the livelihood of more than 60,000 "public servants". In those days, it was planned that 50,000 people would enjoy average living standards and 10,000 people would be treated with preferential livelihood standards. In 1942, the Border Region Government classified the people resident in the Region into 10 categories and 40 sub-categories according to requirements of living standards: the first category was the international friends of the anti-Japanese War and the ethnic minorities, the second category was the education staff, the third category was the soldiers with honorary titles, the fourth category was technical personnel—medical, nursing, engineers, technicians, etc,

---

34 Article titled as "Welcome the Personnel of Science and Art Talents", *Liberation Daily*, June 10, 1941.
35 This part of the writing quotes parts from the work titled as *United Front Study in the Yan'an Period*, Chinese Press, 2010, pp. 318-319.

the fifth category was the financial and taxation staff, the sixth category was the factory workers of the SOEs, the seventh category was the old and sick, the eighth category was the local non-Party intermediaries, the ninth category was party and government officials, the tenth category was the general staff.

In order to ensure the policy of preferential treatment for the cultural and technical cadres, the CPC Central Committee has also formulated certain measures for this policy which stipulated the following: "the standards of preferential treatment for their livelihood shall be determined according to the level of their abilities and knowledge, and that they and their families will have no worries in respect their daily lives, thus can better concentrate on their work." According to this above spirit, the Border Region Government has classified the cultural and technical personnel according to the criteria of "actual ability, current status and according to their performance" and specifically pointed out: "the preferential treatment should mainly depend on their practical and knowledge abilities rather than their backgrounds". According to the above policies, the Shaanxi-Gansu-Ningxia Border Region government classified the cultural and technical cadres into three categories as A, B and C. Class A included those prestigious personalities in the literary and art circles, their monthly allowance was 15-30 Yuans per person, to ensure their food standards they would be given small cooking stoves, the accommodation supplied to them could be different for each. Jobs should arranged for their families, for example they should be assigned to teach in schools, their relatives should enjoy the same treatment if they fail to do so. Field Ministry of Health of the Eighth Route Army, also classified its medical and technical cadres into three classes, the directive of the Field Ministry of Health said the following: "various classes of technical personnel should receive preferential compensation based on their qualifications, experience, job performances". Class A doctors who graduated from medical schools at home and abroad and who have 3 years of practical work experience, would receive a monthly allowance of 60-80 Yuans, those nurses who are specialized in nursing and graduated from nurse schools would receive a monthly allowance of 20-40 Yuans. Those who are above the level of pharmacys are treathed in a favoried way and the family members of class A doctors are treated the same as themselves. In the Border Region, there were two systems of salaries and allowances for the cultural and educational cadres. Their principal salary (which excludes compensation for their part-time work) was 270 Yuans per month. And those full-time teachers received 200 Yuans per month, 3 Yuans for their class hours, and their class hours would not exceed 18 hours per week.

The regulation also included an allowance of 8 Yuans per month, (12 hours per week) 6 Yuan per month for the ordinary teaching staff, the system also provided public clothes, food, and other kinds of material subsidies. According to the stipulations of the Border District Finance Department, the headmaster and the full-time instructor would get 15 Yuan per month to pay for a vegetable dish. In addition, there will be a remuneration of 2 Yuans per thousand words if the lecture notes are not provided by the school.

From the above we can understand that the preferential treatment for those intellectuals engaged in arts and culture, medicine and health, education, science and technology fields, was far better than the Party and government cadres (for example the Politburo members of the CPC only received 10 Yuans per month at that time) which meant that the Shaanxi–Gansu-Ningxia Border Region paid keen attention to the livelihood of the intellectuals.[36]

The Communist Party of China's preferential treatment policy towards intellectuals not only fully demonstrates its care and respect for the intellectuals, but also enabled the Party to fully mobilize the enthusiasm of the majority of intellectuals, and promoted the cultural construction in the Border Region.

III. Education and remolding of intellectuals

In order to give full play to the special role of intellectuals in the Chinese revolution, the Chinese Communist Party, while uniting with and respecting intellectuals, has enabled the broad masses of intellectuals to gain and establish the Marxist standpoint, viewpoint and methodology, the Party especially educated them with Sinicized Marxism. The Party encouraged them to better unite with the masses of workers and peasants, so that they can change themselves from petty bourgeoisie intellectuals to proletarian intellectuals, which meant a change in their values of life and ideals similar to that of the workers, peasants and soldiers, thus the intellectuals were transformed by education.

The majority of intellectuals had come to Yan'an with a high level of patriotic enthusiasm, and most of them pursued for lofty revolutionary ideals. But their world view was essentially still petty bourgeois, therefore there occurred misunderstandings and conflicts between some intellectuals and some cadres with worker and peasant origin. So the intellectuals

---

36 Quoted from CPC Yan'an Municipal Committee United Front Department, *United Front Study in the Yan'an Period*, Chinese Press, 2010, p. 319.

were faced with the issue of how to unite with those cadres with worker and peasant origin, and how to serve the masses of workers and peasants. Many intellectuals were dissatisfied with the half-hearted war performance of the Kuomintang Party against Japanese aggression, they believed that only the Communist Party really fought for the liberation of the country, and they generally adopted an idealist world outlook and high expectations from the CPC when they had arrived at Yan'an. Wang Shiwei was a representative figure who typically demonstrated the serious shortcomings of these intellectuals. He evaluated the things in Yan'an from a petty bourgeois stand and proposed several flawed and incomplete views about the shortcomings he saw in Yan'an. He published an essay titled as "Wild Lily", which typically reflected his world-view. Wang Shiwei wrote: "Some people say, we have no system of ranks or hierarchical system in Yan'an. But that does not square with the facts, since such a system palpably exists. Another argument goes: Yes, we do have a system of ranks, but it is rational. At this point we should all use our brains and think." "Communism is not the same as egalitarianism, and what is more we are not at present at the stage of carrying through the Communist revolution. I am by no means an egalitarian, but to divide clothing into three and food into five different grades is definitely neither necessary nor rational, especially with regard to clothes. (I myself am graded as 'cadres' clothes and private kitchen', so this is not just a case of sour grapes.) All such problems should be resolved on the basis of need and reason. At present there is no noodle soup for sick comrades to eat and young students only get two meals of thin congee a day (when they're asked whether they have had enough to eat, Party members are expected to lead the rest in a chorus of 'Yes, we're full!')."[37]

Wang Shiwei had different opinions with Li Weihan the director of the Central Research Institute and argued that "the speech content and attitude of Comrade Luo Mai who still retain the old style of the Party, which weakened the enthusiasm of the masses in fighting against the Japanese aggressors."[38] Wang Shiwei also argued: "Rickets itself is a kind of evil, we must be tough". He finished his article saying: Attacking a person with rumors is the meanest, dirtiest act. Wang Shiwei is full of self-confidence. "His bones have never been soft and are not softer than anyone else!"[39]

---

37   Wang Shiwei, *Wild Lily*, see book by Liu Zengjie, *Historical Data of the Literary Movement during the Anti-Japanese War Period and the Anti-Japanese Democratic Base Areas*, Intellectual Property Press, 2010, pp. 316-317.
38   Ibid., p. 322.
39   Ibid., pp. 324, 326.

These remarks of Wang Shiwei were imbued with hostile feelings against the leadership, and his remarks had provoked emotional disgust of some leading comrades."[40] Against the mistaken thoughts and attitude of Wang Shiwei, we had adopted a full-blown concentrated criticism, which was an improper method, and after such criticism sessions he was labeled as a "Trotskyist" and counter-revolutionary, I think these were our mistakes under specific historical conditions. In July 1, 1947, he was executed, which was absolutely wrong.

Mao Zedong didn't know about the execution of Wang Shiwei. Just about six months after the event, when he heard about it he was extremely furious, he ordered "I want Wang Shiwei back." Several comrades around Mao Zedong told him about the events related to Wang Shiwei. We know that, Mao Zedong rarely got angry, but once he was angry it would be impossible to control him. Based on the published memories related with these events above, "Mao Zedong was extremely angry, the sharp criticism of the relevant cadres was inevitable.[41] In 1992, the Ministry of Public Security fairly rectified the wrong case of Wang Shiwei.

The above issues in regard to intellectuals were particularly evident among literary and art intellectuals. Before the rectification movement had started, there were several shortcomings in their way of thinking, which was mainly caused by the effect of bourgeois and petty-bourgeois world-view among the literary and art workers, they often unconsciously expressed some views and attitudes which contradicted the interests of revolution and the interest of the workers and peasants. Some of them advocated the establishment of an "artistic view of life," and suggested that "art should guide politics", they openly argued that the petty bourgeois writers had always been the main force of the Chinese literary movement. The essential source of these issues of thinking among them was their separation from the masses, their separation from the reality, serious dogmatism in their works in the fields of education and art, and they inappropriately emphasized "formalism". Lu Xun Art Institute was located in the Dongchuan district of Yan'an 15 miles far from the bridge in the ditch at that time, the tutors lived around the school compound. However, they often worked behind the closed doors and performed and displayed their skills inside the auditorium. In those days, the villagers around the Institute knocked the doors and criticized them saying: "improve behind the doors."

---

40   Fan Wenlan, Speech at the Academia Sinica Symposium on June 11, *Liberation Daily*, June 29, 1942.

41   Zhuan quoted from the book written by Zhang Zhiqing, Sun Li, Bai Juntang, *The Period Before and After Yan'an Rectification*, Jiangsu Literature and Art Publishing House, 1994, p. 194.

When they arranged artistic performances in the countryside, they often chose foreign subjects to perform which villagers could not understand, or grasp fully, which arose their strong complaints. At evening of January 26, 1938, the Poetry Association of War Song" club of the poetry organization held a "New Poetry Reading Evening". Three hundred tickets were issued for the evening and Mao Zedong had attended this "Reading Evening" personally. An embarrassing scene took place during the event, people gradually dispersed, and finally only less than 100 people remained in the venue. As the most important guest, Mao Zedong remained seated and "listened without move," "until the event ended." Afterwards, the organizers of the event ashamedly commented admit: "This has been the worst performance in Yan'an during the last several months."[42]

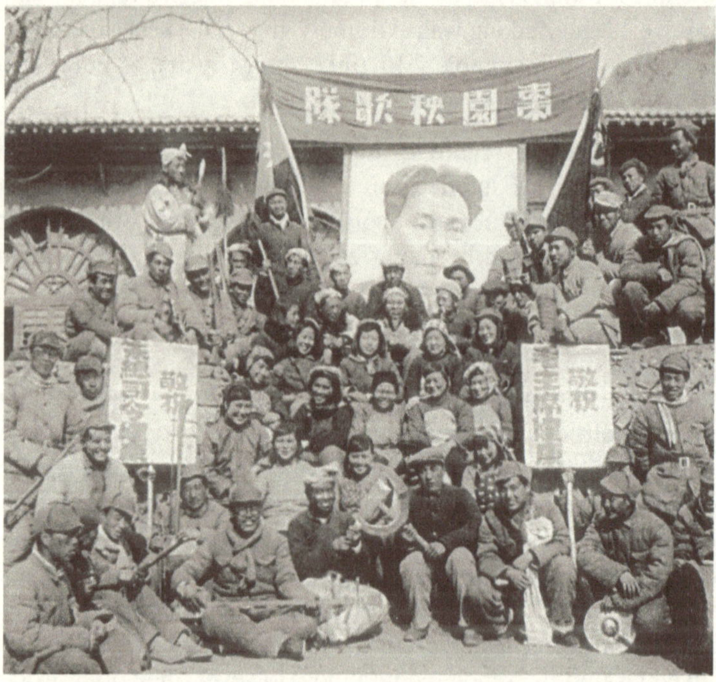

The new Yangge movement throughout the Spring Festival was held in 1944 and 1945, the workers, farmers, soldiers, shopkeepers, students of Shaanxi-Gansu-Ningxia Border Region extensively took part in these Festival activities. The photo shows the "jujube yangko dance team" which was personally named by Mao Zedong.

---

42   Luo Fang, *Poetry Folk Songs Concert Event, Third Period in the Battlefield*, April 20, 1938.

At the same time, we should also see that the revolutionary intellectuals also demonstrated strong willingness to transform themselves ideologically. Lu Xun, the first person in the history of Chinese literature who put a peasant as the main character of his novel,[43] also admitted: "although I tried to explore the souls of people, regretfully I had always kept some distance with them".[44] Such literature and art personalities have taken "individual creation as their central concern, and aimed at a perfect description of individuals' goals in their lives, they ignored the lives of masses," this kind of "thinking only knows heroes, but ignores the masses, they only recognize the individuals, but ignore the collective" we know that "individualism" in creation contradicts with the requirements of "revolutionary literature"[45]. Revolutionary intellectuals demonstrated dissatisfaction with this type of idealistic world outlook which pursued the "marriage between the requirements of literature and requirements of politics."[46]

They took Ding Ling's sayings as an example and believed in them: "A novel is not enough, I want a truly down-to-earth revolutionary work," "I am willing to play the role of "revolutionary screw", "I regard the society as a machine, the revolution is the driving force of this machine, it is necessary to work like a machine and a gear." This passion was general and not only restricted with Ding Ling, alone.[47]

Regarding the problems seen within the literary and art circles, the CPC Central Committee, represented by Mao Zedong, was very concerned and tried hard to guide the literary and art work and sought proper solutions. Mao Zedong in the second phase of the opening ceremony, demanded the following from the educated youth: "Resist to a university like a whetstone, which grinded the petty bourgeoisie, a feeling of impulse, brutal impetuous, impatient, and finally turn yourselves into a sharp knife, in order to innovate the society and fight against the Japanese aggressors."[48]

On May 1938, Mao Zedong warned the literary and art workers of the Lu Yi (Lu Xun Academy): "go deeper into the people's lives," "acting like Northern people" and not "no workers, peasants in the eyes," "Our Comrades do not teach Lin Daiyu, but only cry."[49] Mao Zedong also

---

43   Wang Yao, *Works of Lu Xun*, People's Literature Publishing House, 1984, p. 55.
44   *Complete Works of Lu Xun*, Vol. 7, People's Literature Publishing House, 1981, p. 82.
45   Jiang Guangci, On the Revolutionary Literature, *Sun Monthly*, No. 2, February 1, 1928.
46   Yang Yi, History of Modern Chinese Fiction, Vol. 2, People's Literature Publishing House, 1986, p. 44.
47   Helen Foster Snow (Nym Wales), *Inside Red China*, People's Liberation Army Literature and Art Publishing House, 2002, p. 263.
48   *New China Daily*, July 7, 1937.
49   See He Qifang's article The Song of Mao Zedong, *Journal of Report of the Times*, 1980(1).

carefully studied the works of some influential intellectuals in the literary and art circles and communicated with them. The famous writer Xiao Jun's works were one of them an example. On August 2, 1941, Mao Zedong sent a letter to Xiao Jun:

I have read you two letters and sent you the books that you want. Due to lack of deeper communication with you, I have some suggestions for you, but I am afraid it is not the time since this word is some kind of superficial, which may disturb your future works and can cause some misunderstandings between us. There are numerous bad phenomena in Yan'an, what you wrote to me, are worth considering, these bad phenomena should be corrected. But I advise you at the same time to pay attention to some of your own problems, do not look at the problems absolutely and one-sidedly, be patient, pay attention to conditions that determine the human relationships, consciously and meticulously examine your weaknesses, thus you will see that there is a way out as a result of it. Otherwise you will suffer and feel great pain every day, and will never not feel at ease. You are a very frank person, and I think I can talk to you, above I have given you my suggestions. If you agree, I'd like to communicate with you again.[50]

In June 1940, Zhu De, the commander-in-chief of the Eighth Route Army, pointed to the three deficiencies within the literary and art circles of Yan'an in his speech given at the second anniversary of the establishment of the Lu Yi's (Lu Xun Academy): firstly, the literature and art workers in Yan'an were not "good propagandists"; secondly, their works were only suitable for a few people"; thirdly, most writers dislike the "national and folk" forms and "want to abandon such forms". Zhu De proposed three points: "adapt yourselves to the lives of the collective", avoid to become " narrow" minded individuals seeking small benefits and "be modest and learn from the masses," "Do not think about the old articles 'for your sakes", "we should learn how to fight and the military issues" and also take participate in the actual work armed struggle."[51] In those days, the New China Daily reported the following words of Zhu De:

"In front of us, we take the gun to play very lively, you play with the pen also bustling, but not good enough in this field, and we hope that both the front areas and rear areas, and both the pole of the gun and the pen can be intimately united". "Over the three years of battle, there are so many stories for songs, although a lot of heroic soldiers have sacrificed their lives in the

---

50   *Selected Letters of Mao Zedong*, People's Publishing House, 1983, p. 174.

51   Zhu De, *Three years of propaganda in North China's art work*, see Jin Ziguang, He Luo editor of *Yan'an Literature Series Literature and Art Theory* Volume Hunan Literature and Art Publishing House, 1987, p. 104-107.

battlefields, we do not know their surnames, this is our sin, but also the culprit of your art.[52]

In order to further solve the problems of work within the literary and art circles, the CPC Central Committee held the Yan'an literary forums. There were three consecutive meetings, in May 2, 16 and 23 of the year 1942. In May 23, Mao Zedong delivered his famous speech in the Yan'an Literature and Art Symposium which was later published on the 28th. The speech clearly pointed out: The purpose of our meeting today is precisely to ensure that literature and art fit well into the whole revolutionary machine as a component part, that they operate as powerful weapons for uniting and educating the people and for attacking and destroying the enemy, and that they help the people fight the enemy with one heart and one mind. What are the problems that must be solved to achieve this objective? I think they are the problems of the class stand of the writers and artists, their attitude, their audience, their work and their study. Mao Zedong also clearly put forward the idea that literature and art works should serve the masses, he broadest sections of the people, constituting more than 90% of the total population that is the workers, peasants and soldiers. Evaluating the ideas put forward by Mao Zedong's, the famous writer Xiao Jun commented: "Mao Zedong has analyzed the problems in a profound way, consequently he had a good grasp of the issues prevalent among the literary and art circles."[53]

During the speech at the Yan'an Symposium on Literature and Art, Mao Zedong talked about the sentiments, the works, the actions and the views on the guiding principles for literature and art of the literary and art workers, he said: today, writers who cling to an individualist, petty-bourgeois stand cannot truly serve the masses of revolutionary workers, peasants and soldiers. Their interest is mainly focused on the small number of petty-bourgeois intellectuals. This is the crucial reason why some of our comrades cannot correctly solve the problem of "for whom?" In saying this I am not referring to theory. In theory, or in words, no one in our ranks regards the masses of workers, peasants and soldiers as less important than the petty-bourgeois intellectuals. I am referring to practice, to action." and explicitly demanded that their position, acts and sentiments should change from one class to another, our literary and art workers must accomplish this task and shift their stand; they must gradually move their feet over to the side of the workers, peasants and soldiers, to the side of the proletariat. He added: "Our literary and artistic workers of intellectual origin, in order to make their works become popular among the masses, you have to make a change in your thoughts and

---

52 *New China Daily,* June 18, 1940.
53 *Anecdotes of Mao Zedong,* Central University for Nationalities Press, 2012, p. 124.

sentiments, encounter a transformation. Only by speaking for the masses can he educate them and only by being their pupil can he be their teacher. If he regards himself as their master, as an aristocrat who lords it over the "lower orders", then, no matter how talented he may be, he will not be needed by the masses and his work will have no future."[54]

About the issue of united front in cultural work, Mao Zedong once again stressed the importance of literary and art work for the people and the mass line. He said: "Our cultural workers must serve the people with great enthusiasm and devotion, and they must link themselves with the masses, not divorce themselves from the masses. In order to do so, they must act in accordance with the needs and wishes of the masses. All work done for the masses must start from their needs and not from the desire of any individual, however well-intentioned." "This is true in any kind of work, and particularly in the cultural and educational work the aim of which is to transform the thinking of the masses. There are two principles here: one is the actual needs of the masses rather than what we fancy they need, and the other is the wishes of the masses, who must make up their own minds instead of our making up their minds for them."[55]

Thus, Mao Zedong also proposed brilliant ideas on the two principles of the united front in cultural work: "There are two principles for the united front: the first is to unite, and the second is to criticize, educate and transform." On May 28, 1942, Mao Zedong continued to talk about on the problem of the integration of literary and art workers with the workers, peasants and soldiers in the report of the Central Study Group Meeting held at the Yan'an Literature and Art Symposium. Mao Zedong pointed out in his speech: "The CPC Central Committee already made its decision on the issue of intellectuals, but we still do not have a unified and good decision on the work of literature and art, and now we are ready to make such a decision, so we have convened three symposiums. There are more than a hundred comrades and friends attended these symposiums, among them, some of them were outside the Party, and this was quite well, the purpose of the symposiums were to solve the problem of integration, that is, the unity between the writers, artists, art workers and the cadres of our Party, the integration of the workers and peasants, and the integration of the officers and men of the armed forces." "How do we unite the two?" There are two aspects of work, one is for the writers, artists, workers, they should work with the comrades of the army, the comrades of Party work, the comrades of political work, the comrades of economic work; another is

---

54   *Selected Works of Mao Zedong*, Vol. 3, People's Publishing House, 1991, p. 851.
55   Ibid. p. 1013. Retrieved from http://www.beersandpolitics.com/discursos/mao.

for other people, ask them to contact with writers, artists, In short, we have to do work in two ways, tell the two sides what attitude they should take."[56]

Mao Zedong pointed out in his speech that the literary and art workers should realize the need to integrate with the workers, peasants and soldiers. "One of the fundamental problems in resolving ideological problems is to break the influence of bourgeois ideology and petty-bourgeois ideology, in this way we can promote the proletarian ideology among our ranks and promote the advance nature of the Marxism-Leninist Party. Only, after solving these ideological issues, can we ideologically unite with the proletariat and the masses of workers and peasants. Only with such a foundation, will it be possible to realize the integration with workers, peasants, soldiers, and our Party. If this problem is not resolved, we are always out of their circle. A person engaged in a cause for a long time, will have a lot of habits, including many biases. A number of literary workers were educated and grown up in the feudal society under the rule of the Kuomintang, they bear the influences of the old society, some people were more influenced by the old society, some less, some people are shallower, some are deeper, they have different levels, and if they were not guided properly these bad phenomena will gradually turn to conscious destruction and attack against the proletarian ideology, on the other hand these shortcomings will become an obstacles for the through union of these comrades with the workers, peasants and the Party cadres in their actions, or hinder the pace of this unity process. Therefore, in rectifying the three mistakes, all comrades must be reorganized and unite with the literary and art circles, with the goal of breaking down bourgeois ideology and petty-bourgeois ideology into proletarian ideology."[57]

Mao Zedong hoped that the literary and art workers should learn from the broad masses of workers, peasants and soldiers. "Literature and art workers should learn from the workers, peasants and soldiers, and make friends with them, like brothers and sisters. If we don't value the contempt, it would become a bias, which undermines the revolution (of course the degree of negligence have different levels) if we discuss the case of bias, that is a serious case, but it doesn't mean that everyone have this bias, but there are many people who ignore this revolutionary bias, they ignore the study of Marxism-Leninism, ignore to break the bourgeoisie and the petty-bourgeoisie ideas by relying on Marxism-Leninism, their thoughts and actions are not in unity, and they want to do what they wish and please. This is the separation of theory and practice. Although they work for the workers

---

56   *Mao Zedong Collection,* Vol. 2, People's Publishing House, 1993, pp. 425-426.
57   Ibid. p. 426.

and peasants, those many comrades who come from the petty bourgeoisie origin and being themselves intellectuals, seek friends only among intellectuals On the other hand, these comrades seldom come into contact with the masses of workers, peasants and soldiers, do not understand or study them, do not have intimate friends among them, they have only very few friends from among the workers and peasants, in their minds they want to serve the workers and peasants, but they lack a good understanding of the workers and peasants. In fact, this idea is not complete, they lack a thorough understanding of the revolution. This bias in the minds of comrades within the literature and art circles is very common, and we should conduct a thorough review of it.[58]

After the Yan'an Literature and Art Symposium, a rectification movement was carried out among the intellectual circles. Rectification movement was a profound ideological emancipation and transformation movement within the broad masses of intellectuals. It was also a general movement of Marxist education, especially of the Chinese Marxism – the educational movement of Mao Zedong Thought, which played an important role in the remolding and ideological transformation of the broad masses of intellectuals. Yan Yu-Chang, the president of Yan'an University when evaluating the result of the rectification movement among the Yan'an University teachers and students, said the following: "The rectification movement has been a great exercise and experience for us to learn how to be a human being, how to do things, it can be said that the great transformation of mankind is a great thing." "This rectification movement has a great historical significance.... Consequently it has laid a solid foundation for our school."[59]

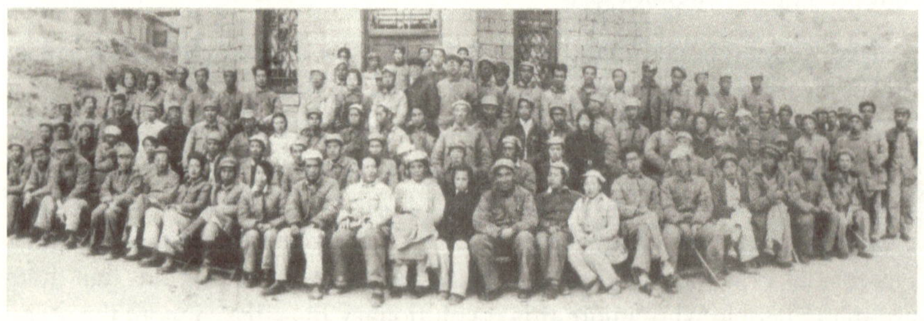

The photo taken in May 1942, includes Mao Zedong, Zhu De,
Ren Bishi, Wang Jiaxiang and other participants who participated in
the symposium of literary and art workers in Yan'an Yang Jialing.

---

58   *Mao Zedong Collection,* Vol. 2, People's Publishing House, 1993, p. 428.
59   Quoted from Zeng Lu Ping's book *Yan'an University History*, People's Publishing House, 2008, p. 73.

At the same time, we have to admit that in the late period of the Yan'an rectification movement, due to Kang Sheng's mistakes, a lot of intellectuals were executed. On May 24, 1944, at the opening ceremony held in Yan'an University, Mao Zedong was there and made an apologetic speech for the maltreatment of intellectuals: "The rectification has been successful, the trialing process has also made achievements, but in regard to rescue movement, I will give you a hat-line trip." Next, Mao Zedong took his hat off and bowed deeply to everyone.[60] "The atmosphere in meeting room suddenly became warmer Mao Zedong's words and gesture was responded with a prolonged warm applause, then all the participants sang the East is Red." "Especially those comrades who were wrongly attacked, they were singing louder with tears of excitement."[61]

Organizationally, in order to guarantee the implementation of popularization of literature and art works, the Chinese Communist Party has adopted a series of measures. The first was to organize a representative conference of labor heroes including the literary and art workers, so that they can better understand the masses, so that they can better approach to creative themes. The Party held a mobilization meeting with the theme of "go to the countryside", and more than 50 literary and art workers took part in this meeting. In October 1943, the speeches made in the Yan'an Literature and Art Symposiums were published, the Central Propaganda Department issued a "decision on the implementation of the Party policy on literature and art", which also determined the slogan of "going to the countryside" and this slogan was widely spread the Shaanxi-Gansu-Ningxia Border Region. "Go to the countryside "to observe, experience, and study." " "Go to the countryside, to factories, and to fighting troops and become part of the masses!" which become the action slogan of cultural workers in the Jiefang District. The broad masses of literary and art workers consciously began to learn from the thoughts and sentiments of masses of the people, consciously studied their language and tastes, and learn to transform the masses of literature and art. In the Shaanxi-Gansu-Ningxia Border Region, many literary and art workers carried their backpacks to the countryside, to the factories and to the fighting troops. Among them were: the poet Xiao San, Ai Qing, playwright (also music composer) Sai Ke went to Nanniwan Gorge, the writers Liu Baiyu, Ding Ling, Chen Xuezhao went to the countryside and lived among the troops, Liu Qing, went to the *Longdong* basin which is located in west of the Loess Plateau to experience life there and

---

60   Quoted from the book edited by Zhang Zhiqing, Sun Li, and Bai Juntang, *Before and After the Yan'an Rectification,* Jiangsu Literature and Art Publishing House, 1994, p. 194.
61   Wang Yunfeng, *History of Yan'an University*, Shaanxi People's Education Press, 1994, p. 95.

improve his creation. Yan'an musicians also put forward the slogan "go to the streets, to the factories". The drama teams often performed their plays in the villages and in forecourts of factories. Painters carried their drawing boards, to the factories and rural areas and took the masses of workers and peasants as the subject of their drawings and paintings.

The Spring Festival of 1943 marked the beginning of Yangko opera[62], performances in the Border Region. On February 9, Mao Zedong watched the well-known Yangko opera called "Brothers and Sisters Wasteland" and was greatly satisfied, he said: "Look, this opera serves the workers and peasants!" He also praised the art workers going to countryside, saying: now the artists that have isolated themselves in the caves have moved to the streets."[63]

The workers, peasants, soldiers, shopkeepers, students widely participated the Yangge activities during the Spring Festivals of the new year 1944 and 1945, in the Shaanxi-Gansu-Ningxia Border Region. According to the data at that time, "Yangko teams" became popular in almost every village and town, even a Yangko dance team consisting of 1,500 people was formed. At the same time, there are 124 music classes, 62 shadow classes, with the audience of 8 million or more.[64]

Mao Zedong had timely encouraged the unity of writers and workers and keenly created the conditions which could enable the unity of literary and art workers with the workers and peasants. On February 23, 1945, Mao Zedong wrote to the famous writer Xiao: "Your first step is quite good. Your attitude is quite different from your first few years in Yan'an, your last article is honest, earnest, lively and vigorous. Of course, your articles in the past were also good, but now they are better, I learned a lot from these articles. In order to spread the spirit of the Yan'an Forum on Literature and Art certain comrades should participate in mass meetings, we should see that Comrade Gao Gang, Jia Tuofu, Tan Zheng, Luo Mai, Li Fuchun and Peng Zhen will participate in them. For such meetings, do not forget to invite these comrades. Please tell them about it, I will also tell them if I have chance.[65]

---

62   This is a kind of national opera which use the folk music as the material and pay equal attention to singing, talking and dancing, is deeply loved by Chinese masses.

63   See the book *Record of the rise of the Yan'an Literary Movement*, Beijing Culture and Arts Publishing House, 1987, p. 419.

64   Quoted from CPC Yan'an Municipal Committee United Front Department, *United Front Study in the Yan'an Period*, Chinese Press, 2010, p. 352.

65   *Letters of Mao Zedong*, People's Publishing House, 1983, p. 258.

The remolding and transformation of intellectuals in the Border Region has enriched the rural cultural life in the liberated areas. Wang Chun made some descriptions regarding the changes in rural culture in the article of continue to seize the position of feudal culture: "We have the labor heroes who turned from the witch, and we have the doctors who voluntarily came to the countryside to serve the people for medical treatment. The tube pot has disappeared, mud master disappeared because the plague of locust is seriously less, so the locust temple did not incense, because the droughts are really hindered, so the ranks of prayer rain meetings are not crowded any longer, instead people participate in the peasant unions, trade unions, there are no meetings of guns and Buddhist. People are enthusiastic to learn more about the current affairs, and no longer use the push back map, they no more read Dongfang Shuo books, they tear the gods together, and replaced it with the portrait of Chairman Mao, and they have also demolished the kitchen god, and replaced it by the farm calendar. And they have given up reading and learning from Mingxianji. And each county has almost fifty or sixty theaters, and more than a hundred or more arts troops."[66]

Famous cartoonist Hua Junwu later recalled the following:

"I most want to say that the "Speeches in the Yan'an Forum on Literature" has solved the question of whom to serve with literary and works, which was the question in our country for thousands of years. This speech has opened an epoch-making chapter. I felt very excited as I have read the speech for the first time but was not fully indulged as those people who usually immediately accept the new ideas. I have pondered on it for several years and gradually grasped its essence."

"First of all, the Speeches solved the question of the position of subject who created the literary and art works. I went to Yan'an with the position of the petty bourgeoisie, my stand was simply the national stand against the imperialism and feudalism. The symposium called us to become acquainted with the people's life and learn their language. The author of the book, "Hero of the New Heroes" properly included the vivid language of the common people in his work, and I also gradually learned to collect the ideas of common people, I realized the importance of Sinicization and popularization of literature and art, both of which have their own connotations and cannot be separated from each other. When creating popular paintings, it is very important for the artists to have a good understanding of the Chinese characteristics, I gradually came to understand that our literary and artistic creation must serve the people reflect the voice of the people and reflect the pulse of times."

66 Quoted from CPC Yan'an Municipal Committee United Front Department, *United Front Study in the Yan'an Period*, Chinese Press, 2010, p. 353.

"In 1942, Cai Ruohong, Zhang E and I held the "Three Man Satirical Cartoon Show" in Yan'an, which caused a sensation in Yan'an, Chairman Mao came to see it. He spoke a lot, I was very astonished, and in some way I felt ignorant and confused. I only remember the cartoon which described of the development of God, and later I drew a cartoon book, "the Tree on the Edge of the Yan River", the photo is only a bare tree. It was a satirical description of trees regardless of cultivation. Chairman Mao said after reading: The trees along the river are dead, but trees of Wang Jiaping are growing up, which is not good to say which paragraph, we should pay attention to distinguish between the individual and general, partial and universal relations. The artists should always consider the people, our purpose is to educate them. Chairman Mao's personal guidance made me become clearly aware that in the creation of cartoons I should not only to solve the problem of service subject, but also how to understand the true problem. For revolutionary writers and artists, the targets for exposure can never be the masses, but only the aggressors, exploiters and oppressors and the evil influence they have on the people."

"Before I thought that the most important thing in my works is to express lives of those I am familiar with, draw cartoons on how they observe things. Now a lot of literary and artistic works lack the required quality, the solution can only be found by strengthening the flesh-and-blood ties with the masses of the people, and sincerely learn from the people. Nowadays, there are few people mentioning the aim of serving the people in literary and art creation and think that the significance of "the Speech" is outdated. Today, while the literary and art circles are confused on these issues, we should use the ideas in the "Speech" advocate the spirit therein and ponder more about it."

"The most memorable was the characteristics of environment and atmosphere in Yan'an. At that time, although the conditions were very difficult the people there were full of optimism. People's ideological level, their national self-esteem, self-confidence were enhanced, first of all the ideological level of literary and art workers, their self-esteem and self-confidence were enhanced."[67]

Famous writer Ding Ling summed up the achievements of literary and art movement which vigorously approached the workers, peasants and soldiers, as follows: "The new wood carving, which closely united with the masses of people and which reflected the struggles of the masses has emerged under the skilled knife of Gu Yuan, Yan Han, and others. Ai Qing wrote a song regarding the *model workers*, Li Ji wrote new folk song about

---

67   Hua Junwu, *Patch Set*, Xuelin Press, 1997, pp. 10-11.

the love between Wang Gui and Li Xiangxiang, Ouyang Shan wrote the interview which praised the heroes from a class aspect and reflected the new life in the northern Shaanxi region. Secondly, many revolutionary authors wrote a variety of works, such as short stories, novels, and folk stories, which depicited the war of resistance against Japan and the twists and turns in the class struggles as the theme, and these works have gradually met with the reader masses. At this time, the Yang song has developed into a lively, fresh little opera from the primary development through the unity and cooperation, transformation, which displayed the level of improvement among the amateur literary workers. When the Yangko opera called "Brothers and Sisters Wasteland" – by Zhao Fugui, Liu Shunqing – was performed or the opera called "Niu Yonggui's Injury" was performed the people who heard sound of the gongs and drums, poured into the square leaving their caves where they lived. Although it was cold winter day in northern Shaanxi, people's hearts became warmer and warmer by the lively and emotional atmosphere of the performance space and that scene have always remained in the memories of actors and the audience, such kind of entertainment enjoy will make people unforgettable. As for the operas called "Blood-and-Tears Revenge" and the "White-haired Girl", I can say that they were indispensable spiritual nurture for the vast rural areas, these works from the old to the fashion, old to the new, both old and fashion were really the new works which on behalf of that era, and have gained great popularity among the masses."[68] "These brilliant cultural achievements which started first from Yan'an has affected all the liberated areas, and also the white areas under the control of Chiang Kai-shek, these brilliant works have made a great contribution to the victory of the revolutionary war, meanwhile, they have laid the building blocks for the development of art and literature in the period after the establishment of new China.[69]

As Yukio Abe said in an article on literature and art published after the Yan'an Forum: "I think that the new literature of China, represented by the literature and created in the Shaanxi-Gansu-Ningxia Border Region, can become a world literature due to its self-creation".[70]

The author Gong Yun is associate researcher in Institute of Marxism attached to Chinese Academy of Social Sciences

---

68   Ding Ling, General Preface in *Yan'an Literature and Art Series*, as part of the Yan'an Literature Series, Hunan People's Publishing House, 1985 pp. 6 7.
69   Ibid., p. 34.
70   See article in *Journal of Yan'an Literature and Art*, 1988(2).

3

Three Issues of State Monopoly in the Purchasing and Marketing of Grain

Tang Zhengmang, Mo Qinghong

The state monopoly in the purchasing and marketing of grain can be considered to be one of the most important policies or systems that are of great concern after the founding of New China. It has existed for about 40 years, involving people across the country, and also has an important effect on China's politics, economy, society and even ideology and culture. Besides, the state monopoly upon the purchasing and marketing of grain had a significant effect on the formation and development of China's economic and political systems, as well as on the changes in the social structure of China. Therefore, studies on this topic are given a lot of attention. However, people hold various opinions on this matter. Regardless of people's comment, we must admit that the state monopoly upon the purchasing and marketing of grain has a close relation with historical facts during China's development:

Firstly, the state monopoly upon the purchasing and marketing of grain has caused the situation of food crisis because of purchasing less and marketing more, which plays a very important role for maintaining social and political stability and consolidating newly-born people's political power during the early days after the nation's founding.

Secondly, it has guaranteed the basic food demand of the nation for a long time (except the years of Great Chinese Famine), and maintains social stability in food demand during those periods which China was in shortage economy mode, including 10 years of the "Great Culture Revolution of China".

Thirdly, the state monopoly upon the purchasing and marketing of grain has effectively supported Three Great Transformations, thus promoted the establishment of the basic system of socialism.

Fourthly, this policy has helped us in accumulating funds for industrialization and accelerated the industrialization process in China, which has played an important role for realizing Chinese people's desire—picking off poor cap and establishing the prestigious status of new China in the world arena.

Besides, there are several basic issues to analyze concretely based on historical circumstances and conditions at that time. First, realizing industrialization was the only way for new China to change its poor and backward situation, and implementing the state monopoly upon purchasing and marketing of grain was also an inevitable choice so as to realize industrialization; second, peasants were not always dissatisfied with the state monopoly upon purchasing and marketing of grain which was implemented for 32 years. With the continuous improvement and perfection of that policy, peasants have begun to understand and support it. Thirdly, after the rural reform, that is, implementation of the system of fixed output quotas for individual households, although the government still conducted the policy of state monopoly upon the purchasing and marketing of grain, the yield of grain continued to increase rapidly, which the negative influences of the state monopoly upon the purchasing and marketing of grain were limited for restricting the effect of law of value or dampening peasants' enthusiasm to produce. This paper intends to make some analysis and discussion on the latter three issues.

I. New China's Industrialization Strategy and the State Monopoly upon the Purchasing and Marketing of Grain

It would be quite easy to see, from the perspective of China's industrialization to interpret the state monopoly upon purchasing and marketing of grain, that a industrialization strategy was an inevitable choice Chinese Communists after the founding of our nation, and implementing the state monopoly upon purchasing and marketing grain was in conformity with the objective requirements of China's industrialization strategy and was also an inevitable choice for Chinese Communists in the face of grain issue. The state monopoly upon purchasing and marketing of grain has provided abundant funds for China's industrialization, making a significant contribution to the industrialization process.

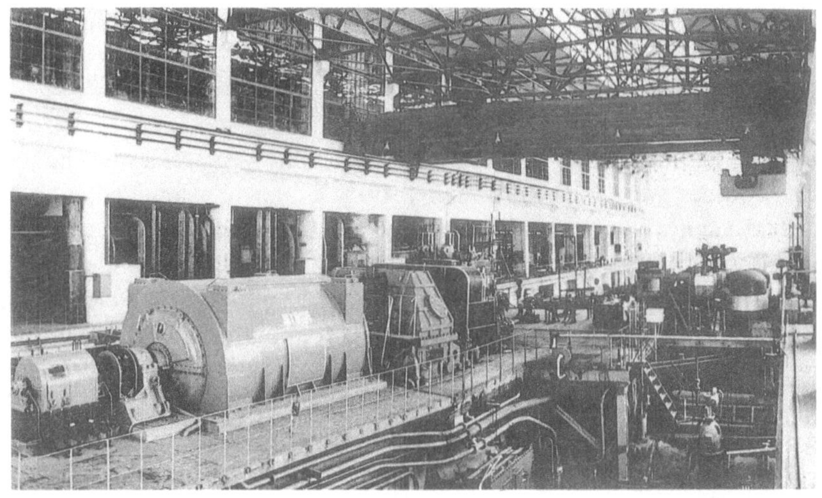

A number of new national key enterprises was built during the "First Five-Plan" period, establishing a relatively integrated basic industrial system. Above is No.1 unit in Wuhan thermal power plant, which was built in November, 1955 and formally started to generate electricity on August 20, 1957.

I. Historical background of the state monopoly of purchasing and marketing of grain: objective requirements of New China's industrialization

Lagging behind leaves a country vulnerable to attacks, which is the most painful lesson the Chinese people have learned since the Opium War. Hence, realizing China's rapid industrialization was the ideal of many progressive who pursued lofty ideals. Since the new democratic revolution period, faced with weak productive forces and backward weapons and equipment, Chinese Communists begin to think about how to realize China's industrialization.

However, having been bullied by almost all advanced countries for centuries, China's powers and people's financial resources were exhausted before she finally won the rights of equal development. As Fei Zhengqing mentioned, "In 1949, China's national economy was near collapse when the Chinese Communist Party replaced the Kuomintang rule. That was a long-term economic structural issue inherited from the pre-modern period, such as low per capita income, short life-span of it population, low fund accumulation and low investment rates, and traditional production methods were prevalent. Those characteristics were interwoven with problems caused by civil and foreign aggression which targeted China for over 20 years, which had caused losses of the manpower and material resources, and hyperinflation."[1]

Above-mentioned factors had led to extreme poverty in China, specifically in the following aspects:

Firstly, the foundation of the national economy was weak and the productive forces were backward. When New China was founded in 1949, the total value of agricultural output across the whole country was only 46.6 billion RMB, which was only 64% of that in 1936. The steel output was 158,000 tons; the output of pig-iron was 252,000 tons; the electric energy production was 4.3 billion KWH; the coal output was 32.43 million tons; the production of cotton yarn was 1.8 million pieces; the crude oil output was 120,000 tons; the cement output was 660,000 tons. Especially in agricultural production, compared with 1936, in 1949, the number of main farm tools around the country had decreased by 30%; the number of farm animals had decreased by 16%; and the food production had decreased by 24.5%. Such low productive forces made it impossible for new China to catch up with the level of productive forces in the developed capitalist countries, and China's productive forces were even lower than that of India which had just achieved independence. By the end of 1952, although the speed of China's economic recovery and development was rapid, the economic gap between the new China and those of the world's major economic powers was still big, since China's economic foundation was too weak.

Secondly, the economic development pattern was extremely unreasonable and imbalanced. From the perspective of regional economic distribution, by the end of 1952, 72% of national industries was concentrated in the coastal areas or Northeast areas of China, and most provinces located in the inland areas, excluding Sichuan, Hubei and Shanxi provinces, were almost blank in industrial development. Across mainland China, 94% of the rail length was concentrated in Eastern China, and 80% of power generating equipment and generating capacity was concentrated in the Northeast and Eastern coastal regions of China. From the perspective of industrial structure, in 1949, the value of agricultural production and the value of industrial output accounted for 70% and 30% respectively of the gross output value of industry and agriculture, especially the proportion of heavy industry was only 7.9%. By the end of 1952, the value of agricultural production and the value of industrial output accounted for 56.9% and 43.1% respectively of the gross output value of industry and agriculture, of which the proportion of heavy industry had increased to 35.5%, which was still relatively low.

---

1   Fei Zhengqing, editor-in-chief, *The Cambridge History of China (1949-1956)*, Shanghai People's Press, 1990, p. 154.

Thirdly, the new China was under severe threats internationally. In the early decades of the founding of new China, the Western capitalist countries headed by the United States adopted the policy of implementing political isolation and economic blockade and sanctions targeting the mainland China. Especially after China joined the Korean War which had erupted in June, 1950, western countries upgraded their blockade and embargo against China. The normal import and export of products and the import of technology were strictly restricted, and it was extremely difficult for China to earn and raise funds for its construction. Meanwhile, the China Communist Party in mainland China and Kuomintang in Taiwan were under serious military confrontation, and the United States united Japan, Taiwan, Philippines and Thailand had encircled China in a half-surrounded pattern, which had put China's under severe threats.

What we have mentioned above in respect to China's environment, situation had forced the central collective leadership of the Communist Party of China led by Mao Zedong to choose the strategy of promoting rapid industrialization. In other words, in the face of such extreme difficult environment, CPC planned to get rid of extreme poverty and to realize rapid industrialization as two elementary goals of economic development. As Stalin mentioned when talking about the urgency of realizing high rate of industrialization in the Soviet Union he had also said: "We are fifty or a hundred years behind the advanced countries. We must make up this gap in ten years. Either we do it or they will crush us."[2] The level of China's economic development was lower than that of the Soviet Union at that time, which had made the Chinese Communists more anxious about China's economic conditions. Mao Zedong once sighed with emotion, "At present, what can we make? We can make a teacup or a teapot, we can grow grains and then grind wheat into flour; and we can also make paper. But, we can't manufacture a car, a plane, a tank, even a tractor by ourselves." It could imagine that if we hadn't completely changed that backward situation or hadn't accelerated the realization of national industrialization, new China couldn't have got rid of or defense against the severe threat or pressure in foreign politics and economy from both international and domestic community. For this reason, the CPC and the people's government hoped urgently to realize China's socialist industrialization as soon as possible in the early years of new China. In March, 1949, the goal of transforming China from a backward agricultural country into an advanced industrial country was put forward in the Second Plenary Session of the 7th National Congress of the CPC. In February, 1951, Mao Zedong proposed his idea of "spending

---

2 *Selected Works of Joseph Stalin*, Vol. 2, People's Publishing House, 1981, p. 274.

three years for economic recovery and next spend ten years for economic development". Later, Mao Zedong systematically put forward the general guideline and task for CPC in the transition period in June and July, 1952, that is, within a long period of time, to progressively realize China's socialist industrialization and gradually achieve China's socialist transformation, reconstruction of agriculture, handicraft industry and capitalist industry and commerce. The general guideline determined the basic strategic goals to realize China's socialist industrialization and indicated the direction for China's economic development. There was only one option for the Chinese Communist Party to change China's poor and backward situation in a short time that is, carrying on the top-down socialist industrialization led by the state. The primary phase of such socialist industrialization in China had the following general features:

Firstly, the government as the engine of industrialization. The government was not only responsible for launching industrialization, but also for organizing, designing, planning and using its power to promote and ensure the smooth development of the industrialization process. There were two major reasons why the government should undertake such hard tasks and directly participate in industrialization. One is that China's backward economic status failed to provide material basis and technological foundation and lacked social and economic forces for implementing such industrialization. Secondly, the state operated economy founded on the basis of confiscated bureaucratic capitalist enterprises has created conditions for government participation in economy. The government should overcome the obstacles encountered in the industrialization process and create the conditions for developing industrialization by using the powerful state apparatus. Besides, the government needed to mobilize and centralize extremely limited industrial foundation and transform them into the most important starting basis of the industrial sector of the economy.

Secondly, China's socialist industrialization was only in the primary phase due to extremely poor and backward productive forces base, that is, China's socialist industrialization was carried out on the basis of inadequate industrial conditions and relatively weak material and technological foundation. The basic task during the primary phase of industrialization was to start China's industrialization, and to initially establish a complete national economic system, which would transform China's economic structure from traditional agriculture which played a leading role into a dual structure which would combine the traditional agriculture with the new machine-building industry. During the primary phase, agriculture should play an important role in the national economy, as the main source of accumulating funds for the whole national economy. And industrial sector would be the main field of investment, and the pattern of industrial development should adopt the mode of extensive development.

Thirdly, China had to undertake a late-developing-and-catching-up-type of industrialization path, that is, China had entered the path of industrialization within the international background wherein some major countries has already realized their industrialization, and needed to implement high-speed development as a primary strategy in its industrialization. China's industrialization path was quite different from those early-developing industrialization mode or path and also was quite different from the mode or path of industrialization chosen by some later-developing capitalist countries (Italy, Germany). The industrialization path of China, in a late-developing socialist country, was formed in the international and domestic background of the 1950s. The main source of construction funds had to rely on domestic savings. China had to take high-speed growth and catching-up as its primary strategies in order to fulfill such an arduous historic task of transforming poor and backward China. Since it had missed the historical opportunity for self-development of industrialization, it was impossible for China to follow the classical sequence of industrialization which develops light industry as the first step and then the heavy industry step, and the only choice for China was to undertake the development of heavy industry as the central task in economic construction, and giving priority to the development of heavy industry. Therefore, the way of implementing China's industrialization path was is designing the process on the premise of fixed objectives, and continuously revising and improving in accordance with those fixed objectives, instead of pursuing goals during the process and continuously revising those goals which is the way to realize industrialization chosen by those early-developed industrialized countries. The basic feature of China's industrialization as described above was the "catching-up" strategy.

Fourthly, to ensure the realization of China's industrialization in the primary stage of socialism, the Chinese Communist Party had to learn from and refer to "Stalin's model" formed by the Soviet Union in the 1930s, and one of outstanding features of such practice in the Soviet Union gave priority to the development of heavy industry at the cost of the agricultural sector. Therefore, it can be clearly seen that carrying out such a socialist industrialization strategy in the primary stage of the1950s was the only reasonable choice for the CPC under the specific historical conditions, which was also the historical background for the implementation of the state monopoly upon purchasing and marketing of grain.

II. Direct causes of the state monopoly upon purchasing and marketing of grain: severe situation that occurred during the grain purchase and sale

After the general guideline to be followed in the transition period was out forward, the first step for the socialist transformation was to design the circulation sphere in respect to agricultural products, instead of changing the relations of production in the production field. In other words, China implemented trade monopoly upon major agricultural and sideline products, such as grain, cooking oil, cotton and cotton cloth. That is, China implemented the state monopoly upon purchasing and marketing. In the beginning, the policy of the state monopoly upon purchasing and marketing was a policy which included grain purchase and sale in, which was first launched in December, 1953, including planned state purchase and supply of grain, as well as management of the grain market. By administrative measures, China has implemented a complete planned control upon grain production, processing, circulation, and residents' consumption, and put the grain production plus the industry and commerce related with the grain processing and circulation into the orbit of state planning. Why was the policy of the state monopoly upon purchasing and marketing of grain implemented in one year after large-scale industrial construction with the heavy industry as its core had begun?

The first reason was the tension that occurred between demand and supply of grain caused by large-scale industrial construction.

Firstly, a large-scale industrial construction would cause a boom in urban population across China. In 1953, the number of urban population had reached 78.26 million, with an increase of 6.63 million compared to 1952, and 20.61 million increase compared to 1949. The urban population boom required China to increase the food supply for urban inhabitants and state staff.

Secondly, due to the requirements of developing the industrial sector, the farming areas of cash crops were rapidly expanded, together with those people who lacked enough food supply which had made the number of rural population which began to consume cash crops increase to 100 million. Therefore, by the end of 1953, nearly 200 million urban and rural residents needed cash gropes (grains) supplied by the state, consequently the domestic grain sales had soared to 61.32 billion catties in 1953 from 46.78 billion compared to 1952.

Thirdly, peasants with more income after the land reform have increased their food consumption. According to available statistics, the figure of grain consumption per capita in rural areas was 370 catties in 1949, and had increased to 440 catties in 1952. Bo Yibo has evaluated after a survey in North China in autumn of 1953, as follows: "In the past, peasants living in the mountainous regions could consume white flour for only ten times a year, and now they can consume for four or five times, even seven or eight times a month".[3]

Due to the increase of self-supporting consumption of peasants, together with peasants' idea of disaster prevention and their reluctance of selling out, the state purchase volume of grain was bound to decrease. The state purchase volume of grain accounted for 28.2% of the total grain output between 1951-1952, and the figure had dropped to 25.7% between 1952-1953.

Fourthly, at that time, the grain market was free, i.e. the grains could enter the market freely after peasants have delivered tax grain to the state. Therefore, that merchants used to raise grain prices and rushed to purchase on purpose which had it difficult to realize the state's purchasing plans. Meanwhile, in order to import machines and equipment needed for the industrial construction, the export of agricultural products, including grain, was also increased in this period.

Given all the above, although the total grain output in China hit a record of 327.8 billion catties in 1952, a crisis of grain purchasing happened and the supply-demand relationship fell into a crisis during the period of July in 1952 to June in 1953. As Chen Yun pointed out, "The demand quantities of grain in urban industrial and mining areas and rural cash crop areas have rapidly increased, but peasants didn't rush to sell out their surplus grain, which is the root cause of the excess demand of grain that occurred in 1953".[4] When China began to implement the "First Five-Year" Plan the grain purchase and sale was under a severe crisis situation. It was estimated that during the period of 1953-1954, the state needed grain more than 70 billion catties. The state could get 27.5 billion catties from agricultural tax-in-kind (as grain) and also needed to purchase 43.1 billion catties, which was hard to realize only depending on the grain market. In order to ensure the smooth progress of the large-scale industrial construction, stable prices, and achieve the basic level of grain supply for urban and rural residents, it was imperative for China to implement the policy of the state monopoly upon purchasing and marketing of grain, as well as cotton and cotton cloth.

---

3   Bo Yibo, *A Review of Several Major Decisions and Events*, Vol. 1, Party School of the Central Committee of CPC Press, 1991, p. 257.

III. Practical implementation of the state monopoly upon the purchase and marketing of grain: The only road to accumulate funds for industrialization

As previously mentioned, realizing the national industrialization was the only way for New China to change its extreme poor and backward situation, which has formed the "dream of building a powerful country" pursued by the Chinese people. After establishing its industrialized development strategy, China was faced with the next tough problem—the sources of funds for industrialization. In other words, there existed the contradiction between the heavy investment funds needed for developing the large-scale industrial construction and the shortage of funds, which was another important reason for implementing the state monopoly upon purchasing and marketing of grain.

Generally speaking, there are two ways for internal accumulation of industrialization. One is "Meiji Mode". Japan adopted the policy of high land rents ant and high agricultural taxes to realize its high level of accumulation after the Meiji restoration, which resulted in a tensioned relation between the state and the peasants, besides, peasants were reluctant to do farm work. Second is the "price scissors" model. The Soviet Union adopted the method of "price scissors" between the industrial commodity prices bought by the agricultural collectives and agricultural product prices sold by them. China chose the latter way, but Chen Yun had commented in June, 1950, "China is an agricultural country. So, investing in industrialization should not sacrifice agricultural development."[4] In August, 1953, he added, "Narrowing price scissors between industrial and agricultural products is our goal, which is the consistent and unforgettable task for the Communist Party. China's revolution aims at improving people's livelihood. But due to the shortage of industrial products, we cannot achieve that goal in a short time. It is my responsibility to make it clear, because we also need to accumulate funds and expend reproduction."[5]

And Bo Yibo also made the following evaluation: "As an economically backward agricultural country, to conduct the large-scale industrial construction, it is necessary and inevitable to ask peasants to provide more accumulation at the beginning. The way adopted by capitalist countries for raising funds for industrialization was primitive accumulation or plundering the colonies or they utilized both methods. We can't do that because we are is a socialist country. However, where will the funds for industrialization

---

4   *Selected Works of Chen Yun*, Vol. 2, People's Publishing House, 1995, p. 97.
5   Ibid, pp. 194-195.

come from, if we don't require the peasants to provide more accumulation in a certain time period? At that time, some people within and out of the Party showed excessive sympathy for peasants and were against the state monopoly upon purchasing and marketing of grain. Although their motives maybe good, their opinions were wrong because they didn't take the actual demands of funds accumulation for industrialization into consideration."[6]

If conducting industrialization construction in an economically backward agricultural country, the implementation of the state monopoly upon purchasing and marketing of grain is an inevitable way to guarantee the grain supply by the state. Meanwhile, the state-fixed prices for agricultural products has provided a support to maintain low wages in the large-scale industrial enterprises and provided low cost of raw materials, and also enabled excess industrial profit earned by the large-scale industrial enterprises and that part of excess profit were handed over to the state and were accumulated as funds for national construction. The model of transferring agricultural accumulation to the industrial sector was achieved through the formation of price scissors between the industrial and agricultural products.

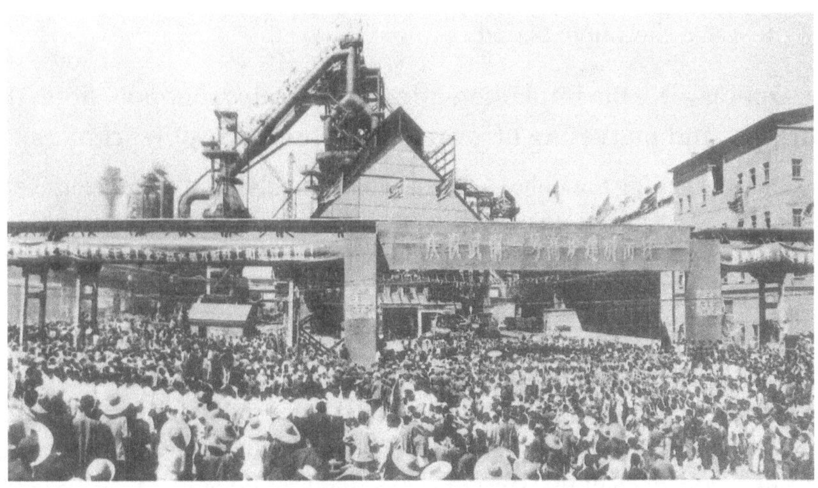

Above is No. 1 blast furnace in Wuhan Iron and Steel Group Company, whose building was started in July 1ˢᵗ, 1957, and was completed and put into use on September 25, 1958

---

6 Bo Yibo, *A Review of Several Major Decisions and Events*, Vol. 1, Party School of Central Committee of CPC Press, 1991, pp. 280-281.

During the "Fist Five-Year" Plan period, the investment in infrastructure had reached 49.3 billion RMB, which was 15.3% higher than the original plan and a large number of national key enterprises were newly built so as to establish a relatively comprehensive industrial system. The number of industrial and mining projects above norm to be constructed was 921. At the end of 1957, 428 projects were fully completed and put into production, as well as 109 projects were partly completed and was also put into use. The sum of newly added fixed assets was 49.2 billion RMB. As for the rate of development, the planned value of industrial output increased at a rate of 7% each year, and actually, the rate of annual increase in industrial development had reached 18%. Therefore, those achievements made during the "First Five-Year" Plan period basically provided a solid foundation for China's socialist industrialization. Since then, during the long-term implementation of the state monopoly upon purchasing and marketing of grain, there were two major goals o to be achieved. One was to ensure food supply for China's increasing population, and the other one was to purchase sufficient industrial raw materials needed by the state enterprises and to provide capital accumulation for the industrial build-up. Without the support of the state monopoly upon purchasing and marketing of grain, China's industrialization construction could not make such a great achievement and the Chinese people could not realize the "dream of building a powerful country" in such a short time period.

IV. Doubts after the implementation of the state monopoly upon the purchase and marketing of grain: "Were there any other choices?"

When evaluating the policy of the state monopoly upon the purchase and marketing of grain carried out during the traditional building period of New China, some people have often raised such doubts even blamed it, such as "was that policy an inevitable choice?" or "were there any other choices". However, people have already considered all possibilities at that time.

First, the state needed more grain output from peasants. Previously, the state provided its grain requirement by the taxes paid in kind and by exchanging its industrial commodities with the peasants, of which, the tax-in-kind had reached its limits. Bo Yibo has explained this situation in his book, A Review of Several Major Decisions and Events, as follows: "During the first few years of new China, the state got grain mainly depending on tax and partially depending on purchases from the markets. The annual proportion of requisition of grain and market purchase was 61:39 in 1951-1952, and was 56:44 in 1952-1953. After considering the criticism on agricultural taxes, on May 25th, 1953, the Party Central Committee made a clear statement in its instruction to Party committees at all levels to faithfully implement the agricultural taxes, which said: "From now on, China has to control the grain circulation, should implement the policy of depending more on purchasing and less on taxes. The number of requisition of grain would be stable as the same as that in 1952 (that is, 34.8 billion catties minus deductible number in special disasters) in a few years. Therefore, it is hard to realize the income growth of commodity grain by increasing agricultural taxes."[7]

Secondly, in the commodity exchange mode, free purchase and marketing didn't work well in the market. Under the circumstance of tensioned supply-demand relationship, since the state didn't have strong financial funds to purchase grain from peasants by offering them higher prices, and since the ordinary peasants wanted to sell their grain at higher prices and speculators have rushed to purchase and hoard grain, the grain purchased by the state was bound to be insufficient, which naturally affected the general situation.

"Between July 1, 1952 to June 30, 1953, the annual figure of grain that entered into the markets reached 34.8 billion catties across China, the purchases by the state and purchases by the supply and marketing cooperatives accounting for 69.6% of that figure and that purchased and traded by private merchants for 30.1%. The severer the grain situation was, the sharper the conflict in getting the grain resources between the private merchants and the state was. In a short period during the winter of 1952, all the rice that entered into the market was purchased by private merchants in the Ji'an City of Jiangxi Province.

In 1953, when the soybeans was harvested in the districts and the counties of the Xuzhou City of Jiangsu Province, many merchants, from North to South, poured into this region. A grain merchant named Wang Yunong purchased 500 thousand catties for one time. In those years when the grain inventory was already nearly exhausted but the new crop was not yet ripe, some merchants rushed to purchase "Qingmiao crops" and "Hehua crops" in some regions of Zhejiang and Hubei provinces. Although those grain purchased be merchants could meet the needs of the market, the grain price was determined by those merchants, which affected the price stability of the whole market. At that time, the market price of grain in those places where trade activities conducted by private merchants was frequent was 20%-30% higher than the government-fixed prices of grain. China's economic

---

7   Bo Yibo, *A Review of Several Major Decisions and Events*, Vol. 1, Party School of Central Committee of CPC Press, 1991, p. 258.

power was weak and people's income was low, people couldn't afford such high prices. Under the circumstances of free grain market, the fluctuations in grain prices was bound to cause a series of price fluctuations in all kinds of commodities. Thus, China had experienced the phenomenon of hyper-inflation for 12 years (1937-1949), and the Chinese people were quite sensitive to price fluctuations. If the state would ignore such phenomena, such fluctuations would make people anxious and cause social instability, and it would be difficult for China to implement its large-scale economic construction plan." And China's industrialization plan would come to nothing.[8]

Thirdly, at that time, Chen Yun had designed 8 policies after considering all the options. Apart from the state monopoly upon purchasing and marketing of grain, other 7 policies included the following: only rationing; only requisition of grain; staying unchanged; making no preparation until the last moment; mobilizing to subscribe to buy; contractual purchase in advance; and each local authority going its own way instead of implementing a unified method. After making a careful analysis, it turned out that other 7 policies hadn't worked and only the 8th policy was feasible, which emphasized the combination of grain requisition from the rural areas with rationing of grain supply in urban areas, namely, the state monopoly upon purchasing and marketing of grain. Thus, it could be seen that the only practical option for China was the state monopoly upon purchasing and marketing of grain. In short, only by evaluating the policy of the state monopoly upon the purchase and marketing of grain within the China's historical environment can we deeply understand the historical basis and inevitability of that policy, and can understand the greatness of the decision made by the CPC and value the rationality of the choice.

II. Periodization of the state monopoly upon the purchase and marketing of grain

We should pay attention to the changes in different periods within about three or four decades when the state monopoly upon the purchase and marketing of grain was implemented. Both the policy's effect on social life and the peasants' attitude towards the policy are quite different in different periods or stages. For example, at the beginning, the state didn't specify the quantity of grain, and all peasants' surplus grain were delivered to the state, which broke liberated peasant's dream of "improving their lives and finding their fortunes", causing their resistance to the policy. But it doesn't mean peasants always complained even resisted the policy of state

---

8   Ibid, pp. 257-258.

monopoly upon the purchase and marketing of grain implemented over the last few decades. With the continuous improvement and perfection of the policy, for instance, requisitioning surplus grain was upgraded to the fixed quotas for production, purchase and marketing of grain (three fixes quotas) which mobilized the initiative of peasants and set their mind at ease, and then three fixed quotas for each county was improved to three fixed quotas for each household. And since 1965, the method of one fixed quota for each year was changed to "one fixed quota for three years" (namely, three years with one fixed quota) which fitted peasants' interests and stabilized their quotas of grain, and then to "one fixed quota for five years" since 1971. Considering several improvements of the state monopoly upon purchasing and marketing of grain (especially "three fixed quotas" in 1955), the general trend of the policy was getting better and better. Hence, peasants' attitudes towards the policy have changed from unwillingness, dissatisfaction and resistance to welcoming, understanding and supporting. We can't only draw a simple conclusion, which was used to be ignored by people. Some just discussed the state monopoly upon the purchasing and marketing of grain implemented at the first few years and ignored features of the policy in the last period, which made their comments be overgeneralized. History was not simple. At different stages of the state monopoly upon purchasing and marketing of grain, it could not be overgeneralized on peasants' attitudes and social repose. Otherwise, it would get into misunderstanding and impact its objective fair evaluation from the perspective of both summing up experiences and learning a lesson. Here we focus on the social response and peasants' attitude towards the policy of "three fixed quotas" in respect to grain. We shall analyze the situation at different stages based on exploring the historical facts.

I. "Three fixed quotas"–improvements in the state monopoly upon the purchase and marketing of grain and changes observed in peasants' attitudes

Because the state monopoly upon purchasing and marketing of grain (especially the state monopoly upon purchasing) involves personal interests of peasants, and breaks peasants' habit of grain, together with the implementation of the policy around the whole country for the first time in 1953, besides, since the policy has been implemented for only one month, China is in face of a heavy task within a limited time, and China lacks experience, the policy has made achievements in putting end to a passive state of grain. In the same time, however, there still exist a few problems, which cause had influences in some places, such as compelling orders.

1954 is the second year of the implementation of the state monopoly upon purchasing and marketing of grain. In the summer of 1954, the Yangtze River basin, the Huaihe River basin and Hebei Province, as China's main grain producing areas, suffered a record-breaking flood disaster of rarely seen proportions. The number of farmland inundated by flood around the whole country was 16.13 million hectares, and the areas of flood disaster was 11.31 million hectares with the flood-hit population of 60 million. The flood caused massive failure in staple crops in those areas, but the requisitioning task load of grain didn't change, and the required task load would increase by each authority, for example, the state planned to purchase 86.8 billion catties grain, and actual amount was 89.1 billion catties grain, exceeding 2.3 billion catties, of which more 7 billion catties grain were requisitioned in non-disaster areas. Those factors caused the appearance of serious compelling orders and the grain shortage of peasants at some places in 1954. Actually, peasants didn't have enough surplus food, but working groups or leaders still forced them to sale their "surplus grain", and even unlawful acts occurred at some places, such as restriction of personal liberty, putting in prison, hang peasants, and beating them, leading to a tense relations and situation in rural areas. In many places, peasants even killed pigs or cattle, were unwilling to collect manure and negatively prepared spring ploughing, which led to peasants be in low spirits for production. With respect to that issue, Mao Zedong gave his opinions in his book *On Ten Major Relationships*, putting that "We have made a mistake on the grain matter. In 1954, some places of China suffered floods disaster, resulting in a reduction in grain yield, while our authority purchased 7 billion catties grain. Such a paradox caused that people complained about the state monopoly upon purchasing and marketing of grain when talking about grain in many places last spring. Besides, our comrades within the Party have a lot of complaints about such an approach."[9]

There emerged some issues on the state monopoly upon purchasing and marketing of grain in 1954, for example, some authorities made a compelling order to excessively purchase peasants' grain, causing the resistance to the policy, which attracted much attention of the Party Central Committee. In January, 1955, Chen Yun went to Qingpu County of Jiangsu Province for on-site inspection. In the seminar, some leaders criticized such measure of excessively purchasing peasants' grain; a lot of peasants complained that the left food was too little for their own. Chen Yun made a special survey in Tingxiu Village of Xiaozheng County, and the half of peasant household were lack of food. The period of food shortage lasted for one to three

---

9   Mao Zedong, On the Ten Major Relationships, *Collected Works of Mao Zedong*, Vol. 7, People's Publishing House,1999, p. 29.

months. Through that survey, Chen Yun felt deeply that there exited some shortcomings and loopholes during the implementation of the state monopoly upon purchasing and marketing of grain, which was needed to be improved and supplemented. And then, he proposed for the Party Central Committee to implement "three fixed quotas" in rural area, that is, the fixed quotas for production, purchase and marketing of grain, which was to eliminate the phenomenon of excessively purchasing grain. On March 3, 1955, the Central Committee of the CPC and the State Council of China issued the Urgent Instruction on An Assignment for Grain Purchase and Marketing and Smoothing Peasants' Emotions, which pointed out some mistakes and made a further analysis. The Urgent Instruction put that the main reason causing peasants' complaint was that they felt helpless about the policy, because the state purchased all amount of increase yield of grain, causing that peasants had not benefited at all. Besides, they put that the amount of purchasing by the state was too larger, while the amount of left grain couldn't meet their actual needs. The Urgent Instruction put forward that it's necessary to further implement the fixed quotas for production, purchase and marketing of grain, that is, before spring planting of each year, taking township as a unit, the planed output of the whole township should be roughly determined and the figure of the state of purchasing and marketing of grain should be published to peasants, making it clear for peasants about the proportion of grain yield by themselves, of grain purchased by the state, and of grain left for themselves, as well as the proportion of supply for grain-deficient household. Such an approach makes peasants clearly know their task and sets their mind at rest, so as to help dealing with the tension in rural areas and develop agricultural industry, as well as implement the state monopoly of purchasing and marketing of grain in a planned and controlled way.

In the spring of 1955, in accordance with the instructions made by the Central Committee of the Communist Party of China and the State Council of China, the "three fixed quotas" of grain was carried out at township, and the figures of grain output and of state purchasing and marketing were determined for each township, eliminating peasants' worry about "unlimited purchase and market of grain". So that, the mass showed their support for "three fixed quotas" and their enthusiasm for production was improved as well. They said that the approach of "three fixed quotas" of grain "could let the state and peasants be prepared in advance". "Once the number of grain monopolized by the state, all peasants would like to produce more grain." A lot of peasants rearranged their production plans. And those who originally intended to kill pigs or sell donkeys or cows replanned to do a good production, make a fortune and live a better life after determining the figures for "three fixed quotas". On March 25, 1955, a news report "Three Fixed Quotas" Inspires Yuexiaoqiao Village's Peasants written by Liu Fancai who was a correspondent, was published on People's Daily, describing that peasants support the policy of "three fixed quotas" in Xiaoshan county of Zhejiang Province. The report indicated: On March 14, the news on the implementation of "the fixed quotas for production, purchase and marketing of grain" spread to Yueiaoqiao Village, Xiaoshan County of Zhejiang Province. All peasants throughout the village were very excited when hearing the news and went around spreading, "the Communist Party is to implement a favorable policy for peasants!" When heard the news, Wang Miaoxing, a middle peasant who was worried about the state monopoly upon the purchasing and marketing of grain, was prying in the field, and then he dropped pinch bar and cheerfully run back home, saying with a laugh, "What a favorable policy launched by the Communist Party. They really know peasants' minds!"[10]

II. The policy of "three fixed quotas" for each household was supported by the peasants

After the implementation of "three fixed quotas" for each township, while the peasants supported the policy, peasants were concerned with another issue which was more important for their direct interests, that is, there wasn't fixed-quotas for each household, although the fixed quotas in the townships level was launched. This issue has bothered them which had made peasants to nurture ambiguous ideas in their minds. Some have worried that in spite of "the fixed quotas" for township, whether the policy would change after the autumn harvest. It is to say, peasants hope urgently that the policy won't change for a long time and it would be better that "three fixes quotas" for each household can be determined, letting them be clear about their tasks.

In order to meet peasants' requirements, and eliminate their doubts, as well as improve the policy of the state monopoly upon the purchase and marketing of grain, in June, 1955, the Party Central Committee and the State Council hold National Food Conference in Beijing, summarizing the work about the state monopoly upon purchasing and marketing of grain from 1954 to 1955, lowering indicators for grain purchase of 1995 set by the Urgent Instruction of March, and drawing up the Interim Procedures for the State Monopoly upon Purchasing and Marketing in Rural Areas. Besides, three principals were made at the conference, including first, subject to peasants' actual output and don't overestimate output; second, based on the peasants' actual demand to deduct

---

10   See *People's Daily*, March 25, 1955.

grain the peasants consume, and calculate the purchasing amount of grin according to a reasonable proportion instead of progressive purchase; and third, determine the figures of the fixed quotas for production, purchase and marketing of grain for each household.

On August 25, 1955, the State Council formally issued the Interim Procedures for the State Monopoly upon Purchasing and Marketing in Rural Areas which was distributed to all cities and countryside across

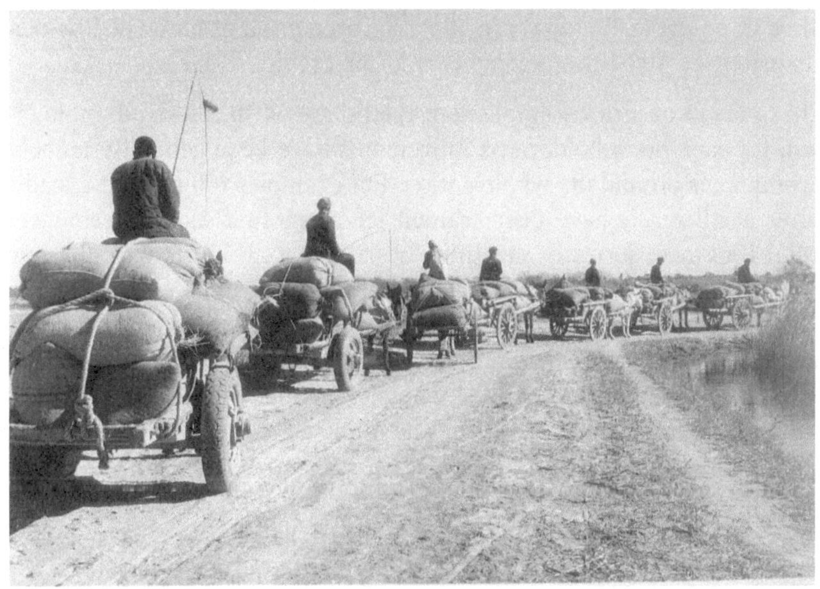

After several improvements (especially "three fixed quotas" of grain in 1955), the general trend of the policy of the state monopoly upon purchasing of grain became better and better. And the peasants' attitude toward the policy change from reluctant, dissatisfied and resistant to welcome, understand and support. Above is the members of an agricultural sub-cooperative sending surplus grain to the state in Dongzhuang of Ninghe County, Hebei Province

the country. The Interim Procedures stipulated: When implementing the state monopoly upon purchasing and marketing of grain in rural areas, the authority should check and ratify grain output of each household, stipulate the standard for peasants' consume and calculate the amount of each household's grin consume; for gain-surplus households, check their grain output and monopolize the purchase of their surplus grain; for grain-deficient households, check their grain supply and monopolize the marketing of their grain; for grain-self-sufficient households, do not monopolize the purchase and marketing of their grain. Besides, once the amount of grain purchase has been determined for grain-surplus households, the amount won't change from 1955 to the next three years, even if their grain yield increase. After fulfilling their task, grain-surplus households have a right to distribute and use the rest of their grain. Such the policy of "three fixed quotas for each household" which "won't be changed in three years" is exactly what peasants hope urgently. Therefore, the Interim Procedures on "three fixed quotas" of grain for each household is welcomed and supported by peasants. According to the statistics, due to the implementation of "three fixed quotas" of grain in 1955, the amount of grain owned by peasants increased 40 catties per capita over the previous year.

In order to accurately implement the policy of "three fixed quotas" of grain for each household, mass movements have been generally launched in rural areas around the whole nation. For example, 400 thousand leading cadres at all levels have been trained for promoting such movements in Anhui Province; series of meetings of cadres at all levels with the number of 1,700 to 4,000 has been hold at all prefectures in Sichuan Province, aiming to carry out the relevant work in each township; and 16 thousand cadres from leading organizations at all levels have gone to the rural areas, and each township has organized a publicity team comprised of dozens of members in Guangdong Province. The implementation of the "three fixed quotas" for each household eliminates cadres' and masses' misunderstanding of the state monopoly upon purchasing and marketing of grain, eases masses' dissatisfaction, improves relations between the Party and the masses, and greatly raises masses' enthusiasm for production.

For example, in Naihai country of Guangdong Province, an experienced peasant told his son, "I have supported the Communist Party. But last year, when they purchased our gain, I felt dissatisfied to what they did. Now, hearing to implement "three fixed quotas" for each household, I will firmly support our Communist Party just as before because they have made a favorable policy for peasants."

In the Sichuan Province, the broad masses had such kind of emotions: "'Three-fixed quotas' are 'four-fixed quotas', even my heart is fixed." "Now, we are sure about what our tasks are and we are full of energy for production." They also said, "The policy of 'three fixed quotas' becomes more reasonable. Even if our production increase, the number of purchase won't change, so that we should make efforts to increase grain yield and don't let our Chairman Mao down."

The suburban dwellers in Xi'an city also spoke highly of the policy of "three fixed quotas", saying that "Now, we are sure about our production. The more grain harvest, the better our life is"; "The policy of 'three fixed quotas' sets us at ease".

In Zhejiang Province, the peasants said, "Our Chairman Mao is so thoughtful, and their policies are more and more reasonable, which solve our problems. Some said, "The policy of 'three fixed quotas' sets us feel at ease", "in the past, we thought grain-deficient households are better than grain-surplus households. Now, we only worry about that the harvest yield of grain is too small."

"Three fixed quotas" of grain for each household was carried out in rural areas around the whole country since August, 1955 and was basically stopped at the end of 1955. In addition to Tibet, Qinhai, and Xinjiang, the checked and ratified amounts of "three fixed quotas" of grain for other provinces, cities and autonomous regions were: 354.7 billion catties for the fixed quotas for production, 108.33 billion catties for fixed quotas for purchase (of which, 42.97 billion catties for requisition of grain and 65.36 billion catties for monopolized purchase of grain), and 20.82 billion catties for fixed quotas for marketing respectively. After the implementation of "three fixed quotas" of grain for each household, the issue of excessive purchase of peasants' grain was corrected in many places, so that more grain was left in their hands than before. What's more, "three fixed quotas" sets their mind at ease. Therefore, all peasants regarded that the policy not only determined the fixed quotas for production, purchase and marketing, but also made them be relieved. So "three fixed quotas" mobilized peasants' initiative of production. A peasant, living in Lugu Village, Shijingshan, a suburban area of Beijing, wrote a couplet for "three fixed quotas".

First line of a couplet: "Chairman Mao Calls for 'Three Fixed Quotas', everyone is pleased."

Second line of a couplet: "Communist Party 'Four Left Grain', each one is relieved."

Horizontal scroll: "Efforts for Production"

That couplet vividly showed peasants' support and welcome for the implementation of "three fixed quotas" for each household.

III. Rural Reform Has Made Limited Negative Effects on Peasants' Enthusiasm for Production

Although they approved the positive effects of the state monopoly of purchasing and marketing of grain, some researchers have pointed out to its negative influence on limiting law of value to play a role in agricultural production and product management, and dampening peasants' enthusiasm of production, which constrains grain production and causes that there is no breakthrough in grain yield over the long term. Although it is quite objective and accord with historical facts, such a conclusion overestimates the negative effects caused by the state monopoly upon purchasing and marketing of grain on law of value and peasants' production enthusiasm over a long period. Actually, in first seven years or eight (that is, the period before 1985 when stop monopolizing the purchase of grain) of reform on rural economic system, namely, the system of fixed output quotas for individual households, the policy of the state monopoly upon purchasing of grain was still implemented (and the monopoly upon marketing of grain lasted longer) in rural areas. However, the implementation of the policy of fixed output quotas for individual households, namely, "enough grain to pay the country, leaving food for the collective, and the rest all in their hands", connected peasants' vital interests with their own production, which aroused their enthusiasm for production. Although monopolizing the purchasing of grain was still carried out, the grain yield increased rapidly and peasants showed no worry about the state monopoly upon purchasing of grain and no resistant to that policy (besides the purchasing price of grain increased at that time, but the price factor was not main reason, because people's income and consumer prices also were increased at the same time). It can be seen that the negative effects of the state monopoly upon purchasing and marketing of grain on law of value and peasants' production enthusiasm is limited and we shouldn't overestimate the negative influence of that policy. Only we abandon equalitarianism and break the "big-pot" system can emancipate the productive forces in rural areas, that is, the implementation of monopolizing the purchase of grain, which speeds up the development of agricultural industry, especially in grain production, and massively increases grain yield. In the following paragraphs, we will restore historical reality from the perspective of reform of rural economic system. Although in first seven years or eight of the reform, the policy of the state monopoly upon purchase and marketing of grain was still implemented, agricultural and grain production developed rapidly as before.

I. Fixed output quotas for individual households and state monopoly upon the purchase and marketing of grain

At the end of 1978, with the support of Party committees in the Fengyang County of the Anhui province, farmers of the Xiaogang Village have initiated a new reform mode—"family contract responsibility system". In the same year, people in Xiaogang Village worked with untiring energy and their enthusiasm for production ran unprecedentedly high, so that the grain output reached a new high. The grain total output reached over 66 thousand kilograms which was more than all grain output in the five previous years from 1966 to May, 1970; and the total output of oil crops had reached 17500 kilograms which was more than all output over the last 20 years. Previously, the state purchase quotas of grain in Xiaogang village had never been realized, and people needed to grain resold by the state to needy grain-producing areas, finally leading to depend on: resold grain for living, relieves for consuming, and loan for producing. However, great changes happened in 1979. In that year, the state purchase quotas of grain for the production team in Xiaogang village was 2,800 catties, but the production team handed over 25,000 catties to the government, which was over 7 times of the original task, over fulfilling its plan. As for the state purchase quotas of oil crops, the task of 300 catties had also never been fulfilled. But in 1979, Xiaogang sold 25,000 catties of oil crops including peanut, sesame and others, which was over 80 times of the original plan, beating the target. It could be seen that Xiaogang's people's production enthusiasm was unaffected by the state purchase quotas of grain and oils. Other places, where carried out the fixed output quotas for individual households to increase their grain yield, had achieved great successes as Xiaogang village.

When Xiaogang village only spent on year in changing itself to be a famous one around the whole county, the reform mode–"household responsibility system or contract responsibility system"—crated by Xiaogang's people rapidly spread to Fengyang County, even to the whole province and nation. In Heze District of Shandong Province, a temporary agency—Disaster Relief Office—was established at each county and city. In spring and winter of each year, the prefectural and county Party Committees would organize a disaster response team to distribute relief grain and relief fund. There is an old village, Liuli Village of Donming County, along the Yellow River. Before the reform and opening up, there were three or four hundred out of over one thousand people leaving home for begging. In the spring of 1978, the production brigade distributed over 600 mu of uncultivated land to its members of the cooperative, and members could kept the harvest. Surprisingly, those alkaline land yielded good crops and the amount of grain output exceeded that of the collective. At the beginning of 1979, the brigade distributed one mu of land again to each member in secret, and the grain harvested could be left at their hands as their rations. After harvest day, the total grain output of the whole village increased 270,000 catties compared with that in 1978, reaching a new high without parallel in history, which made members work with untiring energy. Someone said, "If it is possible to use a bamboo pole for fishing, why don't you use a large fishing net? So, why don't we adopt big contracting?".

At the night of December 17, 1979, in Liuli village, 247 households got together to declare their position about the implementation of big contracting. And all households have agreed with the proposal. The news of the implementation of the fixed output quotas for individual households in Xiaoliu village spread like wildfire around the whole Dongming County. And soon 99% of all production brigades adopted the fixed output quotas for individual households, to realize land reform, liberate the labor force and improve living standards.

When crops were planted in spring of 1979 in Neijing county of Sichuan Province, some production brigades of Yongdong, Tongfu and Guonan communes started to implement the fixed output quotas for individual households in secret. From 1979 to the beginning of 1980, there were 142 brigades around the whole county spontaneously implemented the responsibility system of fixed output quotas for individual households. Xu Wenbing, secretary of the County Committee in Neijing, strongly supported that policy, so that he collected his survey data and asked relevant provincial leaders to extend the limitation on fixed output quotas for individual households. He said, "I would rather support the masses to carry out fixed output quotas for individual households at all costs, even losing my official job." With the support of the secretary of the County Committee and the County Party Committee, peasants' enthusiasm was at an all-time high. A member said, after the implementation of that policy, the cultivated areas became larger and our passion was increased; management became more reasonable and grain yield increased. Because of severe drought and pest and disease damage happened in the spring of 1981, the sown area of grain decreased 34,000 mu around the whole county, but wheat yield increased 77.61 million catties, up 7.4% compared with that in 1980. In the next half year, catastrophic flood occurred and 81,870 mu of agricultural crops were inundated, but the total grain yield reached 704.16 million catties around the whole county with net increase of 74.97 million catties compared with that in 1980, of which, rice yield increased 38.32 million catties, up 14.8%. In February, 1982, when the number of production brigades carrying out the system of fixed output quotas for individual households or contract system only accounted for 60%, all 5,117 production brigades in Neijiang County had implemented the family contract responsibility system.

In Shanxi Province, when leaders of the commune and the production brigade argued and couldn't make up their mind to carry out fixed output quotas for individual households, the masses run to tell their leaders, "There is no need to argue about it. We have already parceled out our land to individual households." After implementing fixed output quotas for individual households, grain production increased greatly, and peasants' resistant to the state monopoly upon purchasing and marketing of grain was gradually eliminated. Besides, many places scrambled to hand over grain to the state just as Xiaogang's people did. In March, 1981, the General Office of the Central Committee issued the document titled as "Some Opinions on Rural Economic Policy" written by Zhao Ziyang during January 1 to 8, 1981, who was a retinue of Du Runsheng, vice director of National Agricultural Council (ROC), which was an investigation report about rural circumstance in several provinces or areas, namely, five prefectures of Hubei, Heibei and Shandong Province, including Yichang, Jinzhou (a severely afflicted area), Nanyang, Kaifeng and Heze (a distressed area). The investigation report put:

"According to what I had seen and heard, I felt deeply that rural situation was much better than we thought." Those members in these areas had solved their problems of food and clothing. Peasants said brightly, "In the past, we worried about no food; now, we worry about finding some room for storing our grain. We don't leave our homes to beg anymore." "Cooperative production makes us closer, and we improve our living standards only in one year. We are affordable for steamed bread instead of sweet potatoes, and a bachelor can take a wife." "We now go to the theater and market, visit our relatives, do farm work and harvest grain." I heard peasants' desire that the policy won't change in three years, namely, "if the policy remains unchanged in one year, we are affordable for food; if the policy remains unchanged in two years, we can have extra money; and if the policy remains unchanged in three years, we will be a well-off family. Therefore, the state should build its own granaries."[11]

11　See the document issued by the General Office of CPC Central Committee: 'Some Opinions on Rural Economic Policy Issues' prepared and delivered by Du Runsheng, (March 27, 1981), in: *Compilation of Important Documents Regarding Agricultural Collectivization (1958-1981)*, CPC Central Party School Press, 1982, p. 1079.

Undoubtedly, "the state should built its own granaries as soon as possible" naturally expresses peasants' desire to hand over grain to the state after harvest. Another historical fact—"the difficulty of selling grain"— covered later in the article also can illustrate that point.

Lankao County of Henan Province and Dongming County in Shandong Province were two counties where they had visited. Those two counties were poverty-stricken areas for a long time, which depended on resold grain for living, relieves for consuming, and loan for production. "Both two counties had implemented the system of fixed output quotas for individual households. Since 1978, the number of production brigades in Kaolan County accounted for 80%, and that in Dongming County accounted for over 90%, with a significant effect in economy. The total grain output in Lankao County reached 200 million catties over the past twenty years, and reached 310 million catties in 1980; the net amount of resold grain was 8 million catties around the whole county in 1978, while in 1979, the situation improved and the net amount of selling to the state reached 32 million catties." In the past, the members of the poorest production brigade needed to beg for living. After implementing fixed output quotas for individual households, the grain ration per capita was 586 catties in one year. "During the past twenty years from 1958 to 1978 in Dongming County, the net amount of resold grain reached 450 million catties. Besides, both its relief fund provided by the state and accumulated loan summed to 78 million catties. Now Dongming County has turned itself into a grain-surplus county. So far, the state has purchased 60 million catties of grain, 3 million catties of cotton, 7.4 million catties of peanuts and 4.7 million catties of sesames from Dongming County." The county not only repaid its loan to the state, but also its peasants had 17 RMB per capita household saving deposit in 1980.[12] The investigation report put that Dengfeng county of Kaifeng prefecture and all counties of Heze prefecture all carried our fixed output quotas for individual households, and their changing circumstance was as same as Lankao or Dongming County.

II. Evaluating the state monopoly upon the purchase and marketing of grain from the perspective of "difficulties in selling grain"

After the implementation of fixed output quotas for individual households, peasants scrambled to hand over their grain to the state, resulting in "the difficulty of selling grain" at the early stage of rural reform. The following cases of "the difficulty of selling grain" could illustrate that issue.

---

12   Ibid, p. 1081.

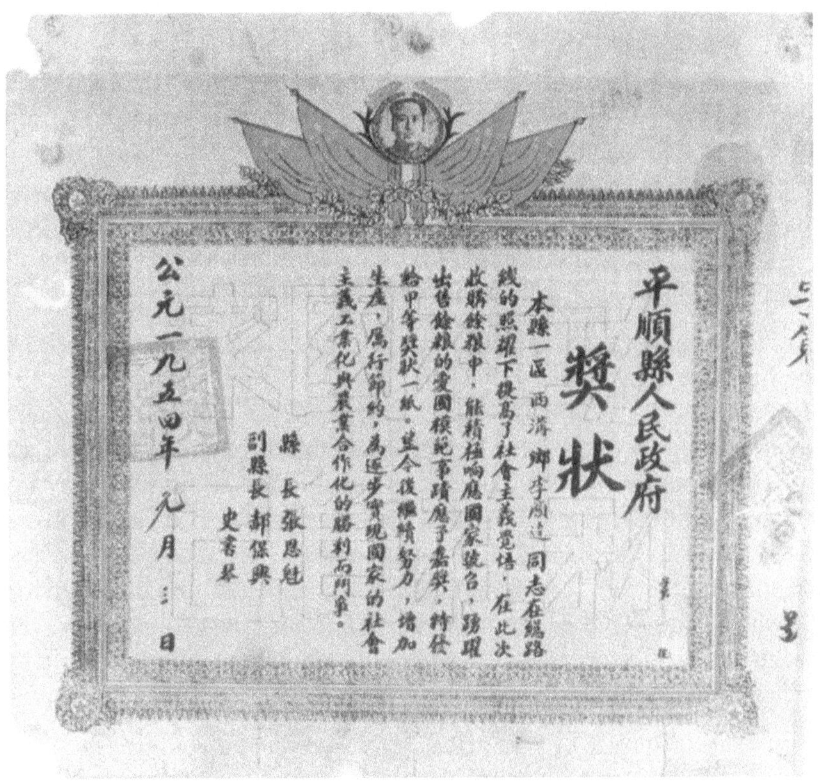

*January 3, 1954, Li Shunda's certificate of merit was awarded
by the People's Government of Pingshun County in Shanxi
Province praising that he actively sold his surplus grain*

Since 1982, "the difficulty of selling grain" had occurred at some places where the developing trend of grain was good. Due to a series of good harvests in 1983 and 1984, the inventory of grain exceeded the needed amount, and that issue failed to be solved timely. Therefore, all those factors led to occur a universal phenomenon—"the difficulty of selling grain", causing the concern of the whole country.

When summer grain crops were purchased by the state in 1984, a fellow-villager from Hunan Province complained at the front of a purchasing station. "In the past, we didn't have surplus grain but the Communist Party insisted on purchasing grain from our hands. At present, we have enough surplus grain but they don't purchase any more!" Such dramatic changes let peasants dumbfounding.

A peasant, who was from Xincheng town of Wanhe District in Suizhou City, Hubei Province, narrated his experience of selling grain. When the old man arrived at the purchasing station in Xincheng town, it was five o'clock in the afternoon. What he saw was a string of handcarts and walking tractors standing in a queue at the purchasing station. People who wanted to sell grain were burning with anxiety while the inspector of grain supply center was totally unconcerned. The sun didn't go down, and there were only four handcarts of grain, but the inspector said, "The order from the top has stipulated that we don't purchase grain at night", and shut the door upon their faces.

An old peasant from a mountainous area had walked about 20 miles to come here. He begged piteously to the inspector at the purchasing station, "Comrade, our home is far away from here. Please purchase our grain!" The inspector gave him a stern look and said, "If everyone comes here and say the same thing like you, I couldn't finish the work until tomorrow." Another peasant provided the second plan and said, "If it doesn't work, please let us put our wheat at the courtyard, and how about you purchase them till tomorrow?" "That is not allowed. You should find place to store your wheat", answered by the inspector. But after repeated pleading from peasants, the inspector reluctantly agreed to let them put their wheat in the courtyard of the purchasing station.

Huaiyuan County was one of key grain-producing counties in Anhui Province. With the promotion of the family contract responsibility system and other rural policies, the situation of a standstill of agricultural production for a long time had been reversed and more and more surplus grain were left in peasants' hands. But because the storage capacity was limited in the previous years, causing that purchased grain couldn't be sent out timely, together with other factors, such as strict restrictions for negotiated purchase and marketing, the grain sector was unwilling to purchase surplus grain from farmers without limit once they fulfilled their tasks. Besides, the supply and marketing department didn't participate in selling grain and peasants couldn't transport sale over a long distance, finally causing that peasants felt "the difficulty of selling grain".

Besides, Xinghua County was one of key marketable-grain-producing counties in Jiangsu Province. Since 1983, the issue of "the difficulty for selling grain" had been happened in that county. Due to a good harvest in 1984, the amount of marketable grain was increase dramatically again. The latter half of June was the peak period for selling grain. Once, there were more than 400 grain carriers in the river next the county grain supply center, leading to a bad traffic jam. Clean ships couldn't come out while grain carriers couldn't come in, often causing disputes. There were hundreds of boats gathered in the river side where was next to a purchasing station of Dazou commune, and people restlessly waited to sell their grain. Generally speaking, the peak period of selling grain was also the busy time for farm work, which was "rush-harvesting and rush-planting season" called by peasants. Therefore, labor and time were very important and if missing the farming season, peasant would waste half a year. But if peasants went out to purchase grain, it would take several days even though their grain met a criterion. A person in charge from County Agricultural Council said, the longest period was seven days.

A peasant from Feidong County of Anhui Province wrote in his letter to his brother working in Beijing, "People always regards that there is a good situation in rural areas, but I think they are wrong. Why? Because peasants are not able to sell their grain. If you want to sell grain, you need to get in through the back door. Sometimes, you are not able to sell grain even if you even wait for a few days and nights." In the past, the grain sector needed to mobilize or order peasants to sell their surplus grain and also required local authorities to transport more grain. At present, the issue of "the difficulty for selling grain" has occurred in many places. Peasants desired that the grain sector could purchase more grain and local authorities hoped that the central authority would transport more grain.

Actually, in the new period ongoing issue of "difficulty of selling grain" has been a negligible factor in determining the increase in peasants' income. Someone says, "The difficulty of selling grain" is a "sweet burden" because hard to sell is much better than nothing to sell. However, we disagree with this opinion. Because "low prices for grain hurt the peasants", which directly affected peasants' enthusiasm for growing grain. The historical fact that the national grain output decreased in 4 years in a row after the issue of "the difficulty of selling grain" can illustrate that point. However, this is an issue at another level. What we want to say here is that, during the process of implementing the state monopoly upon purchasing and marketing of grain, peasants felt "the difficulty of selling grain" and the state could meet all peasants' requirements, which can illustrate the following issues from another perspective, that is, the negative effects of the state monopoly upon purchasing and marketing of grain on the law of value and on peasants' enthusiasm of production is limited. With the promotion of fixed output quotas for individual households and other reform policies in rural areas, such negative effects could be negligible. In other words, in the past, the main reasons of which there was not a breakthrough of grain yield in a long period are that the equalitarianism and the "big-pot" system dampen the peasants' enthusiasm, instead of the state monopoly upon purchasing and marketing of grain.

The peasant, Wang Jiayuan, who lives at a mountainous area in Dabie Mountains about 57 years, writes a central scroll, vividly describing that since the Reform and Opening-up, China has made great achievements in grain work and peasants' happiness. The central scroll put:

Several tile-roofed houses scatter near the mountain and by the river, and I enjoy myself from sunup to sundown; everyone is responsible for its fixed-output-quota farmland, as well as planting, management and harvest; I am affordable for eating rice and wheat flour at three meals; I can afford to wear dacron cloth; I don't do something bad, and enjoy my inner peace; I come back home and chat with my wife and children about ancient and modern anecdotes, policies that aimed to enrich peasants are welcomed and peasants live a better life.

We can feel peasants' happiness from the central scroll. Considering that with the promotion of reform policies in rural areas such as fixed output quotas for individual households, which has increased grain yield during successive years, peasants have showed no resistance or complained against or become worrisome about the state monopoly upon purchase and marketing of grain, they even hope that they could deliver more grain to the state. And peasants' enthusiasm for producing grains wouldn't be affected by the policy of delivering their surplus grain to the state.

The authors are researchers of School of Marxism at the Xiangtan University

4

How to Understand China's Socialist Transformation in 1950s?

Xie Yi

The Communist Party of China has always praised the achievements of the socialist transformation in the 1950's (1953-56). Resolution on Certain Historical Issues of the Party since the Establishment of the PRC approved in the Sixth Plenary Session of the 11th Central Committee of the Chinese Communist Party in 1981 pointed out: in the transition period, the Communist Party of China creatively paved the way for a socialist transformation that suited the unique characteristics of China. Although the transformation had its drawbacks and deflections, it smoothly achieved such complex, difficult and profound social transformation and facilitated the development of the industry and agriculture and the whole national economy in the country with several hundred million people. It was indeed a great historic victory. The victory paved the way for all the later advance and development in China. The report of the 16th National Congress of the Communist Party of China pointed out: since the founding of new China, Chinese Communist Party creatively accomplished the transition from the new democratic society to the socialistic one, achieved the greatest and most profound social transformation in Chinese history, and started the historic course to rejuvenate China via socialist road. The 17th and 18th National Congress of the Communist Party of China further illustrated that, China accomplished the new democratic revolution, implemented the socialist reformation, and established the basic socialist principles under the leadership of the Communist Party of China, which provided fundamental political prerequisite and institutional basis for all the later Chinese development and advancement. They showed affirmative approval to the socialist transformation again. However, someone viewed this transformation in a different light. They thought that, China's socialist transformation was just imitating the Soviet Model and wasn't a success; the transformation wasn't in accord with the tasks and process of industrialization and "was tinged with a color of populism"; "it impaired Chinese productive forces", so it had no positive significance. China's basic socialist economic system was built through the socialist transformation. To take a negative attitude to this transformation was to deny the necessity and correctness of China's basic basic socialist economic system. Therefore, we need to carefully distinguish these opinions.

I.   Insisting on the fundamental principles of Marxism-Leninism or slavish copying of the Soviet Model?

China was faced with two radical historic tasks of fighting for national independence and liberation and to make China prosperous and people affluent in the period of recent history. The founding of People's Republic of China in 1949 signified the accomplishment of the first historic task. Then striving for the second historic task by concentrating on economic construction and development in other fields was placed high on the agenda of the Party and the state day by day. How could China develop its economy and realize the industrialization? If we look into the world history, there were no more than two ways: one was the capitalist industrialization path which EU, America and Japan took and it worked; the other was the socialist industrialization road which the Soviet Union took and it worked too. Russia was an underdeveloped country in Europe before the October Revolution. Since Russia realized the socialist industrialization, it became superpower in the European region and one of the two world leading powers.

Mao Zedong said: "Although the capitalist road can increase productive forces, it is a time-consuming and painstaking process".[1] So it wasn't the right path for China to take. China's capitalist economy was essentially vulnerable. As it couldn't form an independent and integral industrial and economic system, if independent China implemented capitalist system instead of socialist system, China's economy wouldn't get rid of dependence on foreign capitals. Consequently, China would be inevitably reduced to a processing plant of foreign monopoly capitals and solely a supplying place of cheap raw materials and labor just like many countries and regions of Asia, Africa and Latin America. China's economy couldn't prosper rapidly if the

---

1   *Selected Readings of Mao Zedong*, Vol. 6, People's Republic House, 1999, p. 299.

circumstances went on like this. It was hard to imagine such a big country like China should rely on foreign capitals and equipment to pursue development. What's more, if China's economy would remain dependent on foreign countries, its politics would have no strong backing and probably it would lose its independence. As a result, China would again face the subjugation of western capitalist countries if it adopted the capitalist system. For this reason, the Central Committee of the Communist Party of China put forward to carrying out planned economic construction and national industrialization; in the meantime, the CPC suggested implementing the socialist transformation based on private ownership of productive means. "We have to make the socialist reformation, because as long as the transition from private ownership of productive means to public ownership of productive means is realized, it will be beneficial to develop social productive capacity and start a reform in scientific technology. Then the situation that the vast majority of the country use simple and outdated tools to work will be changed into using various machines even the most advanced machines in the factories, so that we can

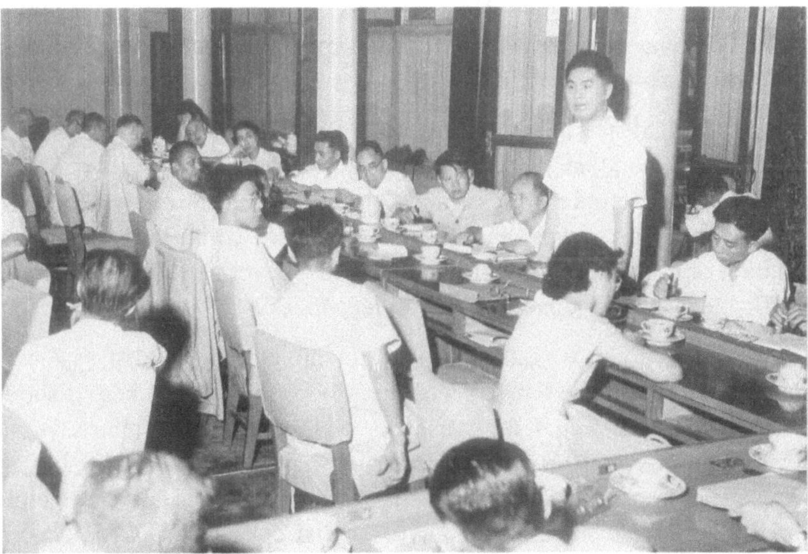

The CPC made proper political arrangement for those representative figures who upheld and made contribution to the socialist transformation. This photo taken in June 27, 1957 recorded that Rong Yiren, the members of Presidium of the National People's Congress and deputy mayor of Shanghai gave a speech in the group discussion of Premier Zhou's Government Work report in the 4th session of the First National People's Congress.

manufacture diverse industrial and agricultural products on a large scale to satisfy people's daily increasing needs and improving their living standard, resolutely strengthen national defense capability to fight against imperialist aggression, and consolidate people's political power in order to guard against revolutionary restoration."[2]

It is one of the basic principles of Marxism that the economic basis of a socialist country should adopt the public ownership of the means of production. Marx and Engels have expounded that the theory for communists can be summarized into one sentence, that's to wipe out private ownership. They said, the proletariat class must "centralize all production tools under the control of the ruling class – the proletarian, and increase the total productive forces as quickly as possible"[3] after gaining the power. Engels had in detail explained that, after the proletarian had established its governance, it can "gradually expropriate the ownership of owners of lands, mills, railways and shipyards through either by the competition way conducted by the state-owned industry or develop the policy of redemption".[4] He also said, "What we should in respect to farmers' production is to transform their private production and possession into cooperative production and possession".[5]

China's socialist transformation adhered to the basic principles of Marxism. It embodied the combination of Marxism and the reality of China, so it was definitely not a simple imitation of the Soviet Model. What should be pointed out was that those who criticize China's socialist transformation of blindly copying the Soviet Model never really understood the specific meaning of the laws of the Soviet Model.

The Soviet Model was an approach to implement socialist system in Soviet Union. A detailed analysis of the Model should be made. It should be noted, the model included two aspects: on the one hand, it referred to the basic system of socialism, mainly referring to proletarian dictatorship and public ownership of productive means. Persisting in the basic principles of socialism should be affirmed. All socialist countries must implement and persist in the basic principles of socialism, or they cannot be called a socialist country; on the other hand, it referred to some specific system or mechanism of the Soviet Union. We should explore the Soviet Model in the consideration of specific historical situation. Mao Zedong said, we should study their merits and avoid their shortcomings. So we cannot simply

---

2   *Selected Readings of Mao Zedong*, Vol. 6, People's Republic House, 1999, p. 316.

3   *Collected Works of Marx and Engels*, Vol. 2, People's Republic House, 2009, p. 45.

4   *Collected Works of Marx and Engels*, Vol. 1, People's Republic House, 2009, p. 687.

5   *Collected Works of Marx and Engels*, Vol. 4, People's Republic House, 2009, p. 524.

imitate their model. It is not proper to arbitrarily regard and label the Soviet Model as negative without making specific analysis. In China, socialist basic economic system based on public ownership of production means was established through the socialist reformation. Deng Xiaoping made it clear that, "the predominance of public ownership and common prosperity are the two fundamental socialist principles that we must adhere to". So, we will by no means agree with those who denied the socialist transformation by "putting a label of copying the Soviet Model". In terms of the realization form and concrete approach of the socialist transformation, China "took a path of socialist transformation suitable for Chinese characteristics rather than just copy the Soviet Model" as the second important resolution of the Communist Party of China pointed out in 1981 (The Resolution on Certain Questions in the History of Our Party since the Founding of the People's Republic of China). China differed with Russia In many ways. The examples are as follows.

The first was its different policies when dealing with capitalist economy.

Soon after the October Revolution, Russia nationalized all banks and large enterprises of metallurgy and mine, metal fabrication and electrical machinery and so on. Lenin once considered "implementing socialist transformation to eliminate bourgeoisie by the method of peaceful redemption". But "the Russian bourgeoisie class insisted on the counter-revolutionary path. They attacked the new state by sabotaging, vandalizing, and rebelling with armed might. The proletarian class of Russia had no alternative but to get rid of them."[6] Things were different in China. The Communist Party of China divided Chinese bourgeoisie into comprador-bureaucratic bourgeoisie and the national bourgeoisie. The Communist Party of China treated the comprador-bureaucratic bourgeoisie as its enemy. The CPC knocked down the comprador-bureaucratic bourgeoisie politically and confiscated their property; the CPC treated national bourgeoisie as friend. The CPC remolded the latter step by step while uniting with them. "For the national bourgeoisie, first, we should gradually rather than abruptly transform their ownership status by the way of compensation rather than unpaid way through redemption and state capitalism methods; second, we should necessarily arrange jobs for the members of the national bourgeoisie class while remolding them; third, we shouldn't deprive them of their voting rights. We should make proper political arrangement for their representative figures who positively support the socialist transformation and make a contribution in the reformation."[7]

---

6 *Collected Works of Mao Zedong*, Vol. 8, People's Republic House, 1999, p. 112.
7 *Collected Works of Mao Zedong*, Vol. 7, People's Republic House, 1999, p. 87.

The second was the different attitudes toward the transformation of the individual peasant farming.

The Soviet Union forcedly implemented collectivization of agriculture from 1917 to 1929. In 1927, the collective socialist farms in the agriculture of the Soviet Union accounted for less than 1%. Right from 1929, the collectivization of agriculture was vigorously carried out nationwide. Till March 1, 1930, the farmer households joining the collective farm had already accounted for 56% of the total sum; in 1934, 75% of the farmer households and 90% of the arable land across the country were given to the collective farms. Only several months were spent to achieve collectivization of agriculture in more than half the country. Steps in haste and improper measures had caused sharp loss of grain output and loss of livestock inventories over a period in the SU.

Things were different in China. The Communist Party of China adopted a policy of "steering a steady course by positive leadership" after the Agrarian Revolution. "The CPC, chose the policy of striking when the iron is hot, led people to unite. The CPC has led people to join the socialist road gradually through several transitional economic forms from producers' mutual-aid teams, to elementary level agricultural producers' cooperative and later to advanced agricultural producers' cooperative". These procedures made farmers gradually raise their consciousness by their own production experience and change their mode of living, so there was less chance for them to be worried from the abrupt changes in their lifestyles. And these gradual steps have avoided grain output loss in the period (for instance, within one or two years).[8] Its feasibility was proved by the fact.

The third was different attitudes towards the further improvement and development of socialist system.

"The formation of the Soviet Model by Stalin had played an important role in consolidating the socialist system of the Soviet Union in specific historic period, it has accelerated the development of Soviet economy and social life, and strengthened the Soviet army in the future war against the fascist forces." (Xi Jinping). But the leaders of the Soviet Union denied the existence of contradictions in socialist society and neglected that these contradictions were the driving force for the development of socialist society. Therefore, they never carried out reforms according to changing situation and never sincerely evaluate the past to accumulate lessons and experience, thus their thoughts tended to be rigid and conservative. As a result, the socialist system could not get further improvement and development.

---

8   *Collected Works of Mao Zedong*, Vol. 6, People's Republic House, 1999, p. 435.

But China followed a different path. After the basic completion of socialist transformation, Mao Zedong immediately pointed out that China had basically established socialism, but not it was not fully completed and consolidated, and far from being perfect. Therefore, "It still needs long time for further completion and consolidation". He later evaluated: "In the early years of New China, we had no experience in economic construction, thus we could only imitate the Soviet's mode. This method was completely necessary at that time, but also had some disadvantages, as it was void of creativity and independence. It was certainly not a long-term solution".[9] After we obtained certain level of experience of our own, we had no choice but to change the things that were unsuitable for Chinese realities.

In 1956, Mao Zedong explicitly proposed "the issues on the whole economic system of socialism" at the meeting of Political Bureau of Central Committee of CPC.[10] He believed that instead of "the Charter of the Masteel", "the Charter of Anshan Iron and Steel Company" should be adopted to manage the state-owned enterprises. The former charter was referred to a set of authoritative one-man management way imposed by joint Magnitogorsk steel mill, a major steel mill in Soviet, while the latter one was some guidelines carried out by the Anshan Iron and Steel Company, namely "cadres participate in productive labor, and workers join the management of enterprises; reform the unreasonable regulations; apply the principle of combining enterprises' leading cadres, technicians and workers in the technical reform". After the agricultural cooperative movement, he also put forward the "issues of democratic management" concerning agricultural production.

In September 1956, at the Enlarged Third Plenary Session of the Eighth Central Committee of the CPC, Chen Yun said: "The situation regarding our socialist economy is as follows: As far as production management in industry and commerce is concerned, state management and collective management are to be central, but there is to be, in addition, a certain amount of individual management. This individual management is to be supplementary to state and collective management. As far as production planning is concerned the majority of the entire country's industrial and agricultural products are to be produced according to planning, but at the same time some products may be freely produced within the permitted spheres of state planning, and according to market changes. Planned production is central to industrial and agricultural production, while free production, within the permitted spheres of state planning and according to market

---

9   *Selected Readings of Mao Zedong*, Vol. 3, People's Republic House, 1999, p. 831.
10   *Collected Works of Mao Zedong*, Vol. 7, People's Republic House, 1999, p. 53.

changes, and is supplementary to planned production. Hence the market in a socialist economy is not in any way the free market of capitalism, rather it is the unified market of socialism. In the unified socialist market, the state market is central, but there is also a free market under state control which will put some specific restrictions upon it."

These ideas of Chen Yun were officially put into the Party resolution. Mao Zedong also proposed openly: "Consider two aspects, while not losing the long-term vision of eliminating capitalism." That meant, regarding the ownership structure, we should first keep the state-owned economy and the collective economy as main body, besides we can also properly maintain and develop private and self-employed businesses and bring in foreign investment from abroad. These cases clearly indicate that it is unreasonable to regard China's socialist transformation as the replica of the Soviet's model.

II. Was It Combining Marxism-Leninism with Chinese realities or was it tinged "with the color of populism"?

The founding of the New China in 1949 marked the end of China's new democratic revolution as well as the beginning of the socialist revolution. It was only in 1956 that China's socialist transformation was basically completed. The socialist state-owned and cooperative economy, and the public-private joint enterprises economy, which basically belonged to socialist nature, amounted to 92.9%, produced the overwhelming part of the national income. This indicated that the basic economic system of socialism based on the public ownership of means of production was established. It was the main result of socialist transformation. Some people have argued: China's socialist transformation didn't match with the process of socialist industrialization, but was "tinged with the color of populism". They also treated the judgment of Mao Zedong "On a blank sheet of paper free from mark, the freshest and the most beautiful character can be written, the freshest and most beautiful pictures can be painted" as "a typical statement" of populism. Mao Zedong viewed that a nation with backward economy and culture can only build socialism under given conditions. Was his idea in accord with Marxism-Leninism or "tinged with the color of populism"? In order to answer this question, it is necessary to examine the discussion of Marx and Lenin on the premises of socialist revolution.

We know that the development of capitalism has transformed human's regional and national histories to a world history. We must observe the problems of contemporary China with a vision of world history, otherwise we are impossible to reach the correct judgement. In the German Ideology, Marx and Engels said: "According to our point of view, all historical collisions are rooted in the contradiction between productive forces and the form of intercourse. Incidentally, to lead to collisions in a country, this contradiction need not necessarily have reached its extreme limit in this particular country. The competition with industrially more advanced countries, brought about by the expansion of international intercourse, is sufficient to produce a similar contradiction in countries with a backward industry."[11] This kind of contradiction, under certain context, may lead to proletarian revolutions. In fact, the prosperity of developed capitalist countries relies on the underdevelopment in undeveloped countries. The developed capitalist countries have blocked the way for those underdeveloped countries to prosper and become strong by following the capitalist development path. It had been proved by the history of many countries. This was one of the critical reasons why proletarian revolutions could occur in backward countries instead of developed countries. Here it is necessary to talk about the correspondence between Marx and Zasulich. In February 1881, Vera Zasulich wrote to Marx for the explanation about "the likely fate of Russian rural commune and his views on the theory that every country in the world must go through each stage of capitalist production because of the inevitable course of history". Marx replied: "The analysis I have made in Capital provides no reason either for or against the vitality

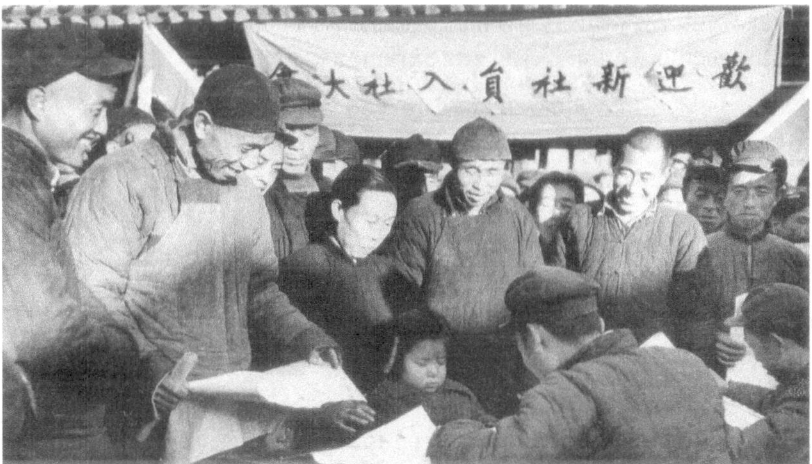

After the Land Reform movement, the CPC adopted the measures of "active leadership, steady advance" and quickly guided farmers to the path of cooperation in production. By the end of 1955, all farmers in the suburbs of Beijing joined semi-socialist cooperatives. Photo shows the farmers of the East Guantou village of Fengtai district applying for cooperative admission.

11   *Selections of Marx and Engels*, Vol. 1, People's Republic House, 1995, pp. 115-116.

of Russian rural commune. But the special study I have made of it, including a search for original source material, has convinced me that the commune is the fulcrum for social regeneration in Russia." Marx had argued that, because in Russia, thanks to a unique combination of circumstances, the rural commune, still established on a nationwide scale, may gradually detach itself from its primitive features and develop directly as an element of collective production on a nationwide scale. It is precisely thanks to its contemporaneity with capitalist production that it may appropriate the latter's positive acquisitions without experiencing all its frightful misfortunes. Russia does not live in isolation from the modern world...." "On the other hand, the contemporaneity of western production, which dominates the world market, allows Russia to incorporate in the commune all the positive acquisitions devised by the capitalist system without passing through capitalism's Caudine Forks [i.e., undergo humiliation in defeat]".[12] One of the requirements for such an achievement was the "Russian revolution" and the assimilation of the positive achievements of the capitalist civilization. In fact, although the rural commune in Russia, didn't become the backbone of revitalization in the Russian society, Marx's statement above still had guiding effect on studying the conditions for countries like Russia to build socialism from a methodological perspective. Russia used to be an economically and cultural backward country, and until 1913, it was still a poor agricultural country. In the total output of industry and agriculture, industry accounted for 42.1%, and agriculture for 57.9%.

Nevertheless, Lenin, on the basis of the "permanent revolution" idea of Marx and Engels and basing himself on the idea of combining revolutionary peasant movement with proletarian revolutionary movement, clearly pointed out on the eve of 1905 revolution that Russia would immediately transit from democratic revolution to socialism, based on the strength of our class conscious and organized proletariat. During the October Revolution, Lenin successfully led Russian people to achieve this transition. In 1923, Lenin wrote a short article titled *A Review of Nikoloai Sukhanov's Notes on the Russian Revolution*.

In his voluminous books "Notes on the Russian Revolution" the author Sukhanov in a chapter had argued that the above-mentioned theories of Lenin "lacked a sufficient analysis of the objective premises of the Russian revolution, namely lacked a sufficient analysis of its social and economic conditions". In his point of view, Russia, as a country with backward economy and culture, lacked the objective premises to carry on socialist revolution. Lenin replied: "You say that civilization is necessary for the building of

---

12   *Selections of Marx and Engels*, Vol. 3, People's Publishing House, 1995, pp. 770-775.

socialism. Very good. But why could we not first create such prerequisites of civilization in our country by the expulsion of the landowners and the Russian capitalists, and then start moving toward socialism?" "If a definite level of culture is required for the building of socialism (although nobody can say just what that definite "level of culture" is, for it differs in every Western European country), why cannot we began by first achieving the prerequisites for that definite level of culture in a revolutionary way, and *then*, with the aid of the workers' and peasants' government and Soviet system, proceed to overtake the other nations?" That is to say, in Lenin's opinion, it is true that socialist system should be based on the highly developed productive forces, but if it is ripe for revolution, the proletariat of underdeveloped countries should also grasp opportunities and promote a revolution, wrestle for political power, establish the Soviet system in order to create the premises of developing productive forces. Do we violate the principles of Marxism? Lenin thought we do not. He believed that the general laws of development of world history would not reject particularity: on the contrary, presumed, that certain periods of development may display peculiarities in either the form or the sequence of this development." "They all call themselves Marxists, but their conception of Marxism is impossibly pedantic. Those people have completely failed to understand what is decisive in Marxism, namely, its revolutionary dialectics."[13] Before this, according to the idea mentioned above, when he evaluated the prospects of revolution in the colonies and semi-colonies, Lenin said directly: "With the assistance of the proletariat of advanced countries, an underdeveloped country could transit into Soviet system without undergoing through the development phase of capitalism and then into communism after several developmental stages."[14]

Therefore, the viewpoint that underdeveloped country could not launch a socialist revolution before capitalism got highly developed is not the genuine Marxism or Leninism. When Chairman Mao unswervingly conducted the socialist transformation (socialist revolution) with the support of Chinese people, he had followed the above-mentioned theories of Marxism. He also developed this theory and creatively combined the historical experiences of revolutions in the world with the Chinese revolution and China's reality. He pointed out that it was a general rule to win the public opinion and seize the state power as the first step, then solve the problem of ownership and develop productive forces greatly as the next and final step. Mao said: "Similarly, from the standpoint of world history, the bourgeois revolutions and the establishment of the bourgeois nations came before, not after, the

---

13 *Lenin Selected Works*, Vol. 4, People's Publishing House, 1975, pp. 775-778.
14 *Ibid.*, p. 279.

industrial revolution. The bourgeoisie first changed the superstructure and took possession of the machinery of state before carrying on propaganda to gather real strength. Only then did they push forward great changes in the production relations. When the production relations had been taken care of and they were on the right track they then opened the way for the development of the productive forces. To be sure, the revolution in the production relations is brought on by a certain degree of development of the productive forces, but the major development of the productive forces always comes after changes in the production relations." … "As to the proletarian social revolutions, this general rule can also be applied."[15]

Capitalist socialized mass production has underwent several development phases including simple coordination, handicraft workshop and large-scale mechanized production. According to this, Mao Zedong pointed out: "Handcraft workshop is the capitalism of non-mechanized production. This kind of capitalist production relations have generated the need for the technological improvement and paved the way for adopting mechanized production. In England the Industrial Revolution (late eighteenth-early nineteenth centuries) was carried through only after the bourgeois revolution, that is, after the seventeenth century. All in their respective ways, Germany, France, America, and Japan underwent change in the superstructure and production relations before the vast development of capitalist industry."[16] He held that socialist productive relations should be systematically established after the victory of democratic revolution in economically backward China, moreover, China's socialism could also undergo a stage of handicraft workshop.

What should be emphatically pointed out is that Chairman Mao affirmed China could and should build socialist system before finishing the task of industrialization, but he never argued that socialism could be built on the basis of small production and could linger based on manual labor for a long time, unlike the populist views. He pointed out, in the climax of agricultural cooperation, we were not only progressing a revolution about social system that is from private ownership to public ownership but also progressing a revolution about technology that is from handicraft production to large-scale modernization machine production, and these two kinds of revolutions were actually hanged together.[17] When he wrote down "on a blank sheet of paper free from mark…" In the article *Introduction of Cooperative*, he wanted to demonstrate the viewpoint "the time for China's industrial and agricultural production to catch up with capitalist great power may not need too long as

15   *Collected Works of Mao Zedong*, Vol. 8, People's Publishing House, 1999, pp. 131-132.
16   Ibid, p. 132.
17   *Collected Works of Mao Zedong*, Vol. 6, People's Publishing House, 1999, p. 432.

we used to consider", which had not any common ground with Populist's ideology that socialism should base on small production. In fact, Mao poured great enthusiasm into industrialization of the country and agricultural mechanization, furthermore, he led the Party and Chinese people to strive hard and basically set up an independent and intact industrial system and national economic system after suffering many difficulties and setbacks, which had laid significant foundation for realizing modernization.

During his talk with Mr. Lin Daguang and his wife from Canada on October 15, 1977, Deng Xiaoping pointed out: "Lenin has argued that underdeveloped country could launch socialist revolution when he was criticizing Kautsky's vulgar productive forces theory. We also opposed this vulgar productive forces theory, so the path of encircling the cities from the rural areas was adopted, which totally differed from the October Revolution. At that time, China have already had an advanced proletarian political party and elementary level of capitalist economy, evaluating all these together with the international condition, we concluded that socialism could be built in underdeveloped China. This is the same as what Lenin had said when opposing vulgar productive forces theory."[18] In order to evaluate China's socialist transformation scientifically, the thinking of vulgar productive forces theory must be rejected. The theory of vulgar productive forces does not belong to Marxism, it is the distortion of Marxism by dogmatism.

III. Did the Socialist Transformation Liberate and Develop the Productive Forces or Hinder Them?

Socialist transformation was a profound revolution which transformed private ownership to public ownership in productive relations. The main standard to measure whether the revolution of productive relations right and necessary or not necessary should be based on whether it can bring about positive effect or hindering effect and destructive effect on the development of productive forces. The purpose of socialist revolution is to emancipate the productive forces. In order to emancipate and develop the productive forces, Chinese Communist Party put forward the socialist transformation on individual agriculture, handicraft industry and capitalist industry and commerce. China's national capital mainly consisted of commercial capital and financial capital, while industrial capital only accounted for one fifth. The industry owned by national capitalists was mainly composed of light textile industry and food industry, but lacked the heavy industry sector. The existing industrial enterprises were in small scale, with poor

---

18 *The Chronicle of Deng Xiaoping's Life (1975-1997)*, Vol. I, Central Party Literature Press, 2009, p. 223.

technical equipment and low labor productivity. According to statistics of the new China, 69.7% of industries only owned less than 10 workers; 79.1% of industries were handicraft workshops. To change the condition, socialist transformation had to be put into practice.

Chinese individual farming economy had many limitations. Individual farmers had little cultivated land and small scale of operation with insufficient instruments of production, poor peasants and farm laborers only occupied 0.47 head of farm animal and 0.41 plow per household averagely; they were also short of fund. On this occasion, farmers confronted with many difficulties in building farmland water conservancy facility, land formation and soil improvement, utilizing improved farm tools and even machine to cultivate, sow and harvest as well as implementing division of labor system to develop diversified economy and so on; they also lacked in the capability to resist natural disaster. Most peasant households were incompetent in maintaining simple reproduction, not to mention expanding reproduction. In order to change the condition, socialist transformation must be put into practice.

The Party and government has paid much attention on boosting revolution of productive relations by adapting requirement of economic development during the process of leading people to implement socialist transformation, meanwhile, development of productive forces was guaranteed when transforming productive relations. Therefore, social and political situation was stable and economy developed continuously even though a profound revolution was proceeded. During the process of socialist transformation (from 1953 to 1956), the national gross industrial output value had an average annual increase of 19.6%, while the total value of agriculture output had increased 4.8% annually. Then, China's economy developed rapidly and economic achievements were relatively good, the proportional relations among several significant economic sectors was relatively harmonious; the market was prosperous and price of commodities was stable; people's life quality had apparently improved. During the process, state-capitalist economy and cooperative economy had showed their obvious advantage. For instance, after the private capitalist industry turning into public-private partnership, the average annual value of production of each worker in the year of 1952, 1953 and 1954 was 9,297 RMB, 10,800 RMB and 13,401 RMB respectively. In 1955, the average worker labor productivity rate of public-private partnership enterprises were two-fold higher than that of private industry. After the industry-wide public-private partnership in 1956, production output value of jointly operated industry had increased by 32% compared to that of 1955. The business volume of jointly operated shop, cooperative shop and co-operative group had increased by 15%. Agricultural production in this time also had been rising year after year. 1956 was a year when agricultural cooperation flourished, but agriculture suffered from a severe natural disaster: about 240 million mu land were influenced by the flood, but the gross value of agricultural output still increased by 4.9%; grain yield increased by 15.4 billion kilogram, which had an increment of 4.4% over the previous year; output of rice, wheat, potato, flue-cured tobacco and tea had surpassed the production target of 1957 (the last year of China's first Five-Year Plan). Those facts vividly manifest that socialist transformation had not hindered the development of productive forces, instead it had become the direct driving force for the development of productive forces. It was a sheer nonsense that socialist transformation had destroyed the productive forces.

It should be particularly noticed that the triumph of socialist transformation had paved the way for socialist construction and it had laid basis for China's progress and development in the future. But on the whole, China had still made historical achievements in building socialism. During this period, we had basically built up an independent and relatively integrated industrial system and national economic system, which brought about economic independence for China after winning political independence. Furthermore, the speed of China's economic development was quite rapid. From 1953 to 1978, average annual growth rate of gross output value of industry and agriculture was 8.2%; the average annual growth rate of total industrial output value was 11.4%. These facts vividly prove that China, a country with backward economy and culture, should and could build socialism; it had preliminarily but strongly showed that socialist system has an inherent superiority. China was a semi-colonial and semi-feudal country which lagged economically and culturally. China's entrance in the socialist path earlier than those developed capitalist countries was the result of China's special historical conditions, plus the correct leadership of Chinese Communist Party and hard work of the whole nation. It was the result of creative development of scientific socialism, the glory of the CPC and Chinese people, the triumph of Mao Zedong Thought.

The author is a professor at the Peking University

5

Aiming to Break the "Poverty Trap" was the Main Reason for the Formation of Planned Economy in China

Wu Li

Why did China set up the planned economy in the 1950s? How was it established? Was it a result of copying the economic mode of former Soviet Union? How to evaluate the planned economy in the first 30 years after the founding of the PRC? Today as China has implemented the socialist market economy, it is necessary for us to comb and examine these questions so as to clarify confusion and mistakes on this aspect caused by the historical nihilism thought of trend.

I. China faced "poverty trap" in early years of the founding

"Poverty trap" is a self-perpetuating condition where an individual, family, group or region, caught in a vicious cycle, suffers from persistent underdevelopment. Based on his research of the root cause of chronic poverty of developing countries, the renowned development economist R. Nurkse put forward the "vicious cycle of poverty" theory. He detailed the theory in this way: the persistent poverty of developing countries is caused by numerous interconnected and interacted "vicious cycles of poverty". Of that, the vicious cycle of poverty is on the dominant position; from the aspect of capital supply, the developing countries suffer from the vicious cycle of "low income–low savings–low capital formation–low productivity–low output–low income"; from the aspect of demand, the developing countries face the vicious cycle "low income–low investment attraction–low capital formation–low productivity–low income". The reason that the two vicious cycles of supply and demand is because the per capita income is very low which is caused by the capital rareness which in return result in low per capita income. The low income and poverty cannot produce savings needed for the economic development and consequently there is no investment or capital formation, which in return causes the low income and chronic poverty of the country. China was facing such a challenge in early years after founding.

When the PRC was founded, due to its encounter with severe wars for more than a century, imperialist aggression and plunder and oppression and exploitation of feudal bureaucratic capitalism, China's already backward economy became even worse. Take the best development period from 1931 to 1936 for example, the consumption rate and investment rate were 104.1% and -4.1% , 97.5% and 2.5% , 102.0% and -2.0% , 109.1% and -9.1% , 101.8% and -1.8% , 94.0% and 6.0%, respectively. These figures reflect the very low investment rate and it was even negative in four years.[1] Therefore around the time of victory of War of Resistance against Japanese Aggression, the economist circles of China, when discussing the post-war recovery and economic development, almost reached consensus that China could not independently solve the shortage of capital. In 1949, the white paper of the United States on policies towards China also concluded that the CPC could not solve the food problem. Dean Acheson, Secretary of State of the United States, said in a letter to President Truman on the white paper United States Relations with China with Special Reference to the Period 1944-1949 on July 30, 1949, "In forming the fate of modern China, two elements play an important role. The first element is China's population, which had doubled in the 18th and 19th century, and consequently formed an unbearable pressure to China. In modern history the top question that every Chinese government must face is to solve the problem of people's food supply. To date no government has succeeded."[2]

China was a typical agricultural country at the beginning of founding, and the vast population has been one of the basic conditions of the country. The huge population size has determined that the per capita resource is relatively scarce. Because of the long history and developed agricultural civilization, the contradiction between population and arable land has long been existing. Since the Mid-Qing Dynasty, the population growth further

1   Quoted from The Evolution of the Proportional Relation between Investment and Consumption in China and Its Problems and Countermeasures, Wang Haibo, *Collected Works of Wang Haibo*, Vol. 10, Economy and Management Publishing House, 2011, p. 361.

2   *Relations between the US and China with Special Reference to the Period (1944-1949)*, Vol. 1, p. 4, compiled by China Modern History Information Committee, published in September 1957.

worsened the contradiction between population and agricultural resources and resulted in excessive development and outstanding environmental problems. In the days after the founding of the PRC, China had a population of 541.67 million, and 484.02 million of them were farmers and lived on traditional agriculture. But the per capita arable land was only 2.65 mu, and per capita food supply was only 209 kg. In 1952, the primary industry employment accounted for as high as 83.5% of the economically active population, and the per capita agricultural means of production was very scarce, in addition to the difficulties of a large population and relatively little arable land, and agriculture could provide very little surplus for industrialization. Moreover, the industrial output value only accounted for 17.6% of the domestic gross product (GDP) and its self-accumulation capacity was very poor.[3] In the same year, the per capita output was only 2 kg steel, 115 kg coal, 0.8 kg crude oil, 13 KWh electricity. In contrast, the per capita industrial output of main countries and regions of the same period was: 82 kg steel, 724 kg coal, 242 kg crude oil, and 448 KWh electricity. Just as what Mao Zedong said, "What can we produce? We can produce tables and chairs, teapots and teacups, grains and grind grain into flour, and make paper, but we cannot produce even a car, an airplane, a tank or a truck."[4] The very low accumulation capacity and highly scattered surplus made the PRC to easily fall into what the economists call as the "poverty trap".

Formation of the planned economy was highly related to the international environment of the period. The influence of the international environment mainly manifested in the following three aspects: first was the blockade and embargo implemented by the United States-led Western developed capitalist countries. In order to break the economic blockade and avoid losses, we must use the governmental forces, make overall arrangement and take a unified attitude in the foreign trade to the western countries. Meanwhile, the blockade also made China's foreign trade to shift focus to Soviet Union and Eastern Europe. But these countries were only willing to trade in the form of agreement trade. Not only the private importers and exporters were excluded, but also local state-owned enterprises could hardly directly participate in. Second, since the outbreak of the Korean War, the national defense pressure increased significantly together with the national defense expenses. In consideration of the historical lesson of "lagging behind leaves one vulnerable to attacks", China must accelerate development of the heavy industry even for the consideration of national security. This

---

3   Annual Statistical Data publicized by the National Bureau of Statistics on the official website: www.stats.gov.cn.
4   *Collected Works of Mao Zedong*, Vol. 6, People's Publishing House, 1999, p. 329.

required not only increasing accumulation as much as possible, but also keeping the surplus in the government, specifically the central government. Therefore, it was unavoidable to implement the highly centralized planned economy. Third, in the 1950s, Soviet Union was the only country that was willing to and capable of aiding China in a large scale. The Soviet Union's

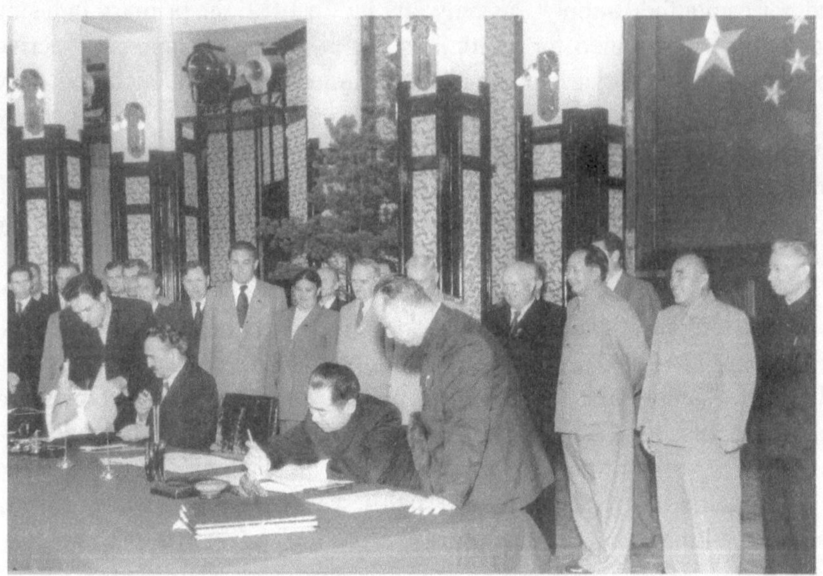

In the 1950s, Soviet Union was the only country that was willing to and capable of aiding China in a large scale. The Soviet Union's aid was preconditioned: China should adopt the socialist system and ally with the socialist camp. On the evening of October 11, 1954, Zhou Enlai (right) and A. I. Mikoyan (left) signed the Joint Declaration and Joint Communique between the Chinese and the Soviet Union governments. People attending the signing ceremony include (Front row of the standing people from the right): Liu Shaoqi, Zhu De, Mao Zedong, N. Khrushchev, I. Eugene and N. Bulganin

aid was preconditioned: China must approve the socialist system and stand at the side of the socialist camp. Meanwhile, the economic system of Soviet Union decided its aid was only to the Chinese government instead of private enterprises. The aiding mode and the industrial construction priorities and layout of the First Five-Year Plan and the Second-Five Year Plan facilitated China's transfer to the planned economy.

The Korean War has erupted in 1950, and the following Taiwan Strait Crisis, Vietnam War, Sino-Indian border conflict, and Sino-Soviet border conflict, among others, forced the CPC to put the national security on the top of the agenda when choosing the economic development strategy. The act that the United States attempted to prevent reunification and directly threaten the security of China was based on the remarkable difference of weaponry power between China and the United States, furthermore the remarkable difference of the industrialization level. That the United States dispatched troops to Taiwan after the outbreak of the Korean War and threatened China with atomic bomb in 1955 to prevent the national reunification of China, which have all reinforced the Chinese policymakers' determination to give priority to heavy industry. Just as what Mao Zedong said when amending the general publicity guideline of the Party in the transition period, "since our foundation of heavy industry was very poor in the past, and we were not economically independent, and our national defense was not solid, the imperialist countries have bullied us. We Chinese people have suffered much. If we do not set up our heavy industry, the imperialism will make attempts to bully us in future."[5] To establish an independent and strong national defense industry, the country had to give priority to the development of heavy industry which is featured by large amount of investment and which possesses a long construction cycle.

There was a huge gap between the limited financial resources and the massive capital needed for upcoming economic construction. Moreover, the Korean War, Vietnam War and the first Taiwan Strait Crisis forced China to accelerate the speed of industrialization. At that time, Soviet Union agreed to comprehensively aid China's economic construction. That was a hard-won historical opportunity. Under the severe situation, the political and economic isolation and blockade of the western countries, economic isomorphism with Soviet Union and Eastern European socialist countries also determined that China had to develop an inward-oriented economy in a semi-closed situation. This meant that China had to rely on its own capacity to implement rapid and large-scale capital accumulation to launch the industrialization process. The limited and scattered agricultural surplus was almost the only way for China to realize such accumulation. In order to accelerate industrialization, China needed to set up a highly centralized planned economic system to ensure the government to own strong resource mobilization and allocation capacity. The new democratic economic system could not meet such requirements. Therefore, China soon started the transition from the new democratic economy to the socialist economy of the Soviet Union model.

---

5 Struggle for Mobilizing All Forces and Build China into a Great Socialist Country, December 1953. CCPCC Party Literature Research Office: *Selected Works of Important Documents since the Founding of PRC*, Vol. 4, Central Party Literature Press, p. 705.

Therefore, when the task of national economic recovery was basically completed and China shifted its efforts to large-scale economic development in 1953, the challenge of how to solve shortage of the construction funds and the hindering of agriculture to industrialization became outstanding. Giving priority to development of the heavy industry when the problem of food and clothing was not solved, the planned economy showcased its superiority on "concentrating our limited resources on large projects". In the First Five-Year Plan, China had concentrated all of its resources on 156 major construction projects and 694 other construction projects which were all ambitious targets. Thus China set up factories for aircraft manufacturing, automobiles, tractors, power generation equipment, mining equipment, heavy machinery and precision equipment and other industries through renovating the original industrial structure and also by establishing a new industrial basis, thus significantly improved the internal coherence of its industrial structure. From 1958 to 1965, China established a series of emerging industries such as electronic industry, petrochemicals, and atomic energy; from 1966 to 1978, the industry had maintained a rapid growth and the iron and steel sector and the heavy industry were given priority. With more than 20 years of industrialization construction, "China set up an independent and relatively complete industrial system and national economic system on the 'poor and blank' base left by the old China."[6]

II. Formation of the planned economy

As for the planned economy, the Encyclopedia of China makes the following definition: "Based on the premise of socialized production, on the basis of the public ownership of the means of production, the socialist countries, according to the requirements of the objective economic laws, in particular the requirements of the law of planned proportionate development, manage and regulate the national economy through directive and guiding plans. It is not only a method and a system for administrating the national economy, but also an economic system and one of the basic characteristics of the socialist society."[7] The planned economy of China experienced three phases in the first 30 years after the founding of the PRC: (1) 1949-1952, the first phase, that was the phase for creating conditions for establishment of the planned economy; (2) 1953-1957, the second phase, that was the phase for the planned economy to take shape; (3) 1958-1978, the third phase, that was the phase of complete form of planned economy.

---

6   Ye Jianying, Speech at the Ceremony Marking the 30th Anniversary of the Founding of the People's Republic of China, *People's Daily*, September 30, 1979, p. 1.

7   *Encyclopedia of China* (electronic version), China Encyclopedia Press, 1999.

The PRC government, established through the new democratic revolution, not only possessed a strong power of governing the state, but was also ideologically and culturally tended to be an "omnipotent government". The state concept in the traditional culture of China, the huge bureaucratic capital that controlled the national economy and people's livelihood left by the old China, and the worries on the national security after outbreak of the Korean War and strong belief in the socialist economic theories expounded by Lenin and Stalin has forced the CPC to naturally affirm that government would be the main propeller of industrialization. After the founding of the PRC, the ruling CPC made the rapid industrialization as its unswerving struggle goal. In early years of the founding of the PRC, the CPC set forth, based on its understanding and legacy of old China, to realize industrialization as soon as possible through controlling capital and the foreign trade and implementing the "all-round policy" (that is, giving consideration to both the public and private sectors, benefiting both the labor and the capital, urban-rural mutual assistance and domestic-foreign exchange) on the basis of the coexistence of various economic components under the leadership of the state-owned economy. After the outbreak of the Korea War in 1950, the military conflicts between China and the United States made the international environment grim. For the industrialization aiming at growing stronger and prosperous, the Chinese government emphasized the strength growth, i.e., establishing a heavy industry as soon as possible that could reinforce the national defense. Therefore, the CPC naturally accepted the economic mode of Soviet Union, which was cognized as a successful model.

In the 1950s, the economic system of China changed from a system which gave equal importance to planned economy and market economy to the first phase planned economy system which was characterized by the administrative management, and gradually abandoned the market system from China's economic operation mode. It was no doubt that there were theoretic and cognitive reasons for such change. But if we look from the aspect of economic system changes of that time and trace back the historical development of economic thinking and policy evolution of the CPC, we can comfortably see that subjective cognizance of the time was the manifestation of the objective reality and the repulsion of the market function was the result of the economic foundation, development requirements and international environment in combination at that time rather than the result of learning from the socialist mode of Soviet Union. Specifically, the following elements contributed to the formation of the planned economic system: (1) "Market failure" element. The chronic chaos and predatory policy of the KMT government caused the distorted economy and twisted market regulation. Therefore in the early years after the founding of the PRC, the market did not show its positive regulation effect, in contrary, because of excessive expansion of the private financial industry, the living necessities were short of supply and the demand elasticity was very low, the urban unemployment was serious and foreign trade was blocked, making the market regulation hardly to work by adjusting the supply-demand relationship through price. Take the living necessities such as food, cloth and coal that had little demand elasticity for example, the government had to guarantee the livelihood of urban residents and protect the social stability through establishing the state-owned commercial companies and implementing "listing price" (making the market price close to the listing price). (2) National security element. The lesson of being bullied for more than 100 years of old China and the severe international situation after the outbreak of the Korea War, and the threats of the United States on China's reunification forced the PRC government to give priority to the development of the heavy industry to set up a strong national defense for the consideration of national security. (3) Breaking "poverty trap" element. The traditional agriculture based poor and weak industrial structure and the large population made the per capita means of production in serious scarcity and farmers had no surplus after feeding themselves though with the land reform China had enabled land to tiller. It was hard to break the low income "poverty trap" and realize the industrialization take-off in a short time relying on market. When the PRC was founded, it implemented the combined planned and market regulating system on the basis of coexistence of various economic components. Therefore, from the very beginning the PRC was faced by the issue of how to handle the relationship between planned economy and market economy, the issue of status, means and scope of the planned management in essence. The planned economy, as a basic economic system of socialism, was practiced in the first socialist country Soviet Union. After the founding of the PRC, China chose the socialist industrialization path and learned from Soviet Union on the economic management system to set up the planned economic system. In fact during the economic recovery period of China, it made the planned management a means of the government for the economic management. As a means of the economic management, the planned management consisted two methods: mandatory plan and instructive plan. It started in the 1930s when Soviet Union completed the socialist reform for regarding the planned management as the supreme and the only economic management means. The reason that the planned management became the only or the major resource allocation and economic operation means after the socialist reform could not be separated from the unitary public ownership and the top-down administrative economic management system, under which enterprises could hardly

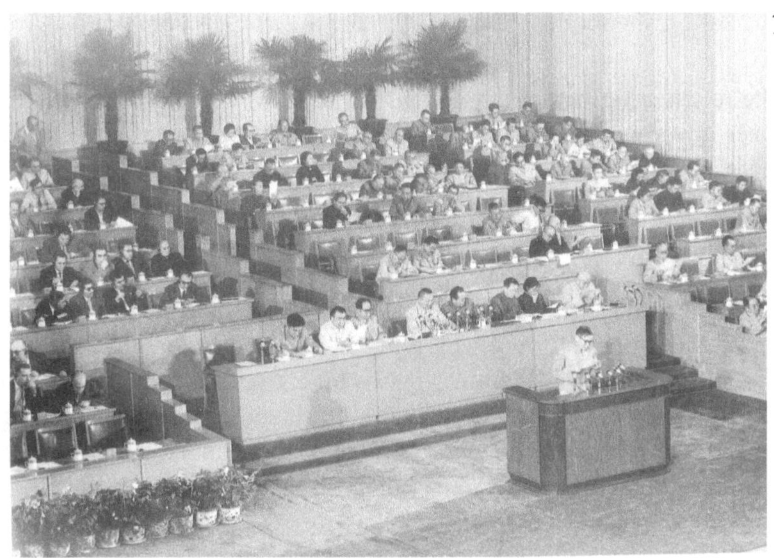

*At the 8th National Congress of the CPC in 1956, Chen Yun proposed
to employ the market regulation to make up for the deficits of the
planned management and Li Fuchun set forth the idea to employ both
the mandatory and instructive planning, and these proposals were
agreed by all the delegates. On September 20, 1956, Chen Yun made the
speech On the New Issues after the Capitalist Industrial and Commercial
Reform Tide, and set forth a relatively complete and creative concept of
socialist economic system that suited the actual conditions of China*

utilize the real decision-making rights, and although they had certain opera-
tional space, they lacked guidance to access the necessary market information and had restricted capacity of utilizing market competition mechanism.
Therefore, the scope of market regulation and its extent were in an inferior
status in the traditional planned economic system of China.

The process within which the traditional planned economic system was
formed was also the process wherein the market regulation function has
declined. It had actually started with the financial market controls and
price regulations by the government on the living necessities such as food,
cloth and coal in early days of the founding of the PRC. Latter the country
completed the socialist reform of private financial industry by the end of
1952, established the urban labor force planning and allocation system and
launched the system of "controlled procurement and distribution" of the
major agricultural and sideline products in 1953 and abandoned the free
market of urban consumer goods, in 1957.

The relationship between plan and market was actually the relationship between governments at all levels and enterprises (also included the relationship with individual economy). Because the government-led economic development mode was not changed basically, the formulation and implementation from the First 5th Five-Year Plan to the 10th Five-Year Plan, i.e. the economic operation procession, had centered on how to handle the relationship between the planned management and market regulation. This issue has nibbled the CPC and the Chinese government for over 50 years. Before the Opening-up and Reform, or before the Chinese government set the goal of establishing the socialist market economic system in 1992, many could not distinguish the essence of the planned economy from that of the planned management. As the unitary public ownership must implement the planned economy (in another word, the planned management was only the major means), and in the transition period (1949-1956 transition from the new democratic economy to the planned economy, or 1978-1992 transition from planned economy to market economy), the administrative planned management played a leading role in the economic operation and therefore caused the following illusion: it seemed the planned economy was the part under the administrative planned management of the government, and the necessity of planned management was confused with the planned economy and both their means and basic system were treated as the same. When in 1992 China made the market economy as the goal of the economic system reform the past debates on the planned economy and market economy has vanished in a puff of smoke.

In fact, from the day when the planned economy was established, the CPC had realized the defects of the planned economy and attempted to reform and improve it. Mao Zedong, Liu Shaoqi, Zhou Enlai, Chen Yun, Li Fuchun and other leaders have made many improvement opinions for the formulation and implementation of the plan since 1956. For example, Liu Shaoqi pointed out the drawbacks of the unitary planned management: "The socialist economy was characterized by planning and the planned economy, but actually the social economic activities included all walks of life and all aspects, several thousands, tens of thousands and hundreds of thousands. The national plan could not be detailed to the several thousands, several thousand, tens of thousands or hundreds of thousands, but only the catalogues. In the end the social economic life was made simple and stiff."[8] Therefore at the 8th National Congress of the CPC in 1956, Chen Yun's proposal to make up deficiency of the planned management with market regulation and Li Fushun's proposal of employing both the mandatory plan

---

8   Liu Shaoqi, How to Properly Handle the Contradictions among the People, April 27, 1957, *Selected Works of Liu Shaoqi*, Vol. 2, p. 147.

and instructive plan were adopted by the whole Party. However, during the 20 years from 1958 to 1978, the market regulation and instructive plan method were basically excluded from the government's means of economic regulation. The Five-Year Plans in these period, although none was officially adopted and determined, actually contained mandatory plans and became the reference for the governments at all levels and the planning management departments within the economic administration.

After 1958, the mandatory planned management was strengthened in the rural economy after the launch of the People's Commune Movement and the management mode tended to be single. Farmers had little independent decision-making rights and free marketing of agricultural products became nearly impossible. After several economic setbacks, the role of market and free trade was tapped for a while in the adjustment stage from 1961 to 1964, the State Development Planning Commission once proposed to diversify the planned management, including mandatory, instructive and referential (indicative) management modes to respond to the requirements of streamlining the markets and requirements of improving planning. It was proposed to differentiate the plans made for collectively-owned enterprises from those made for enterprises owned by the whole people. Direct planning should be implemented for the enterprises and undertakings owned by the whole people while the indirect planning for collectively-owned agriculture and handicraft production units. The government should only assign the purchase plan of agricultural products to the rural communes and give referential opinions for the major agricultural production indexes of grain, cotton, and oil plants. As for the supply, production and marketing plan of the handicraft, the central government should only control several important products that were related to national welfare and people's livelihood, and the rest products were subject to the local governments. The petty commodities produced by handicraft producers and agricultural and sideline products produced by the rural people's communes and farmers should be under the centralized leadership of the commercial department and used for promoting production and exchanges through the supply and marketing contracts and country fair trade by employing the value law to meet national production and consumption requirements.[9] But in a situation when the economy was just recovered and the above mentioned measures were not fully implemented yet, the "Cultural Revolution" was launched. The Movement of "Cutting the Tail of Capitalism" abandoned the small-scale farming by farmer families nearby their homes. Under the encouragement

---

9 CPC Central Committee approved and issued the Provisions for the State Planning Commission on October 7, 1961.

of slogans "learning from the Dazhai-type institution in agriculture" and "taking grain as the key link", the rural production teams were controlled by the planning authority even in the selection of crop kinds, allocation of planting area and output amounts. Farmers had no decision-making rights and the production teams lost the right in the system of "three-levels of ownership and production team as the basis". In urban areas, the state-owned enterprises were also controlled rigidly. However, under the system that the planned economy controlled the whole country and the market role vanished before 1978, it was true there were problems mentioned above, but the system also helped realize part anticipated goals, for example ensuring the surplus claim and investment to the highest level and setting up an independent industrial system and strong national defense industry. According to the development economics and "poverty trap" hypothesis, one of the important conditions for a country's economic take-off is investment exceeding 11% of GDP. In the best economic period of old China from 1931 to 1936, the rate of capital accumulation in four of the six years was negative, and only 6.0% the highest in 1936.[10] It was much higher than 11% before 1978 in new China, and reached 22.7% the lowest in the period from 1963 to 1965, and 33.27% the highest in the 4th Five-Year Plan period, and 24.2% in the First Five-Year Plan period that was regarded the most reasonable.

III. Characteristics and effects of the planned economy in China

Compared with the Soviet Union, China's planned economy showed apparent differences in its economic development level and per capita resources. These facts have determined the unique characteristics of China's planned economy and choice of reform path which is different from Soviet Union.

(I) Basis and characteristics of China's planned economy. According to the basic principles of Marxism, socialist planned economy should be developed upon the capitalist socialized mass production, and the high-level of industrialization, marketization and urbanization would provide the necessary conditions for the implementation of the planned economy, thus it would fully give play to its advantages. However, China's planned economy was formed in the stage of backward agricultural country, in which the industrial system was not yet established, and when the majority of the population made living from was the traditional agriculture and lived in the countryside, and when the majority of the population had not experienced a

---

10   Chief editor Wu Baosan, *National Incomes of China (1933)*, Vol. I, Zhonghua Book Company, 1997, p. 20.

relatively developed market economy stage. The level of productive forces was very low and the economic development among different regions was seriously unbalanced; the traditional agriculture, handicraft and small industry took a high proportion, and agriculture was basically lived on the mercy of elements; and the production socialization level was very low. All these conditions made China's administrator of planned economy to face much more difficulties in implementing the planned management than Soviet Union and Eastern European socialist countries. For example, due to level of socialization of the production, any accurate, complete economic data, statistics and economic information collection was very difficult. Therefore, the government faced great constraints in the management of the national economy, especially when leading the mandatory plan management.

The planned management was manifested in the high authority and low quality (i.e., very high government power and authority, but the quality of government officials at all levels were very low; the plan was far from the reality, and the plan was highly fickle and arbitrary. It was mainly caused by economic backwardness and development unbalance).

The planned management was divided into the urban and rural sections. In the rural section, as it was mainly under the collective ownership (state-owned farms accounted for a very low proportion), therefore the agricultural plan was mainly estimated and arbitrary, lack of accurate and reliable statistics, and could not be used as the rural basic unit production and benefit appraisal index. The economic plans for the urban area, especially the plan for state-owned enterprises and public institutions and the basic construction plans, were under strict control and supervision.

The planning authority swung back and forth between the central government and local governments ("line and block"). China has the largest population of the world, and the economic development was highly unbalanced from place to place. The excessive centralization of authority resulted in constrained enthusiasm and insufficient vitality locally; but under excessive decentralization, unrealistic comparison among difference areas and characteristics not undertaking the national macro balance would result in chaos. Therefore in the planned economy period, the planned management authority division was characterized by the periodic cycle "power delegating results in disorder, and when disorder appears, delegated power would be taken back, but when the power is taken back, the situation would become rigid, and force power delegating again".

The market elements were lower than Soviet Union and Eastern European socialist countries of the same period. Because of the backward productive forces and unbalanced economic development, the planned economy could never be a monolithic whole no matter in the formation period or after its establishment except for some years (for example the three-year "Great Leap Forward" period). The serious shortage and high management costs forced the government to loosen control. But compared with the planned economy of Soviet Union and Eastern European countries, the market elements were much lower, mainly manifested in the labor force mobility, independent decision-making of enterprises and disposal of people's communes (collective farms) on the surplus products. China's exploration and reform of enlarging the scope of market regulation which was decided in 1956 was abandoned in 1957 after "Anti-rightist" campaign was launched. Although the economic recovery achieved during the economic adjustment period had not yet reached the economic levels in the year 1956, economic adjustment policies were also abandoned.

(II) Two inherent elements of the planned economy have the natures that can give play to its anticipated superiority. According to description of classical theory of Marxism on the planned economy, the planned economy was to arrange production and consumption under a unified plan of the state according to the social demand wherein all the members of the society have an equal share on the means of production. This system could avoid the waste caused by private ownership, avoid the anarchy of production and destructive market competition under the capitalist system and "polarization" in the society and increase the social and economic fairness to unprecedented levels.

However, once the planned economy was established, it was discovered that it was very difficult to realize this anticipated superiority. As for China, first, China was in the early stage of industrialization and the traditional agriculture and small producers took a high proportion and could not reach the socialization level of production. Therefore, the key for the planned economy to give play to its superiority–timely collection of sufficient information and timely handling of problems- became the largest challenge for formulating a right plan. And the difficulty seemingly could not be apparently improved through progress in industrialization and strengthening of the plan makers. The plan makers could not have access to sufficient and timely socio-economic information, due to the complicity of economy itself and backwardness of information tools. More importantly, the information was collected and forwarded through many institutions or people and in the process, the related institutions and personnel naturally filtered or even distorted the information due to their cognitive levels and personal

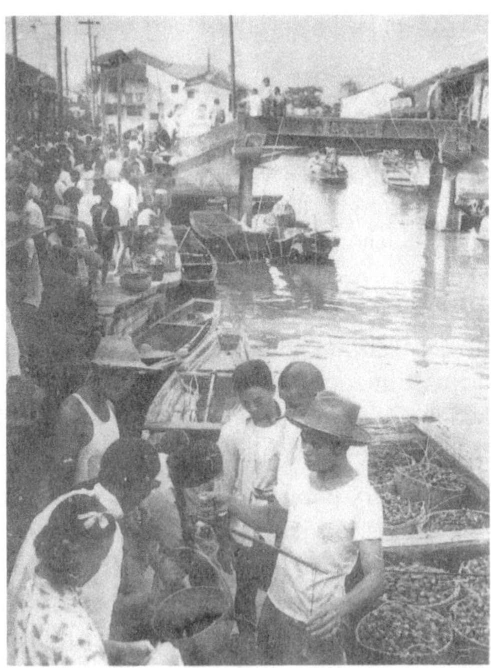

In the economic adjustment period from 1961 to 1964, the role
of market and free trade was once given play for a short period.
The photo shows the members of Guanshu Commune of Shaoxing
County, Zhejiang Province selling agricultural products

preference (in addition to personal interests, the class, group, unit, industry and region and many other elements played a role). For example, Chen Yun said when presided over the formulation of the 4th draft of the First Five-Year Plan in February 1954, "The current problem is that the fiscal revenue is lesser after repeated calculation while the investment amount becomes higher. Therefore, we really need to calculate the unit cost of each project. All departments concerned should not include those sub-items of investments and purposely omit important projects."[11]

Objectively, there were problems with method of the plan formulation. During the First Five-Year Plan period, we borrowed the plan formulation method from Soviet Union that was to formulate the Five-Year Plan and annual plan with the main product balance method. But at that time China's agriculture lived on the mercy of elements, and accounted for a high proportion, there were many uncertainties even the planned figure was accurate. Just as what Mao Zedong said when discussing the 3rd Five-Year Plan in June 1964, "In the past the plan formulation method was basically learned from Soviet

---

11 Compiled by Party Literature Research Office attached to CC of CPC, *Chronicle of Chen Yun*, Vol. 2, Central Party Literature Press, 2000, p. 198.

Union. We first decide the quantity of steel, and then calculate the quantity of coal, electricity and transportation, and urban population and welfare that should be increased. When the output of steel becomes smaller, the others would be reduced accordingly. It was the hand computer method and not realistic and practical. Such calculation did not take account of the heaven. When any natural disaster occurs, we could not obtain that many grain and the urban population could not grow that much, the others would be void."[12] Since the 2nd Five-Year Plan, we attempted to explore the planning methods meeting China's actual situation. But the exploration failed. Till 1978 when China had launched the Reform and Opening-up policy, China was not able to formulate an official Five-Year Plan except the first one.

Second, under the unitary public ownership and planned economic system, the society was in the top-down pyramid-like power system and had little decision-making. And enterprises and individuals could hardly give play to their capability. Moreover, their working performance could hardly be pegged with their incomes. For example, Duan Zhenting, director of Dushanzi Oil Refinery of Xinjiang Petroleum Administration said in 1979, "Two retired workers who were doormen of the swimming pool of our factory built two roofless locker rooms with discarded bricks collected during their leisure time. It was a good deed, but a bank came and criticized that we haven't submitted a feasible financial plan."[13] Therefore under the planned economic system, there was a widespread lack of economic incentives. It was just as what a couplet described, "labor force, finance and property are under different administrations, production, supply and marketing do not meet each other", and the horizontal scroll bearing, "secretary faces challenges".[14] The CPC Central Committee also realized the defect and once implemented reform of delegating power to the lower levels for two times, but failed and had to resume centralization of authority.

(III) Impact of planned economy on the Reform and Opening-up and China's economic development in the new period

Since China's planned economy was not based on the highly developed capitalist economy, the task anticipated from it was not to solve the "anarchy" caused by the lack of socialized production and private ownership of means of production but aimed to accelerate industrialization. In fact, the main goals of China's planned economy, was to solve the shortage of funds needed for industrialization, give priority to development of the heavy industry and

---

12   Quoted from *Bo Yibo's Reviews on Important Decisions and Events*, Vol. 2, People's Publishing House, 1997, pp. 1235-1236.
13   Compiled by CPC Central Committee Secretariat, *Research Materials for Economic Issues (1979)*, China Financial and Economic Publishing House, 1983, pp. 212-213.
14   Ibid., pp. 46-47.

properly resolve the issue of urbanization. The above-mentioned goals under the planned economic system made the role of the planned economy itself to some extent not embodied in how to accurately calculate balance between social production and demand and the best allocation of resources, but on how to mobilize social resources to the largest extent, accelerate industrialization paces and realize the catch-up strategy. From this aspect, the low level, extensive and arbitrary management of the planned economy seemed not that important. What is important is the characteristics of concentrating resources to the largest extent for industrialization of the top-down administrative management. That can be said the main reason for the planned economy to be formed and implemented in China for 20 years, and also an important reason for we to have different opinions of the historical role of planned economy. To put it simple, the planned economy formed in the 1950s at least adapted to the requirements of rapid industrialization and establishment of an independent industrial system at that time, it had undertaken the following two functions that market economy could not offer in a short period of time:

Under the conditions of backward economy, planned economy ensured high accumulation and the rapid development of heavy industry could be prioritized, and establishment of a relatively complete and independent industrial system and infrastructure (the most prominent was the water conservancy works).

Under the condition of backward economy and high accumulation, it ensured the people's basic livelihood and social stability in general except for some special periods. Moreover, the strict urban-rural isolation formed in more than 20 years of the planned economy period objectively provided the institutional foundation for the rural reform and for the vigorous development of township enterprises in the later period: since the rural population could not move to the urban areas freely, this situation have urged them to develop non-agricultural light industries in the rural area, which provided a foundation for the reform out of governmental system and rapid economic growth.

We should also notice that the over the 20-year planned economic system, although it was featured by a low management level, had after all improved the economic management capability of the Chinese government, accumulated rich lessons and experiences on the planned management economy. This experience has played some positive role in the macroeconomic control and maintaining rapid and sustained growth of national economy of the Chinese government, in the next period.

The author is deputy director and fellow member of the Institute of Contemporary China Studies attached to CASS

6

USSR Had Indeed "Debited China for the Weaponry" in Those Years

Shi Yun

On April 15th, 2013, an article titled *Did the USSR Debit China for Payment in Those Years* under the name of Shi Tiefu was published in the Yangcheng Evening News. The article has proposed three main points. First, "China's debts to USSR (Union of Soviet Socialist Republics) were mainly caused by imports of weaponry"; China's "second major debt" was for "USSR's machine and equipment aids". Second, "there aren't any documents that can prove that 'USSR dunned China for payment'". Third, the debt payment to USSR "exacerbated China's economic difficulty was not true". This article was reprinted by some other papers and web media and created considerable influence. I believe that the data and historical record quoted in the article are incorrect and the conclusions are biased. Next, I'll make some corrections to the descriptions in the article.

I. What was the amount of debt owed by China to the USSR?

There are different data on the amount of the total loans that USSR has granted to China, i.e. China's debts to USSR. Neither China nor USSR has publicized the loan details. The 2nd volume of *Diplomatic History of the People's Republic of China* compiled by Wang Taiping from the Diplomatic Office of the Ministry of Foreign Affairs of the PRC presents comprehensive record: During the whole 1950s, USSR offered 11 loans to China, amounting to 5.676 billion old rubles. The classifications were: Category I, economic development loans (4 loans in total) of 1.25 billion old rubles;

Category II, the loans for the War to Resist U.S. Aggression and Aid Korea (5 loans in total) of 3.425 billion old rubles; Category III, the goods sold when USSR's army withdrew its troops from Lyushun and Dalian (1 loan in total) of 723 million old rubles; and Category IV, the loans on USSR's shares in China-USSR joint companies (1 loan in total) which amounted to 278 million old Russian rubles.[1]

As a matter of fact, USSR had provided 13 loans to China in the 1950s with the total amount of about 6.6 billion old rubles instead of the said 5.676 billion old rubles. Because no official agreement was signed for the additional military loans dated April 10 and September 12, 1951 for the War to Resist U.S. Aggression and Aid Korea. The loan issues were settled between Stalin and Mao Zedong in telegraphs and not included in the official statistics. According to the records filed by Yang Shangkun, in 1960, USSR requested China to pay back the loans of 6.6 billion old rubles. So, the additional military loans should also be paid back.[2]

The loans of 6.6 billion old rubles, together with USSR's sugar trade loan of 329.6 million new rubles (1 new rubles = 4.45 old rubles) to China in March 1961, has increased the total loans to about 8.0 billion old rubles. If we include the interests of loans in previous years into consideration, from the 1950s, China's debts to the USSR was about RMB 8.6 billion in total. According to the article "Did the USSR Debit China for Payment in Those Years?", "during the 1950s, China's debts including loan interests to the USSR was about RMB 5.743 billion in total", which was one third lower than the aforesaid amount. The error was possibly caused by data gathering and can be regarded as an acceptable mistake made by the academy.

But, the major problem was the argument on the mature of the loans. The article titled *Did USSR Debit China for Payment in Those Years?* said that the loans were mainly caused by "import of military equipment and weapons" and "acquirement of machines and equipment-aid to China from the USSR". It didn't mention the War to Resist U.S. Aggression and Aid Korea as the cause of the loans. Thus, it gave an impression that China raised loans to strengthen its military and economic construction and it was reasonable to pay them back afterwards. Then, it becomes necessary to discuss the second questions below.

---

1   The 2nd Volume of Diplomatic History of the People's Republic of China compiled by Wang Taiping, World Affairs Press, 1988, pp. 257-258.
2   Dairy of Yang Shangkun, Part I, Central Party Literature Press, 2001, p. 566.

II. Why was China indebted to the USSR?

First, the article titled *Did the USSR Debit China for Payment in Those Years?* said, "In November 1950, Zhou Enlai, on behalf of China, signed a loan agreement with USSR which stipulated that the China's orders before the date October 19, 1950 when China sent troops for the War to Resist U.S. Aggression and Aid Korea will be paid in full while those orders after that event to be paid in half". There are several mistakes in this description. In November 1950, there was no loan agreements signed between USSR and China. On February 1, 1951, China and USSR signed an agreement, defining USSR's 1.235 billion old rubles loan (986 million old rubles offered in fact) to China for purchasing military equipment, ammunition

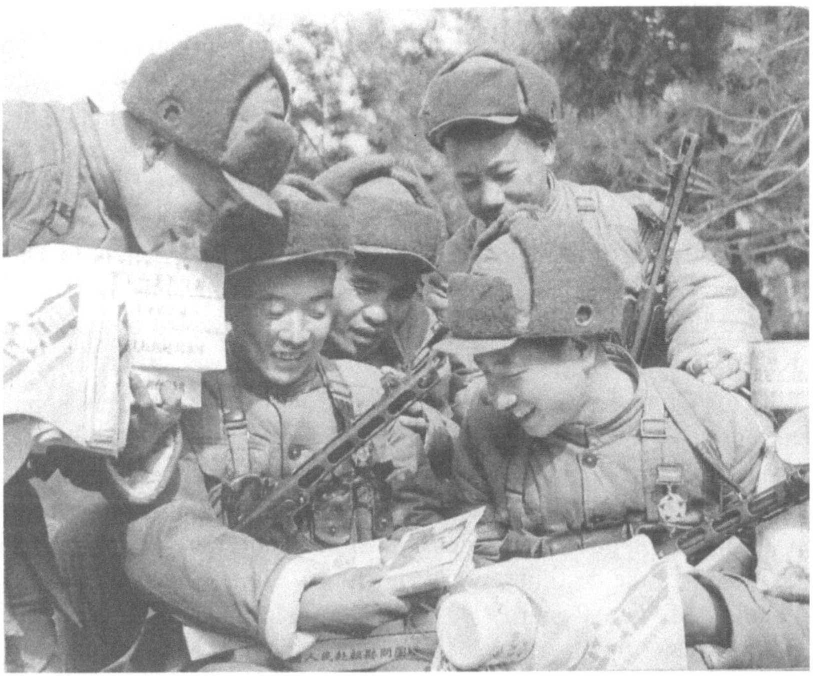

On February 1, 1951, China and USSR signed a 1.235 billion old Rubles loan agreement, (in fact 986 million old rubles was offered) for China's purchase of military equipment, ammunition and railway facilities needed for the War to Resist US Aggression and Aid Korea. The photo shows soldiers of Chinese People's Volunteer Army armed with USSR-made submachine guns, reading books, pictorials and photos brought by Chinese 2nd Consolation Delegation to Korea

and railway facilities necessary during the War to Resist U.S. Aggression and Aid Korea, and the payment for these goods to be made in full before October 19, 1950 while for the military equipment and ammunition to be made in 50% and for the railway facilities in 75% after October 19, 1950 (short for 50% Payment Agreement hereinafter). The price discount in this agreement was only valid for the 1.235 billion old rubles loan.

Second, the article titled *Did the USSR Debit China for Payment in Those Years?* said, "during the War to Resist U.S. Aggression and Aid Korea, USSR had offered military equipment and weaponry for 64 army divisions and 23 air divisions, which had mostly favorables price with 50% discount. China owed RMB 3.0 billion, equivalent to USD. 1.3 billion". This description also has several mistakes. On November 9, 1952, China signed a 1.036 billion old rubles loan agreement with USSR to purchase equipment for 60 divisions, which was just a small part of China's military loan from USSR during the Korean War and was totally irrelevant with the 50% Payment Agreement inked on February 1, 1951. In 1951, USSR offered equipment for four divisions. But China only delivered military equipment and weaponry for three divisions to the Korean People's Army. And the payment for the equipment for 60 divisions was not "mostly made at 50% price discount" as mentioned in the Did USSR Debit China for Payment in Those Years? Because USSR didn't offer preferential prices any more. Zhou Enlai suggested the equipment for 60 divisions to be fully paid by China and concluded the loan agreement with USSR.

Why did China require additional loans from USSR to purchase equipment for the 60 front line army divisions of China after the 50% payment agreement? It was mainly for the War to Resist U.S. Aggression and Aid Korea. After the founding of the People's Republic of China in 1949, reduction of military expenses and recovery of economy were the most urgent issue in face of the destitute, war-torn country. So, on December 5, 1949, the Central Military Commission issued an instruction and requested the PLA to shoulder the production tasks besides combat and on-duty trooping tasks. The military area commands and No. 13 Corps of the national defense tactical units joined the production and construction of land reclamation works, construction of railway and water conservancy facilities. In 1950, the Central Military Commission decided to release 1.5 million of troops and service men to join the production work. On June 24, a day before outbreak of the Korean War, the Central Military Commission and the Government Administration Council Joint Meeting adopted a resolution and requested the Northeast, Northwest and North China Military Area Commands to complete the demobilization mission before September and the East China, Central South and Southwest Military Area Commands to complete the mission before the end of the year. Since then a nationwide military demobilization started.[3]

While China was in urgent need to concentrate very limited funds and materials for the large-scale economic recovery, China had no plan or ability of financial payment for rapidly arming large batches of troops.

After the Korean War erupted on June 25, 1950, the United States militarily occupied Taiwan and then organized the "United Nations Command" (UNC) to enter Korea. After making a careful analysis the Central Military Command decided to put off the plan of liberating Taiwan indefinitely and establish the Northeast Frontier Forces with the No. 13 Corps as the main body. In order to cope with the threat of Korean War, the national defense meeting in August started to deploy the arms and formulate the three-year development plan.

In October 1950 after entering Korea, the People's Volunteer Army had suffered high number of casualties due to backward military weaponry and equipment. Therefore, the need to arm the armies and air forces with modern weaponry and equipment was put on the top agenda soon. On November 7, Mao Zedong called Stalin and requested USSR to provide infantry equipment for the 36 divisions that China planned to send to Korean War in January and February, 1951, and delivered the list of weaponry that was needed. On June 1951, the loan under the "50% Payment Agreement" for military equipment, ammunition and railway facilities had been totally used up.

In June 1951, Gao Gang, Peng Dehuai and Xu Xiangqian went to Moscow to negotiate and arrange the purchase military weaponry and equipment for the 60 divisions. The USSR said it could only provide for 16 divisions (including three divisions of the Korean Army). Mao Zedong in his urgent telegraph, said: the 8-month experiences of our army in Korea have clearly showed that there is a large gap of military weaponry and equipment between ours and the enemy and we urgently need to improve ours. The arrangement of USSR is in conflict with the need and timing of the battlefield of Korean War. Mao Zedong had urged that all the needed military weaponry and equipment should be delivered in the same year (1951) as soon as possible. But after repeated discussions, USSR only agreed to deliver equipment for 10 divisions and later reduces it four divisions, and the delivery of the rest was postponed to 1954.

---

3   Complied by the Military History Research Department of PLA Academy of Military Science, *History of the War to Resist U.S. Aggression and Aid Korea*, Vol. 1, Military Science Publishing House, 2000, pp. 7-8.

Of course, Korean Armistice Agreement was signed in 1953 and the expansion of the war was prevented. The military equipment provided by USSR played an important role for the PLA to reinforce the national defense. Although a part of the military weaponry and equipment delivered by the USSR was partly outdated which was leased by the United States to USSR during WWII,[4] it was better than "millet and rifle" owned by China. But it could not be predicted or controlled by China when the large-scale war between China and the United States—the world's best military power-would come to an end or whether the war would expand to the territory of China at the beginning of the war. Just as what Zhou Enlai said in August 1950, "On our side, we must fight one war after another launched by it (the United States)."[5] From this aspect, that China purchased large batches of military equipment was forced on the consideration of the possible expansion and chronicity of the War to Resist U.S. Aggression and Aid Korea. In fact, except the Navy, the Air Forces, Armored Force and Artillery had gone to the Korean battlefield in 1950 and 1951 according to the three-year development plan of the arms deployed at the national defense meeting in 1950. If without the Korean War, China should use the valuable funds for the most needed economic development. The debts China undertook should also be evaluated as sacrifice which China made for the War to Resist U.S. Aggression and Aid Korea.

The article titled *Did USSR Debit China for Payment in Those Years?* said, "The second major debt to USSR was the machinery and equipment acquired from USSR during the 1st and the 2nd Five-Year Plan period, in turn China had agreed to provide agricultural and sideline products for USSR which were in urgent need, besides minerals and raw materials." In fact, in addition to the military needs, the majority of the loans China obtained from USSR for the economic construction in the 1950s were directly or indirectly used for the War to Resist U.S. Aggression and Aid Korea. The Diplomatic History of the People's Republic of China pointed out: Among the loans from the USSR to China, "the loan for the War to Resist U.S. Aggression and Aid Korea accounted for above 60%".[6] This refers to the purposes of the loans only, and actually the proportion of the loans used for the war was much higher. For example, the 1.2 billion old rubles acquired on February 14, 1950, although designated for the payment of the machinery and equipment and devices delivered by the USSR for the economic rehabilitation and development, the

---

4   Xu Yan, *The First Contest - History and Review of the War to Resist U.S. Aggression and Aid Korea*, China Radio and TV Press, 1990, pp. 31-32.
5   Compiled by CCPCC Party Literature Research Office and PLA Academy of Military Science, *Selected Military Works of Zhou Enlai*, Vol. 4, People's Publishing House, 1997, p. 45.
6   Wang Taiping, editor-in-chief, *Diplomatic History of the People's Republic of China*, Vol. 2, World Affairs Press, 1998, p. 258.

240 million old rubles granted in the first year was basically used for the military purposes and should be attributed to the loan for the War to Resist U.S. Aggression and Aid Korea. The economic development loans accounted for less than 3.3% of China's total debts to USSR in the whole 1950s. In the 1950s, China and USSR signed several trade agreements and USSR committed to export technology and equipment for totally 304 turnkey projects to China. USSR actually committed 142 items (generally known as "156 Items) in the 1st Five-Year Plan period, and 162 items in the 2nd Five-Year Plan period. China repaid the loans for equipment with exporting agricultural products and mineral products that USSR was in urgent need. In 1960, China had exported 7.2 billion rubles worth cargo and planned to export 7.9 billion rubles worth cargo in future. The barter trade in import and export was different from the loans and debts used for the War to Resist U.S. Aggression and Aid Korea and belongs to the deferred payment items in today's international trade practices. On January 5, 1964, Mao Zedong said when talking to a member of the Central Committee of the Japanese Communist Party that China owed more than 7 billion rubles to USSR in total, of which only US$ 300 million was loan, and the rest was for purchasing weapons for the Korean War. This figure and proportion basically accorded with the facts.

III. Did USSR Debit China for the Weaponry?

The article *Did USSR Debit China for Payment in Those Years* said, "The view of 'USSR Debiting China' was a long-standing public opinion. It was especially in those years during Sino-Soviet Split. But to date, there is no historical literature to testify the view "USSR Debiting China" and no official documents had officially condemned USSR for its "dunning". The article further explained, "How the rumor of 'dunning' did appeared? In 1960, China orally informed the SU that the 2 billion rubles debts to USSR might be repaid in five years, and was criticized by Patolitshev, then the Minister of Foreign Trade who declared China had unilaterally delayed the debt repayment time to 'five years" without negotiation with USSR and USSR would not supply gasoline to China in a short time."

Why did China consider to delay the repayment of the trade debts to a five-year period? The article *Did USSR Debit China for Payment in Those Years?* avoided to mention the important reason for that. Because the CPC did not approve Khrushchev's rude attack against the CPC in front of other communist parties at Bucharest Conference in June 1960, Khrushchev hadn't been successful to succumb China after increasing pressures upon China, consequently he had decided to elevate the ideological differences to state-to-state relationships. USSR had delivered a notice to China which informed calling back of Soviet experts working in China. The Chinese government had presented repeated notices to the USSR and expressed its hope that USSR would reconsider the unilateral breach of the agreement between the two countries, but USSR ignored China's demands and called

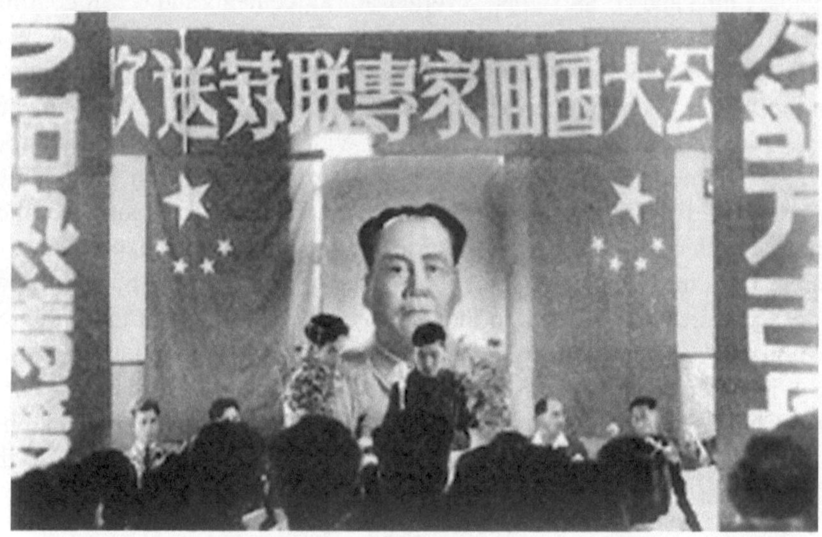

On July 16, 1960, USSR government delivered a notice to the Chinese government which included its decision to unilaterally call back Soviet experts working in China. On July 25, it further notified China that it would call back all the 1,390 experts in China from July 28 to September 1, terminate the dispatch of more than 900 experts, and tear up the 343 contracts and supplementary contracts, and annul 257 scientific and technological cooperation projects. The photo is a scene from the No. 135 Factory holding a farewell party for the Soviet experts.

back all of its 1,390 experts till September 1, also packed back the design drawings of the ongoing projects and other technical materials and stopped the delivery of machinery and equipment and key components. It refused to supply gasoline and truck that China were in urgent need, instead ordered "to stop deliveries of gasoline to China" as the article said. Such a unilateral act severally hit China's economy. As for the above mentioned 304 projects that USSR agreed to deliver machinery and equipment to China, China had completed or basically completed 149 before USSR withdrew its experts in 1960, and the rest 155 were not completed yet. After USSR called its experts back, it stopped to supply technology, equipment and materials, most of the 155 projects were paralyzed. China made heavy investments in these projects by exporting agricultural products and mineral products, but these projects were faced with the risks of "cancellation".

Therefore on October 31, Ye Jizhuang, Minister of Foreign Trade of China, met with Soviet officials and made the following oral statement: Due to natural disasters and economic difficulties caused by the USSR's withdrawal of experts from China, the export plan of China must be adjusted and that China needed to reconsider USSR's orders; the past loans from the USSR would be paid back including both principal and interest in the period between 1961-1965; in terms of trade, the debts amounting to about 2 billion rubles might be paid back within five years.[7]

It was a retaliatory action to USSR's unilateral withdrawal of experts and violating the agreements between two countries, and it's normal. Since the USSR did not honor its promises in the agreements, China of course needed to consider an adjustment. Even so, China did not unilaterally fix the repayment conditions of five-year period, and only said that "it might occur so". But on December 17, Soviet Minister of Foreign Trade Patolitshev, said USSR agreed to China's suggestion to hold negotiations on the issues, but on the other hand accused China by "unilaterally fixing the repayment term of five years" without negotiation, and forced China to pay off all trade debts within three months upon the expiry of the contract. At the end of the year, China made an oral statement to USSR again and refuted its request of paying back the trade debts within three months which included the following ideas: in line with China-USSR agreement, when the contract could not be fulfilled due to force majeure reasons, the liabilities that were not fulfilled could be relieved.[8] This argument was quite polite, and in fact Khrushchev first "purposely" broke the agreement between the two countries. In this period, remarks and behaviors of some foreign trade officials of USSR have gone beyond the line of "criticism" as what the article *Did USSR Debit China for Payment in Those Years?* said, but nasty "dunning". China's official documents did not publicize these "dunning" behaviors, but this doesn't mean such behaviors did not exist, for example:

Gu Ming, the secretary of Zhou Enlai responsible for economic issues, recalled, "Once a Soviet Deputy Minister of Foreign Trade negotiated with our Premier at the People's Grand Hall and requested us to pay back the loans. Our Premier said we were in difficulties temporarily. After the negotiation, when Premier was seeing him off the Soviet official saw a large quartz stone weighing more than 300 kg. He said, if you do not have something else, this is good enough. Premier rejected him, if you desire you can

---

7 Wang Taiping, editor-in-chief, *Diplomatic History of the People's Republic of China*, Vol. 2, World Affairs Press, 1998, p. 241.

8 Ibid, pp. 241-242.

take it with you."[9] Some officials of the Eastern European countries which aligned with the USSR led socialist camp also joined the "Debiting" acts. The Foreign Trade Bulletin of the Ministry of Foreign Trade on December 26th, 1961 noted when reporting the trade negotiations: "Germany and Czechoslovakia (these Eastern European countries) have been extremely rude towards China. The German Democratic Republic sent Mattner, one its members in the Political Bureau of the SED (the German Socialist Unity Party), who has put on a solemn face to collect the debt from China."[10]

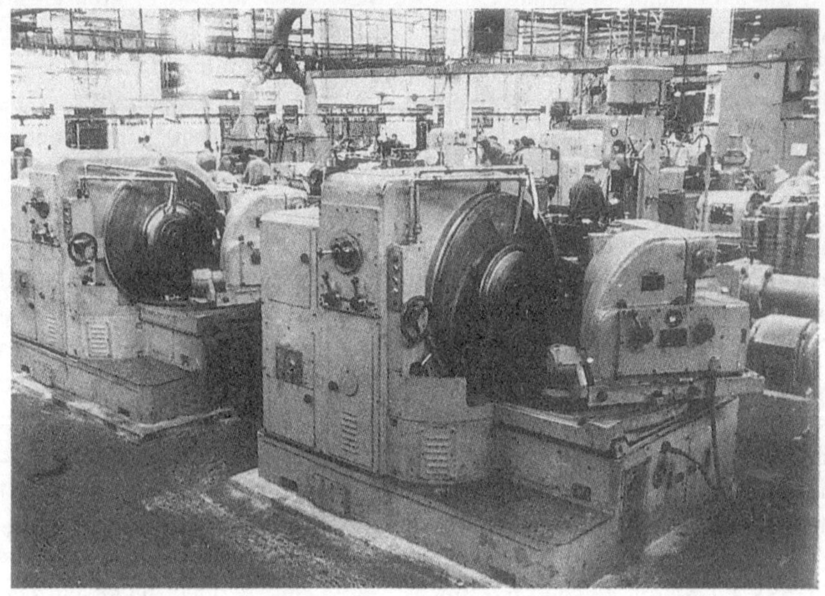

Among the 304 projects constructed with the machinery and equipment imported from the USSR, 149 were completed or basically completed in 1960 before the USSR withdrew its experts, and the rest 155 projects were not completed. After the USSR withdrew its experts, it stopped supply of technology, machinery, equipment and materials and most of the 155 projects were paralyzed. The photo shows a factory that was shut down after the USSR withdrew its experts, stopped supply of technology, equipment and materials.

---

9   Compiled by CC of CPC Party Literature Research Office, *Biography of Zhou Enlai*, 1998, p. 1548.

10   Ministry of Foreign Trade: *Circular on the Trade Negotiation and Trading with Six East European Countries in 1961 and Application for Canceling Purchase Orders of Goods and Set Equipment and Negotiation Postponing Plan with Six Eastern European Countries after 1962*, Dec. 31, 1960- July 11, 1961, Archives of the Ministry of Foreign Relations, 109-02992-01.

People's Daily hadn't reacted as what the article said: "The People's Daily made no response". On the contrary, Li Qiang, Zhou Huamin and Jia Shi, who were leaders of the Ministry of Foreign Trade and attended the USSR debt negotiations, published articles and recalled Ye Jizhuang, Minister of Foreign Trade, and mentioned the intense situation: "When USSR had annulled contracts, called back its experts and humiliated China and increased pressure on us," Ye Jizhuang "worked day and night regardless of his venerable age and illness and led the trade negotiations personally, and often listened to the reports over telephone from the first-line staff members during the late night."[11] These are the recordings and memories of the parties concerned, not as what the article "Did USSR Debit China for Payment in Those Years? said "whitewashed by the Chinese media, the view of "USSR Debiting China" had become quite popular among the general public."

Although the attitudes of the USSR officials were quite bad, it was perfectly justified for the debtor to pay back the debts. China never planned to stop exporting agricultural products and minerals to the USSR in exchange for debt service in order to retaliate against Khrushchev who had unilaterally cancelled USSR's commitments. Three days after receiving the notice from USSR about the withdrawal of experts, Mao Zedong said at the meeting of Political Bureau of the Central Committee: "Anyway in the past we agreed to purchase weapons and ammunition with 50% discount, and now we repay back the debts at the same rate and repudiate not a cent. We will not repudiate even a cent for the debts we have acquired for machinery and equipment for the economic construction and will pay back the debts in full. Since the money belongs to the USSR people we cannot let them down because they helped us when we were in difficulties. Today their leaders are against China, but the money belong to USSR people and we should repay in full. All region and all departments should make a resolution to squeeze the use of materials.[12] This is the reason why no official documents of China used the term of "dunning". In order to repay the debts, On August 10, less than one month after the USSR decided to withdraw its experts, the CPC Central Committee released the Instructions of the Party for Vigorously Launching Foreign Trade Purchase and Export Movement.

However, it was against the accepted codes of human conduct. The reason that the Chinese people was angry with "such humiliation" was because the second point in the article, i.e., most of these debts were in fact

---

11   Li Qiang, Zhou Huamin and Jia Shi, in: Deep Memory of Excellent "Red Butler" Comrade Ye Jizhuang, *People's Daily*, April 24, 1980.

12   Wu Lengxi, Ten-Year Debate, Vol. 1, Central Party Literature Press, 1999, p. 337.

related to the loan agreements for the War to Resist U.S. Aggression and Aid Korea that China had sacrificed for others and upon the suggestions and promises of the USSR and sent troops to the Korean War and made great sacrifice in the face of additional conditions set by the USSR.

On September 30, 1950, Korea was in an urgent situation and the party and government of the Korea requested USSR to send troops for assistance. USSR did not agree, but called Mao Zedong on October 1 and suggested China to send several divisions to quickly push to 38th Parallel in the capacity of a "People's Volunteer Army".[13] On October 4 and 5, leaders of the CPC Central Committee made the decision to resist U.S. aggression and aid Korea and to protect our homes and defend our motherland after hard discussion and from variety of choices. On October 10, the CPC Central Committee sent Zhou Enlai and Lin Biao to request the USSR leaders to send USSR Air Forces to provide air cover for the People's Volunteer Army and provide weapons. USSR agreed to provide weapons but said that USSR was not immediately ready for the air cover, but promised to order USSR Air Forces aid in two to two and a half months. On October 13, the Political Bureau of the CPC Central Committee made a resolution after discussion, which stipulated that even without the USSR Air Forces air cover, China would send People's Volunteer Army to Korea and take the risk of due losses. USSR replied to provide military equipment for China's troops marching to Korea, linked this aid with a loan agreement, and the USSR Air Force would provide air cover but would not enter the territories of Korea, i.e. remain in the Chinese territory, this operation would occur in two to two and a half months-time.[14]

USSR originally had said that it would support Korea by means of China's sending troops and USSR providing funds and equipment, but later it changed its position to offer 50% discount and loan agreements based on full price. In respect to the loan conditions, it requested China to pay back the loans with rare strategic materials, "exporting all the surplus tungsten, antimony, lead and tin to USSR, which China will not use", and the repayment duration was set as 14 years, the first four years in the form of barter trade and supplying such goods for repaying debts starting from the year 1955. Although it mentioned that "all the surplus that China will not use", the annual export requested by the USSR was much higher than the average annual output in history of China, and beyond China's capacity even if it exported all its production. In respect to the economic construction loans, USSR demanded that China should repay

---

13 Complied by the Military History Research Department of the PLA Academy of Military Science: *History of the War to Resist US Aggression and Aid Korea*, Vol. 1, Military Science Publishing House, 2000, p. 148.
14 Compiled by CCPCC Party Literature Research Office, *Chronicle of Zhou Enlai* (I), Central Party Literature Press, 1993, p. 87.

back with rubber, which China's production was quite low and had to import from other countries to export to the USSR. China was afraid of this condition due to economic blockade of enemy forces, in that case China could not be able to fulfill its agreement due to failure in transit purchase, USSR said frankly: if China could not be able to export the amount of rubber as agreed, USSR could only reduce the truck order deliveries to China.

The unreasonable and unfair historical elements, and arrogance of the USSR officials has jointly resulted in the strong reaction of the Chinese people who were faced with such "humiliation". Just as what Deng Xiaoping recalled when he met with Gorbachev in May 1989, "Glaring examples were the Korean War and then the Vietnam War. In the first, China sent volunteers to fight the United States. The Soviet Union supplied us with arms but asked us to pay for them, albeit at half price. In the following years Sino-Soviet relations deteriorated, and China was beset with economic difficulties. But no matter how serious our difficulties were, we were determined to pay that bill, and we paid it two years ahead of time." [15]

In fact, repaying back the debts to USSR had certainly worsened the three-year economic difficulties. In these years, the increased export of agricultural products meant reduction of the valuable needed food of the Chinese people. It is a question that does not need to be discussed. But the Chinese people did not attribute these to the debt repayment and the official documents never mentioned that "dunning" led to the three-year extreme economic hardship, and later shouldered the responsibilities honestly. China did never forget the important aid given to it by the USSR. Deng Xiaoping said when recalling the reasons for Sino-Soviet Split, "I don't mean it was because of the ideological disputes; we no longer think that everything we said at that time was right. The basic problem was that the Chinese were not treated as equals and felt humiliated. However, we have never forgotten that in the period of our First Five-Year Plan the Soviet Union helped us lie an industrial foundation."[16] When we look back into the history, we should carefully consider the complex reasons for the occurrence of the historical events. It would be bound to be one-sided and would cause the suspect of hype if the historical narration emphasizes only one side and deny the rest facts, or even claim that USSR did "not debit" at all or that China didn't encounter the "three-year long natural calamities".

Shi Yun is a renown scholar in Center for Contemporary Chinese Cultural Studies

---

15   *Deng Xiaoping Selected Works*, End the Past and Open up the Future, May 16, 1989, Vol. 3, People's Publishing House, p. 294.

16   Ibid.

7

Mao Zedong's Poems:
A Model for Contemporary Poem Creation

—And a Discussion about the Guiding Role of Mao's Poetry on Contemporary Reform and Innovation of China's Poetry

Yi Xing

As a "professional revolutionist" and an "amateur" poet Mao Zedong has left us for more than 40 years. In addition to his political merits and demerits, his poems have been a hot topic of public discussion. It is widely recognized that Mao's poems play a significant role in leading the development of Chinese poems. His accomplishments in poems and the spirit shown in the lines won high public praise. Mao's poems are precious cultural heritage to the Chinese people and the common wealth of the nation, worth to cherish and inherit but not to slight or neglect. Inheriting the quintessence of classic literature critically, Mao's poems should be a model for contemporary poetry.

I. Aesthetic transcendence of Mao's Ci poems

Mao's poems are as much praised as criticized. As a founding leader of the People's Republic of China, Mao Zedong accepted support and criticism with individual sentiments. A Chinese author of foreign nationality wrote: "I want to tell the Chinese readers that, even people with the most counter-views against Mao and the communism in the world will read Mao's poems and then can't help admiring his talent in poetry." Of course, there are exceptions. For example, Hu Shi said in his diary dated March 11, 1959: "I feel a little bit nauseated when I saw the nine-page Nineteen Poems by Mao Zedong published by Cultural Relics Press in the Chinese mainland. The last one of these poems is the Love of Butterfly, which is highly praised by the Chinese scholars. However, no line reads smoothly. I discussed with Zhao Yuanren about the rhyme of poem. He said it was not of a Hunan style." It is not strange for Hu Shi, who was hostile to the CPC and the new China, to have such extreme view. He even hated classic poems and also all contemporary poems created based on classic poem styles. Even today, there are still many people who dispraise Mao's poems based on Hu's views. Is that true? Take the Love of Butterfly: Reply to Li Shuyi for example. Is it the truth that no line read smoothly? The answer is no. Every line read smoothly. In addition, it is so romantic, graceful and moving that few poems in the history can be on a par with it. The Dreaming of My Deceased Wife on the Night of the 20th Day of the First Month by Su Shi, a great scholar in the Song Dynasty and the leader of the Unconstrained Song Poetry School, may be one of the "few":

Ten boundless years now separate the living and the dead,
I have not often thought of her, but neither can I forget.
Her lonely grave is a thousand li distant, I can't say where my wife
lies cold.
We could not recognize each other even if we met again,
My face is all but covered with dust, my temples glazed with frost.
In deepest night, a sudden dream returns me to my homeland,
She sits before a little window, and sorts her dress and make-up.
We look at each other without a word, a thousand tears now flow.
I must accept that every year I'll think of that heart breaking place,
Where the moon shines brightly in the night, and bare pines guard the tomb.

It is a poem to the deceased wife. It is recognized as a masterpiece depicting the poet's deep love to his wife. However, Mao wrote the Love of Butterfly to his wife Yang Kaihui and his friend Liu Zhixun in a more positive way:

I lost my lovely wife Yang,
You lost your dear husband Liu.
Their souls flew up to the highest place in the heaven,
They asked Wu Gang what he has in the Moon Palace.
Wu Gang brought out a drink of flowers of cherry bay.
Lonesome Chang E extended her wide and big sleeves,
She danced for their loyal souls in the 10 thousand mile vast sky.
Suddenly, it was reported that the tigers in the human world had all
been caught;
Their happy tears poured down like a cloudburst.

He imaged that the martyrs for the revolution were treated well in the heaven and they were very excited when hearing the success in the revolution. How solemn and inspiring it is! Su Shi's poem sounds sad, while Mao's poem sounds more solemn and stirring. The beauty of Chinese literature includes masculine beauty and feminine beauty. However, it is hard to have a clear boundary between them. Yao Nai, a literary theorist in the Qing Dynasty, believed that, the masculine beauty and feminine beauty may co-exist in a work and one of them may play a dominant role; however, neither of them should be lacked in a work (Preface for Zhu Ziying's Poems). Liu Xie showed the similar attitude in the Literary Mind and the Carving of Dragons: masculine beauty and feminine beauty should be adopted commonly and applicably. The Mao's poems mainly show masculine beauty, but they do not lack feminine beauty. The Love of Butterfly is the best testimony. It won high praise soon after it was created. Guo Moruo, a Chinese scholar, wrote in his article: "This poem doesn't show any decadent tone that is usually contained in the classic poems. What's more important, it manifests more highlighted heroism than the poems by Su Shi and Xin Qiji. For this poem, romantic and exaggerated expression techniques were used to serve as a foil to the reality. It is natural, lively, profound and moving. It is really a masterpiece through the history." Even today, more than 40 years after Mao's leaving us, such opinions without personality cult are still being widely accepted. Concerning the rhyme of the poem, Mao refused to change the words for strict adherence to the rhyme principles. In fact, there are historical examples for adopting different rhymes in the neighboring two lines, such as the Love of Butterfly: Standing on High Building amid Breeze by Liu Yong. Such rhyming method is based on the "13 Rhyme Categories", which were identified by Jia Fuxi (Qing Dynasty) based on the Central China Phonology edited by Zhou Deqing (Yuan Dynasty) and the folk pronunciation, especially the verses popular in the Yuan Dynasty. The "13 Rhyme Categories" include the most simple and authentic rhymes in the northern areas of ancient China. These rhymes are basically the same with those in today's mandarin. However, poets in the Song Dynasty, especially lyricists, used rhymes more flexibly. According to the sixth volume of the third edition of "Helin Yulu" by Luo Dajing: "Yang Chengzhai (Wanli) said that the "Rhyme of the Ministry of Rites" is to restrict the rhyme of the scholar Cheng Wen because it is difficult to see his work ear. As for the sentiment of chanting, we should take "The Book of Songs" and "Lisao" as the method, and ridicule the restraint of "Libuyun"!" It can be seen that the poets in the Song Dynasty did not complete their poem writing in accordance with the libuyun based on "Guangyun" (Broad Rimes), let alone the "Cilin Zhengyun" compiled by Ge Zai in Qing Dynasty. If every poet in the Song Dynasty strictly followed the formulas on rhymes, there would not be these famous works such as the Love of Butterfly: Standing on High Building amid Breeze by Liu Yong. In addition, Liu Xie believed that creation of literary works should be flexible based on established methodology according to actual conditions. Mao Guangsheng, a famous expert in Song Poems, pointed out: "To rigidly adhere to certain ways is to cocoon oneself like a silkworm. How can a poem be created by shackling the mind? The Song Poems had a peak development in the Song Dynasty, when there were no books about tunes of poems, principles for writing poems or rhymes." In other word, even if there were not these early examples, was it wrong for Mao Zedong to change the way to make poems? So far eight forms of Prelude To Water Melody poems have been identified, so have 28 forms of Water Dragon Chant poems, 12 forms of Niannujiao poems, at least 16 forms of Manjianghong poems and five or six forms of Love of Butterfly poems. These poems prove that the forms and rhymes of Song poems are changeable. Even new forms of poems can be created. Actually the first poem of every category of poems was created by someone. Why can't contemporary people do the same as the ancients did?

Another popular Mao's poem is The Spring Comes to a Happy Garden (Qin Yuan Chun): Snow.

It is so hard to deny the excellence of this poem. Therefore, some people tried other ways. Based on some irrelevant information, an American author deduced that the poem was written in August 28, 1945 and thus believed that the "heroes" mentioned in the poem might probably refer to Chiang Kai-shek. He said Mao intended to flatter Chiang during the Chongqing Negotiation held in 1945. If that was true, both the poem and its author should be disdained. However, according to this American author, Mao wrote the poem in summer. Was it possible for Mao to write a poem about snow in summer? Even if it was true that Mao wrote the poem in summer, why it should be deemed as a poem to eulogize Chiang? Anyway, the assumption has confused the public. Therefore, the truth should be made clear.

In fact, Mao mentioned the poem in his letter (dated October 7, 1945) to Liu Yazi: "(I wrote it) when I saw the heavy snow in Shaanxi." To be specific, On August 28, 1945, Mao Zedong went from Yan'an to Chongqing by air to attend the peace negotiation with Chiang. During Mao's days in Chongqing, Liu Yazi, a Chinese poet, asked Mao whether he could write a poem for him (Liu). Under such a circumstance, Mao presented him The Spring Comes to a Happy Garden: Snow to Liu as a gift. The poem was written at Yuanjia Ravine, Yulin, northen Shaanxi, in February 1936, when there was heavy snow. On November 14, 1945, the third day of the Chongqing Negotiation, Xinmin Bao Evening published the poem. Later, Ta Kung Pao reprinted the

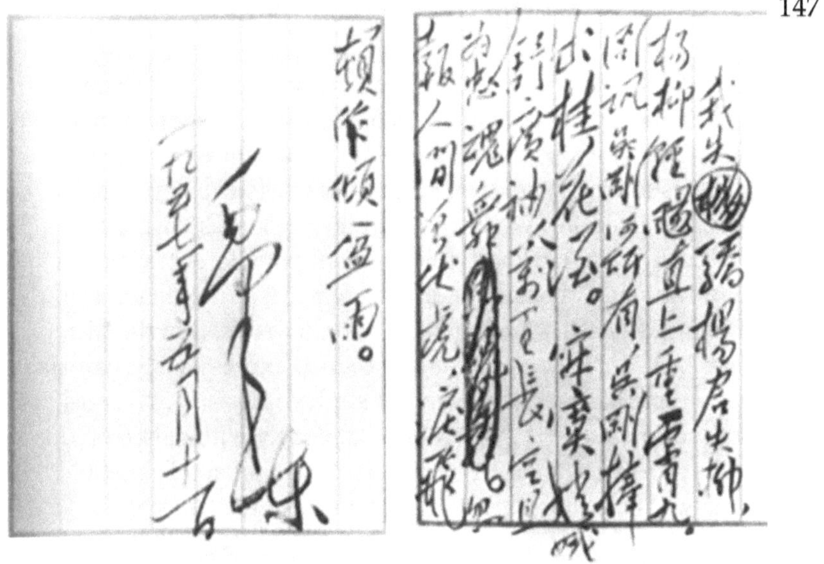

In the photo is the handwritten copy of the Love of Butterfly:
Reply To Li Shuyi written by Mao Zedong in May 1957.

poem together with the Liu Yazi's replying poem published on Xinhua Daily. Mao's poem soon aroused great response in Chongqing and even the whole country. Many people wrote replying poems to praise or criticize it. It was said that Chiang also secretly instigated some poets to write similar poems, trying to overshadow Mao's poem. A "war of poems" broke out. Wu Zuguang said, "It was a wonder in the contemporary political and literary history of China. The military and political conflicts between the CPC and the Kuomintang even extended to the literary circle." The "war of poems" was ended with the success of Mao's poem. What's more, the people in the area under the rule of the Kuomintang were surprised by the talent of Mao, whom they had believed to a bandit chieftain. They became to know that the Kuomintang had been telling lies and began to have new understanding of the CPC. Mao changed people's attitude towards the CPC just with a poem. Many democrats in neutral position turned to the CPC. Liu Yazi was one of them. Liu was known as supercilious and idiosyncratic scholar. Even though he had known Mao since 1925, he did not show any admiration for Mao until he was presented this poem. He was so excited that he soon wrote a replying poem, evaluated Mao as a great talent surpassing numerous classic poets, even including Su Shi, Xin Qiji and Nalan Rongruo. In an article, Liu said: "The poem by Mao ranked as a masterpiece throughout the ages, better than the poems by many classic poets." At that time, it needed great courage to praise the "bandit chieftain" in the area under the rule of the Kuomintang. The courage was from the excellence of Mao's poem.

There is another poem by Mao: The Spring Comes to a Happy Garden: Changsha, which was written in 1925. "Ask the boundless land: who is governing the historical ups and downs?" The poem won a high reputation among poems to the tune of the "Spring Comes to a Happy Garden". Then, the "Snow" created in 1936 mentioned above surpassed the accomplishment of Su Shi's The Spring Comes to a Happy Garden: Cold Lamplight in Longly Inn and was even on a par with Su's Niaonujiao: The Mighty River Flows Eastward, which has been highly praised in the history. Su's poems are known for bold and unconstrained expressions. Yuan Haowen, a famous expert in Song poems in the Jin Dynasty said, "Su was good at incisive description about the country and people with only more than 100 words. His works are masterpieces." The Niaonujiao: The Mighty River Flows Eastward, of course, is the masterpiece of the "masterpieces".

Why is Mao's poem believed to be on a par with such a masterpiece? Su's poems usually show a kind of pessimistic attitude toward his country and the people. On the contrast, Mao's poems show a positive attitude toward the world and high evaluation of contemporary heroes. "For truly great men, look to this age alone." The heroes may refer to a number of top leaders of the CPC, including Mao Zedong, Liu Shaoqi, Zhou Enlai and Zhu De and other representative proletarian revolutionaries, who showed great talent in military and state governance and made unprecedented contributions to the development of China. On the other hand, Mao portrayed more magnificent and powerful natural sceneries. For example:

"A hundred leagues locked in ice, a thousand leagues of whirling snow.
Both sides of the Great Wall, one single white immensity.
The Yellow River's swift current is stilled from end to end.
The mountains dance like silver snakes, and the highlands charge like
wax-hued elephants, vying with heaven in stature.
On a fine day, the land, clad in white, adorned in red,
grows more enchanting."

To evaluate the aesthetic accomplishment of a poem, focus should be first laid on its sublimation, and then the unconstrained personality of the poet, the graceful wording, solemn tone and stirring emotions (Of course, sublimation may include all the latters). Based on such a standard, Mao's Snow transcends many classic works. In fact, Mao had written a poem comparable with Su's Niaonujiao: The Mighty River Flows Eastward before writing the Snow. It was Niannujiao: Kunlun. Both the two poems mentioned above boast an extraordinary beginning. Take Mao's Kunlun as an example. The first line is: "Far above the earth, into the blue, you, wild

Kunlun, have seen all that was fairest in the world of men." However, the two poems show different attitudes at their ends. Su's poem is ended with: "The World of Men is like a dream." It is a lament. Mao's poem is ended with: "Peace world then reign over the world, the same warmth and cold throughout the globe." What lofty sentiments and aspirations. It transcends Su's poem in terms of sublimation. Mao also has another two poems to the tune of Niannujiao: Jinggang Mountain and Two Birds: A Dialogue, which were written in spring and autumn 1965. The Jinggang Mountain includes such lines: "The country is like a photo," "And the world of man has changed, as if the sky and sea are overturned." The Two Birds: A Dialogue includes the lines: "The roc wings fanwise, soaring ninety thousand li and rousing a raging cyclone. The blue sky on his back, he looks down to survey Man's world with its towns and cities." These lines are undoubtedly quotation of Su's poem based on contrary intention.

Su has another widely well-known poem, namely the Prelude to Water Melody; Bright Moon, When Did You Appear? (Hereinafter referred to as the Bright Moon). Hu Zi in Song Dynasty praised it as a mid-autumn poem overshadowing all other similar poems. In the Song Dynasty, Hu Zi commented on the poem: "the Mid Autumn Festival Poem came out from Su-Shi's "Shui Diao Ge Tou", and the rest of poems were abandoned." That may sound like a bit of an absolute, but the evaluations of this poem, like clear, sparse, plain and elegant, follow his inclinations without the aid of refinement, great, upright and brilliant attainments are appropriate. A story indicated its popularity: Emperor Shenzong of the Song Dynasty was moved by the poem and therefore ordered to provide better conditions for then exiled Su Shi. This made Su famous throughout the country. Therefore, Su's Bright Moon really deserves the fourth place on the List of Song Poems. Mao wrote two poems to the same tune respectively in 1956 and 1965: Swimming and Reascending Jinggang Mountain.

Swimming

I have just drunk the waters of Changsha
And come to eat the fish of Wuchang.
Now I am swimming across the great Yangtze,
Looking afar to the open sky of Chu.
Let the wind blow and waves beat,
Better far than idly strolling in courtyard.
Today I am at ease.
It was by a stream that the Master said —

"Thus do things flow away!"
Sails move with the wind.
Tortoise and Snake are still.
Great plans are afoot:
A bridge will fly to span the north and south,
Turning a deep chasm into a thoroughfare;
Walls of stones will stand upstream to the west
To hold back Wushan's clouds and rain
Till a smooth lake rises in the narrow gorges.
The mountain goddess if she is still there
Will marvel at a world so changed.

Reascending Jinggang Mountain

I have long aspired to reach for the clouds
And I again ascend Jinggangshan.
Coming from afar to view our old haunt, I find new scenes replacing
the old.
Everywhere orioles sing, swallows dart,
Streams babble
And the road mounts skyward.
Once Huangyangjie is passed
No other perilous place calls for a glance.
Wind and thunder are stirring,
Flags and banners are flying
Wherever men live.
Thirty-eight years are fled
With a mere snap of the fingers.
We can clasp the moon in the Ninth Heaven
And seize turtles deep down in the Five Seas:
We'll return amid triumphant song and laughter.
Nothing is hard in this world
If you dare to scale the heights.

Both the two poems should not be second to Su's poem to the same tune.

The second-place winner on the List of Song Poems is The River All Red: Hair on End by Yue Fei. It is a poem full of combat spirit, featuring very straightforward expression. Yue Fei was a national hero who, however, was framed to death. The poem is full of the spirit of patriotism to fight against foreign aggression and resentment for being pushed aside. It is encouraging. Mao also has a poem to the same tune, even with the same purpose to encourage the people to fight against aggression. However, it was written in a different way, describing the problems in an easy, humorous and profound way and showing the confidence of the proletariat for the final success. See the details:

Reply to Comrade Guo Moruo

On this tiny globe
A few flies dash themselves against the wall,
Humming without cease,
Sometimes shrilling,
Sometimes moaning.
Ants on the locust tree assume a great-nation swagger
And mayflies lightly plot to topple the giant tree.
The west wind scatters leaves over Chang'an,
And the arrows are flying, twanging.
So many deeds cry out to be done,
And always urgently;
The world rolls on,
Time presses.
Ten thousand years are too long,
Seize the day, seize the hour!
The Four Seas are rising, clouds and water raging,
The Five Continents are rocking, wind and thunder roaring.
Our force is irresistible,
Away with all pests!

It is more sublime and profound than Yue's poem.

Li Bai had two poems known as the "ancestor of Song poems". One of them is the Dream of Maiden Qin (Yi Qin E):

The flute is mute,
Waking from moonlit dream, she feels a grief acute.
O moon, O flute,
Year after year, do you not grieve
To see 'neath willows people leave?
On Merry-making Plain, on Mountain-Climbing Day,
She receives no letter from ancient Northwest way.
Over ancient way,
The sun declines, the west wind falls
Over royal tombs and palace walls.
It is well-known for the expression of sad and dreary emotions.

Mao has a poem to the same tune, namely:

The Dream of Maiden Qin: Loushan Pass

Fierce the west wind,
Wild geese cry under the frosty morning moon.
Under the frosty morning moon
Horses 'hooves clattering,
Bugles sobbing low.
Idle boast the strong pass is a wall of iron,
With firm strides we are crossing its summit.
We are crossing its summit,
The rolling hills sea-blue,
The dying sun blood-red.
It is more grand and heroic.

To the tune of Waves Washing the Sand (Lang Tao Shao), the best-known poems include the Reminiscence by Li Yu, and the Beidaihe by Mao Zedong. Both the two poems mentioned rain. Li's poem said, "The rain is murmuring outside the curtain, and the spring is waning." Mao's poem said, "A rainstorm sweeps down on this northern land, white breakers leap to the sky." Li's poem said, "It's easy to depart but hard to reunite. We are far away from each other, just like flowing water takes away the withered flowers with the leaving of spring". Mao's poem said, "Today the rustling autumn wind comes back again, but the world has changed!" Obviously, Mao's poem showed a more positive attitude. In addition to long and medium poems, Mao was also good at writing lucid and lively short poems, such as Xi Jiang Yue: Jinggang Mountain, Cai Sangzi: the Double Ninth Festival, Yu Jia Ao: Against the First Besiegement, Qing Ping Yue: Liupan Mountain and, especially, the Sixteen Chinese Characters: Mountain, which has been recognized as a model for the poems to the same tune. Nearly all Mao's poems should be edited into the Classic and Contemporary Poem Models. Therefore, it is not an exaggeration to say that Mao's poems overshadow those by many historical poets. Is that strange for Mao, a man with outstanding abilities, an encyclopedic mind, unprecedented high spirit and romantic moods, to have higher accomplishments than the earlier sages did?

II. Aesthetic transcendence of Mao's Shi poems

Some people criticized Mao's Shi poems for violating the regular rules on making such poems. Some people even quoted part of Mao's Letter to Chen Yi as support to their criticism: Mao said in the letter, "I sometimes wrote several eight-line poems with seven characters to a line, but I'm not satisfied with any one of them." In fact, it was just kind of modesty to say that. In the same letter, Mao said, "I know a little about the Ci poems". Is that the fact? Due to ideological sublimation, grandness and ingenious wording, Mao's Ci poems have won high praise from many professionals. Can you believe that he just "knew a little about" such poems?

Then, how to evaluate Mao's Shi poems? The answer is that they are unprecedented!

At the 12th Annual Meeting of the Mao Zedong's Poems Research Society, I made a speech themed "Mao's Poems: Imperishable Works Linking the Past and Future". A comparison between several Mao's eight-line poems and several historically best-known poems of the Tang Dynasty was made. The conclusion was the poems that Mao was not satisfied with are on a par with the best-known ones. The formers even transcend the latters in terms of ideological pursuit, artistic conception and language art. Take the Yellow Crane Tower by Cui Hao for an example. It was highly praised by Yan Yu as the best eight-line poem with seven characters to a line and now still ranks the first on the List of Tang Poems. However, it can't compare with the Reply to A Friend by Mao, whether in terms of ideological pursuit, artistic conception, and wording or expression ways. Sui's poem said, "The trees on Hanyang side stood out in the sun. The grass on Parrot Shoal had grown abundant." Mao's poem said, "Tungting Lake's snow-topped waves surge skyward. The long isle reverberates with earth-shaking song." Sui's poem said, "At dust I asked myself which way led home. The misty waves on the River made me groan." Mao's poem said, "And I am lost in dreams, untrammelled dreams of the land of hibiscus glowing in the morning Sun." Sui said, "The yellow cranes, once more, were gone forever. Millenniums of white clouds have drifted idly by." It is kind of lament. Mao said, "Riding the wind, the Princesses descend the green hills. Once they speckled the bamboos with their profuse tears, now they are robed in rose-red clouds…And I am lost in dreams, untrammelled dreams of the land of hibiscus glowing in the morning sun." He showed a positive and heroic attitude through his romantic and splendid expression.

Li Bai wrote a poem in similar format:

On Phoenix Terrace at Jinling

On Phoenix Terrace once phoenixes came to sing;
The birds are gone, but still roll on the river's waves.
The ruined palace's buried 'neath the weeds in spring;
The ancient sages in caps and gowns all lie in graves.
The three-peak'd mountain is half lost in azure sky;
The two-fork'd stream by Egret Isle is kept apart.
As floating clouds can veil the bright sun from the eye,
Imperial Court, now out of sight, saddens my heart.

In history, many people compared this poem with Cui's poem. Some people, such as Liu Chenweng, believed that Li's poem was based on Cui's poem but better than the latter, and it showed greater love to the whole country but not just nostalgia. Some people believed that Cui's melancholy was from the surrounding environment, while Li's melancholy his own experience as an exile. So they believed that Cui's poem was better. Some people, such as Fang Hui, took a neutral stand, believing that "there should be ranking of poems in terms of emotional expression". The Choice Poetry of Tang and Song edited under the order of Emperor Qianlong of the Qing Dynasty said, "Cui's poem boasts direct emotional expression and Li expressed his feelings by virtue of a number of scenarios. Both the two poems showed similar concern. There should be no rankings." Since the poems by Li and Cui are on a par, and Mao's poem is better than Li's poem. Du Fu, another famous Chinese poet, is believed to the best at writing eight-line Chinese poem with seven characters to a line, with five such poems on the List of Tang Poems, including On the Height, which ranks the 15th. Hu Yinglin, a well-known Chinese scholar in the Ming Dynasty, said, "No poems before or after it can be comparable with it, whether in terms of composition, sentence structure or wording." Emperor Qianlong of the Qing Dynasty had high comments on the poem and believed that it was a rare work. Yang Lun believed that it is unique in history and the best one among similar poems. It is really extraordinary, but it is still overshadowed by Mao's Ascent of Lushan, which is also a poem created when the poet was standing on a mountain.

On the Height

Du Fu

The wind so swift, the sky so wide, apes wail and cry;
Water so clear and beach so white, birds wheel and fly.
The boundless forest sheds its leaves shower by shower;
The endless river rolls its waves hour after hour,
A thousand miles from home, I'm grieved at autumn's plight;
Ill now and then for years, alone I'm on this height,
Living in times so hard, at frosted hair I pine;
Cast down by poverty, I have to give up wine.

Ascent of Lushan

Mao Zedong

Perching as after flight, the mountain towers over the Yangtze;
I have overleapt four hundred twists to its green crest.
Cold-eyed I survey the world beyond the seas;
A hot wind spatters raindrops on the sky-brooded waters.
Clouds cluster over the nine streams, the yellow crane floating,
And billows roll on to the eastern coast, white foam flying.
Who knows whither Prefect Tao Yuanming is gone
Now that he can till fields in the Land of Peach Blossoms?

Du's poem shows the depression and bitterness of the poet, while Mao's poem shows excitement and aggressiveness. Some people said that Mao was defending the Great Leap Forward through the poem, because "Tao Yuanming is tilling fields in the Land of Peach Blossoms". In fact, Mao ended the poem with a question concerning the complicated and intense international and domestic struggles. What he really meant was: facing intense struggles, we can't escape to the Land of Peach Blossoms to till fields.

Du also had another poem titled Recapture of the Regions North and South of the Yellow River, which won high praise of Li Yindu:

Tis said the Northern Gate is recaptured of late;
When the new reach my ears, my gown is wet with tears.
Staring at my wife's face, of grief I find no trace;
Rolling up my verse books, my joy likes madness looks.

Though I am white-haired, still I'd sing a drink my fill.
With verdure springs aglow, "it's time we homeward go.
We shall sail all the way through Three Gorges in a day.
Going down to Xiangyang, we'll come up to Luoyang.

This poem ranks the 28th on the List of Tang Poems and has been highly appreciated by many classic and contemporary readers. As Huang Zhouxing said, it depicts an unimaginably grand photo. Coincidentally, Mao also wrote a poem about taking a city:

The People's Liberation Army Captures Nanjing

Mao Zedong

Over Zhongshan swept a storm, headlong,
Our mighty army, a million strong, has crossed the Great River.
The City, a tiger crouching, a dragon curling, outshines its ancient glories;
In heroic triumph heaven and earth have been overturned.
With power and to spare we must pursue the tottering foe
And not ape Xiang Yu the conqueror seeking idle fame.
Were Nature sentient, she too would pass from youth to age,
But Man's world is mutable, seas become mulberry fields.

Does it depict a grander photo? Du is well-known for subtle and vivid expression, while Mao for aggressiveness and magnificence. Both of the two poets were excited when hearing the success. One showed his excitement in a gentle way, while the other showed it in an aggressive way. Of course, the latter is more exciting and encouraging.

On December 26, 1962, at the age of 69 years, Mao wrote the very encouraging poem titled,

Winter Clouds

Winter clouds snow-laden, cotton fluff flying,
None or few the unfallen flowers.
Chill waves sweep through steep skies,
Yet earth's gentle breath grows warm.
Only heroes can quell tigers and leopards
And wild bears never daunt the brave.

Plum blossoms welcome the whirling snow;
Small wonder flies freeze and perish.

The poem was created during a period when China suffered great difficulties domestically and internationally. It shows revolutionary optimism, confidence in socialism, and the determination and courage of a revolutionary for final success. It makes the readers excited.

Du Fu's Autumn Meditations (I) seems to be comparable with it:

Jade dew withers and wounds the groves of maple trees,
On Wu Mountain, in Wu gorge, the air is dull and drear.
On the river surging waves rise to meet the sky,
Above the pass wind and cloud join the earth with darkness.
Chrysanthemum bushes open twice, weeping for their days,
A lonely boat, a single line, my heart is full of home.
Winter clothes everywhere are urgently cut and measured,
Baidicheng above, the evening's driven by beating on stones.

Huang Sheng of the Qing Dynasty said, "The Autumn Meditations poems should be the best poems by Du." The Autumn Meditations (I) should be the best of the best. Therefore, Mao's poem should be comparable with the other well-known poems of the Tang Dynasty.

Mao once wrote the Reply to Comrade Guo Moruo. Some people believed that Mao wrote it because of misunderstanding of Guo's poem.

This is the poem by Guo Moruo:

On Watching the Monkey Subdues the Demon
Confounding humans and demons, right and wrong,
The monk was kind to foes and vicious to friends.
Endlessly he intoned "The Incantation of the Golden Hoop",
And thrice he let the White Bone Demon escape.
The monk deserved to be torn limb from limb;
Plucking a hair means nothing to the wonder-worker.
All praise is due to such timely teaching,
Even the Pig grew wiser than the fools.

Guo wrote it after watching the opera show titled Monkey Subdues the Demon in October 1961, when many Chinese people hated centrism more than the American imperialism and the Soviet revisionism. So, many audiences who watched the show hated the "monk" in the opera. Mao knew that it was wrong. So, he wrote a poem to refute Guo Moruo's opinions:

A thunderstorm burst over the earth,
So a devil rose from a heap of white bones.
The deluded monk was not beyond the light,
But the malignant demon must wreak havoc.
The Golden Monkey wrathfully swung his massive cudgel
And the jade-like firmament was cleared of dust.
Today, a miasmal mist once more rising,
We hail Sun Wu-kung, the wonder-worker.

Mao said, "Guo Moruo criticized the monk. Actually, it is the demons that should be criticized. The monk just doesn't know the truth. He is deceived."

The replying poem shows profound insight and is very convictive. Guo was completely convinced. However, some people believed that Guo submitted to Mao's comments against his own will. Since Guo has passed away, he could not tell us whether he was against his own will at that time. Mao meant that the enemies (the white bone demons) but not the centrists that should be blamed. His poem indicated his philosophy and political policy. Why should it be criticized?

In addition to the poems mentioned above, Mao also wrote many other excellent poems, such as The Long March and the Farewell to the God of Plague, which was written to praise the local government and people of Yujiang County's efforts in eliminating blood flukes. These poems can arouse new perceptions of the readers, deserving high praise. Imagine, is that a scientific, objective and fair way to classify Mao's poems into the mid-level or even lower-level classes just because they were made by Mao? Literary and art works can be praised or criticized by different people with different views. However, heartfelt praise should not be deemed as over-praise or flattery, and ungrounded conjecture and defamation and cavil should not be turned into truth. The truth will never be on the side of the minority trying to win fame by pleasing the public with claptrap.

To sum up, Mao poems are at least on a par with the classic ones. Famous poet Zhao Puchu once said, "Only someone who is calm, experienced, confident, far-sighted and open-minded and looks at the domestic and international situations as well as the current conditions and the future at the same time can discover the charm of the broad and splendid nature and then write down these poems." When evaluating Mao's The Long March, Famous writer Yao Xueyin said, "It is fluent and easy-to-understand, and ingeniously worded to express high spirit." This is truly a sincere evaluation.

It is of great significance to admit that Mao's poems reach a higher aesthetic level and comparable with or even better than the poems by many historical famous poets. First, it will break the legend that the poems of the Song and Tang Dynasties are unparalleled so that contemporary people will be more confident in making poems. Second, Mao's poems should be used as examples for making innovation and reform in writing poems. This will be greatly helpful for the further development and revitalization of the Chinese poems. Some people may be deemed this as "personality cult". If it is really a kind of cult, it should be cult of the splendid classic and contemporary literature and art. Those who created the literary and art works should be immortal as much as their works.

III. A model for contemporary poem creation

Mao Zedong has quite clear perceptions of reform and innovation of traditional poems. First, emphasis should be first laid on innovation of content to serve the reality and the masses. Second, the innovation of forms and rhymes is also very important. However, to make reform and innovation doesn't mean complete replacement. Instead, it means improvement based on the original poems. Mao clearly pointed out: "An art work should have content, which should meet the demands of the times and the public…I believe that any form of art, including poetry, should meet the demand of the public…Now, many things can't reflect the people's lives so that the people can't understand them." Mao wrote many poems during the wars. These poems were created to reflect and serve the reality. After occupying Nanjing, Mao wrote the occupy The People's Liberation Army Captures Nanking to "encourage the CPC officers and soldiers to go ahead and root out the remaining forces of the Kuomintang reactionaries." After the liberation of the whole China, Mao wrote a replaying poem to Liu Yazi's poem, trying to persuade Liu not to seclude himself from the others because of complaint about little frustrations. The poem said, "Beware of heartbreak with grievance overfull, range for your eye over long vistas. Do not say the waters of Kunming Lake are too shallow, for watching fish they are better than Fuchun River." (Reply to Mr. Liu Yazi). Mao was trying to retain talents for the People's Public of China to be founded. One and a half years later, Mao wrote another poem to the same tune: "The red new China, however, is at dawn when the cock crows; so many nationalities including Xinjiang play with music tonight; the poets have even more pleasure to write down wonderful poems." It describes a prosperous circumstance of the new China. Mao wrote the Beidaihe in 1954: "Today the rustling autumn wind comes back again, but the world has changed!" He wrote

Swimming in 1956: "Great plans are afoot… A bridge will fly to span the north and south…Till a smooth lake rises in the narrow gorges…The mountain goddess if she is still there, will marvel at a world so changed." In May 1957, he wrote the Love of Butterfly: Reply to Li Shuyi, which said, "Suddenly, it was reported that the tigers in the human world had all been caught; their happy tears poured down like a cloudburst." All of these lines were about the huge changes of China after the founding of the People's Republic of China.

Especially, on July 1, 1958, Mao wrote two poems titled Farewell to the God of Plague, which directly reflected the reality. In the afterword for the two poems, Mao said, "The two poems I had written are like pictorial posters, aimed at providing my support for Yujiang County (which had made great success in eliminating blood flukes)." In these two poems, the poet said, "The spring wind blows amid profuse willow wands, and six hundred million in this land all equal Yao and Shun." It eulogizes the power of the country.

In the Shaoshan Revisited, Mao wrote: "Happy, I see wave upon wave of paddy and beans, and all around heroes home-bound in the evening mist." In Militia Women, he wrote, "China's daughters have high-aspiring minds. They love their battle array, not silks and satins." Facing complicated domestic and international problems, Mao gave free rein to his imagination in his Reply to A Friend: "And I am lost in dreams, untrammelled dreams of the land of hibiscus glowing in the morning sun." In another poem, he wrote: "The boundless vista is at the perilous peak." (To Photo of Fairy Cave at Mount Lu by Li Jintong) In addition, in the Reply to Comrade Guo Moruo, Mao pointed out: "The deluded monk was not beyond the light, but the malignant demon must wreak havoc." He believed that the enemies and the friends should be distinguished clearly.

To praise the revolutionaries, Mao wrote: "Sweet and fair, she craves not Spring for herself alone, to be the harbinger of spring she is content." (Bu Suan Zi: Ode to the Plum Blossom). When China suffered unprecedented difficulties, he wrote: "Plum blossoms welcome the whirling snow; small wonder flies freeze and perish." (Winter Clouds) In The River All Red, Mao compared the domestic and foreign enemies to ants: "Ants on the locust tree assume a great-nation swagger, and mayflies lightly plot to topple the giant tree." In the Reascending Jinggang Mountain, the poet wrote: "We can clasp the moon in the Ninth Heaven, and seize turtles deep down in the Five Seas: We'll return amid triumphant song and laughter. Nothing is hard in this world, if you dare to scale the heights."

There are a great number of examples that prove that Mao wrote these poems to reflect and serve the reality. These poems set a model for making innovation of content of poems.

The content needs innovation, and the language needs new elements. Just as Mao said, "Poems should be made following imaginable thinking but not direct statement as that used for proses. Therefore, bi (metaphor)

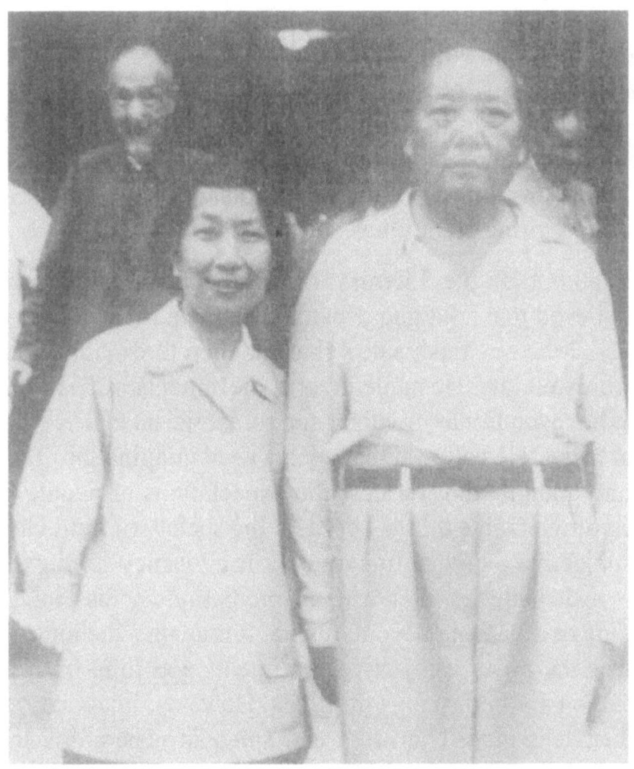

Mao Zedong meets with Li Shuyi, wife of martyr Liu Zhixun, in September 1959.

and xing (to express one's feelings with the help of other matters) should be used. Fu (direct statement) can be used, too. For example, Du Fu's North watch Expedition." (To Chen Yi) Although Mao was erudite and very good at classical Chinese, he wrote poems mostly with spoken and vulgar language, trying to avoid rarely used words and literary quotations. For example, "Gleaming mattocks fall on the Five Ridges heaven-high; mighty arms move to rock the earth round the Triple River." (Farewell to the God of Plague) "Who knows whither Prefect Tao Yuanming is gone, now that he can till fields in the Land of Peach Blossoms?" (Ascent of

Lushan) "Today, a miasmal mist once more rising, we hail Sun Wu-kung, the wonder-worker." (Reply to Comrade Guo Moruo) "When the mountain flowers are in full bloom, she will smile mingling in their midst." (Ode to the Plum Blossom) "On this tiny globe, a few flies dash themselves against the wall, humming without cease, sometimes shrilling, sometimes moaning." (Reply to Comrade Guo Moruo) "Gunfire licks the heavens. Shells pit the earth. A sparrow in his bush is scared stiff. 'This is one hell of a mess! O I want to flit and fly away.'" "Don't you know a triple pact was signed under the bright autumn moon two years ago? There'll be plenty to eat, potatoes piping hot, beef-filled goulash." "'Stop your windy nonsense! Look, the world is being turned upside down.'" (Two Birds: A Dialogue). These poems made a breakthrough in language application. This should be attributed to the proficiency of the poet in using imaginable thinking and the bi and xing writing techniques.

Liu Xie, author of the Literary Mind and the Carving of Dragons: Wording, believed that a language cannot be spread widely if it is not easy to understand. Mao obviously knew that and therefore made great efforts in using the words vividly. He made great achievements in this aspect. He incorporated the revolutionary realism and romanticism to meet the scholarly and popular tastes. He believed that poems need imagination. Tao Wenpeng believed that "imagination reflects the expectations of people for unrealized or even unrealizable things based on the society or individual dreams, wish and subjective feelings. Imagination is a journey from experience to the unknown. It includes memories or predictions across time. It is also brainstorming or dreaming beyond reality. It is against the logical thinking, but expresses the poets' subjective sentiments and thinking. Association and imagination are both wings of minds. However, imagination takes the minds higher. It is more charming and splendid. Therefore, imagination should be deemed as a mark of talented romantic poets". (Romantic Art in Mao Zedong's Poems).

Mao is the romantic poet who was best in association and imagination. His works are full of revolutionary realism and romanticism. Commenting the Love of Butterfly: Reply to Li Shuyi, Guo Moruo said, "It is a typical poem for integration of revolutionary realism and romanticism, showing great revolutionary thoughts between lines. It is an imagery expression of revolution." Concerning The Spring Comes to a Happy Garden: Changsha and other poems by Mao, He Qifang said that they were "the best model for proletarian literature and art with integrated revolutionary realism and romanticism." (See Guangming Daily, September 17, 1977)

In addition to the innovation in content, language and expression ways, Mao also made innovation in rhymes:

First, Mao did not support too strict rhyming. He believed that it is fine to keep the rhymes similar in a flexible way. For this, the Love of Butterfly: Reply to Li Shuyi is a good example.

Second, some people believe that Mao sometimes broke the rules on tones when creating poems. However, sometimes, it was unavoidable, even for other great poets, such as Du Fu. The applicable principle for this is to avoid breaking the roles as much as possible. However, when it cannot be avoided, violation of the rules should be allowed to guarantee the expression of the poem lines.

Third, some people criticized Mao for repeatedly using synonyms in his poems. For example, "Only heroes can quell tigers and leopards, and wild bears never daunt the brave." Those people believe that it was a repetition. However, logically, the couple of lines are in progressive relations. It is not a repetition but a good example that should be spread through ages. What's a repetition? For example, "Only heroes can quell tigers and leopards, and the brave can defeat wild bears."

Fourth, some people criticized Mao for making mistakes in wording, for example, use the same words in a couple of lines. However, to make a poem of four lines, repeated words in two neighboring lines are allowed. There are many examples in the history. The ancient Chinese poets even use the same word in their poems of eight lines, despite such repetition was required to be avoided when making such kind of poems. Two examples are Cui Hao's Yellow Crane Tower and Du Fu's Baidi. Of course, for any kind of poem, repeated use of the same word should be avoided as much as possible. However, sometimes, for better expression, it should be allowed. Some experts believed, "A main reason causing the traditional Chinese poems to gradually fall into a recession was that some (feudal) aristocrat scholars adhered too strictly to the set rhymes and forms for poems so that the poems could be understood by the people. Apart from the grassroots culture, the poems could be only spread among the scholars and therefore had a smaller potential for development. That's why poetry has a decline." (Wu Guochen, Mao Zedong's Reform and Innovation in Theories on Traditional Chinese Poetry) They believed that Mao greatly changed the declining tendency of traditional Chinese poetry. First, Mao changed the thinking mode to make poems, from individual perspective to a wider perspective, such as the revolution, the country and even the world. Second, Mao changed the attitude to make poems, from a negative attitude full of depression and compassion to a positive attitude to pursue successes and achievements. Third, Mao changed the aesthetic consciousness for traditional Chinese poems, from the sentimental and sophisticated beauty to grand, simple and lofty beauty. In fact, Mao's poems incorporate the beauty of painting and music arts. Many of his poems show masculine beauty and beauty of personality. Therefore, some experts believed: "The readers will not only be strongly affected by the artistic attainments contained in Mao's poems, but also will be spiritually enlightened and encouraged, so that they will have higher spiritual pursuit and be more motivated to resist various decadent thoughts and fight against ideological aggression by enemies. The poems serve as great ideological weapon and driving force." (Zhang Ke, Mao Zedong's Poems and Construction of Core Socialist Value System) "Mao Zedong's poems fully manifest his sublime spirit and patriotism against imperialism and hegemonism and firm belief. The poems show his revolutionary spirit to work hard to seek truth from facts and find a new way to victories relying on the masses, his long-march spirit to overcome all difficulties even by sacrificing his life, take an overall perspective and strictly obey the disciplines to enhance the unity and work together to seek a success, as well as his spirit of serving others while seeking self-development by hard learning, fulfilling due responsibilities and living a thrifty life." (Wu Haikun, On Positive Energy and Spirit of Patriotism in Mao Zedong's Poems) Highlighting the national spirit centering on patriotism and the spirit of the time centering on reform and innovation, Mao's poems have a number of positive effects, such as inspiring the fighting spirit, raising awareness and consolidating belief. Therefore, even today, they will play an important role in leading the Chinese people to bring about a great rejuvenation of the Chinese nation and realize the "Chinese dream".

Mao showed his "Chinese dream" in his poems. He had the dream of changing the world, for example, he wrote: "Bitter sacrifice strengthens bold resolve which dares to make sun and moon shine in new skies." He had the dream of seeking a strong economic development, for example, "A bridge will fly to span the north and south, turning a deep chasm into a thoroughfare." "We can clasp the moon in the Ninth Heaven and seize turtles deep down in the Five Seas." He had the dream of popularizing knowledge among the people, for example, "The spring wind blows amid profuse willow wands, six hundred million in this land all equal Yao and Shun." He also had the dream of Great Unity of the communist world, for example, "In a peaceful world young and old, might share alike your warmth and cold!" The "Chinese dream" is a dream of the great rejuvenation of Chinese nation and also a dream of world peace and prosperity. The following leaders of China also have a "Chinese dream". In February

2005, Hu Jintao, then General Secretary of the CPC Central Committee, said, "To realize harmony between human beings and build a wonderful society has been a social ideal of all the people. It is also a social ideal of the Marxist political parties, including the CPC." In March 2013, Xi Jinping, current General Secretary of the CPC Central Committee, called to realize the "Chinese dream" in a peaceful way to benefit the world and contribute to the realization of the "world dream", which pursues for new global order, long-term peace and mutual prosperity. The poems by Mao Zedong provide great ideological weapon and driving force for the realization of the "Chinese dream" and the "world dream".

IV. Mao's theories on poetry guide the contemporary poetry reform and innovation

Mao's theories on poetry are praised and criticized as much as his poems. Some people believed that Mao's theories should be deemed as basis and guidance for contemporary poetry reform and innovation, while others believed that his theories hinder the development of poetry, especially the ancient-style poetry. There are also some people who believe that Mao's theories have little significance, because the Chinese poetry has had an integrated development that leaves no space for any new forms of poems. The reason for some people to believe that Mao's theories hinder the development of the ancient-style poetry is a letter dated January 12, 1957, from Mao to Zang Kejia and other poets. In the letter, Mao said, "Of course, the contemporary poems should play a main role. The ancient-style poems can be written, but should not be popularized among the young, because such types of poems restrict the thoughts and are hard to learn." Actually, such idea is unblameable. Ancient-style poems follow strict rules on rhyme, anti-thesis, number of lines and Chinese characteristics. It is true that it is hard for the poets to free their mind when making such poems. For the same reason, it is really hard to learn. That's why Mao proposed to make reform and innovation and required to write ancient-style poems in a "prudent way" to set good examples for the young. People who believe that Mao's theories have little significance must misunderstand Mao's opinions. Mao believed that there had been some successes in writing free verse written in the vernacular in the past several decades of years. Therefore, he pointed out, "Some ballads are very good. In the future, a new set of new-style poems may derive from the ballads." (To Chen Yi) He hoped that new-style poems could have national characteristics and be popularized among the masses. In January 1957, Mao had a conversation with Zang Kejia and Yuan Shuipai. He said, "New poems should be concise and generally follow the rules on antithesis and rhyming. That's to say, the new-style poems should be developed based on classical poems and ballads. On the one hand, we should inherit the traditions manifested by excellent poems. On the other hand, we should meet follow the development over time to seek for development of new-style poems." (Comrade Mao Zedong and Poems, by Zang Kejia, See Red Flag, 1984(2)). In summer 1965, Mao talked with Mei Bai about poems: "The ancient-style poetry follows many rules on rhyme and forms. It is not easy to learn and restricts people's mind. It is not as free as new-style poetry. On the other hand, the ancient-style poetry has a long history, winning the favor of both the elderly, such as me, and the middle-aged people, such as you. I believe that, through further development and reform, the ancient-style poetry will never be out of date, because it plays the most important role to reflect the characteristics and behaviors of the Chinese nation and Chinese people. It is a mirror for us to know better about the masses!" (See Anecdotes about Mao Zedong, Kunlun Publishing House, 1989.) In June 1957, when talking with Mao Guangsheng about poems, Mao called to make new-style poems based on the ancient-style poems and ballads and develop the ancient-style poetry by drawing the strength of ballads and new-style poems.[1]

Some scholars said: "Conciseness and generally following the rules on antithesis and rhyming are the most scientific concept on creation of innovative new-style poems." They believe that Mao's such concept is similar with Lu Xun's concepts on poems and basically keeps in line with the contemporary poem making practices and theories. For example, Lu Xun once pointed out, "Poems must be in certain format and should be easy to memory, understand and recite. However, there should not too many restrictions on format. There should be rhyme, but not according to the rules adopted for making classic poems. It is ok to read smoothly." (Letters of Lu Xun, Volume 2). He also said, "New-style poems should generally follow certain rules on tune and rhyme." (Lu Xun's Opinions on Literature and Art, Volume 2, Letter to Dou Yinfu). Hu Shi, a representative founder of the new-style poetry school, said, "New-style poems should break the restrictions in formats and tune. They should not be restricted by rules on form, rhyme and length of poems."[2]

Wen Yiduo, another founder the new-style poetry school, said, "I believe that Hu Shi should be the person guiltiest for the new poetry movement of China. The biggest mistake he has made is to claim that writing poems should be like writing essays…For people good at making poems, the rules

---

1   Shu Yan, I Met Chairman Mao Zedong again in summer 1957, the Journal of Xinhua Wenzhai, 1989(1).
2   Collected Works of Hu Shi III: On New Poems.

on form and rhyme has never been a barrier…Visually, poems should have symmetrical strophes and well-organized lines. In terms of auditory effect, poems should follow certain rhyme rules. This is because, what poems manifest is not only the beauty of music (syllable) and drawing (rhetoric), but also the beauty of architecture (symmetrical strophes and well-organized lines)." (Wen Yiduo's Opinions on New-style Poems: Rules on Making Poems). Guo Moruo, who was also a main participant in the May 4 New-style Poetry Movement, said, "Rhythm is the appearance of a poem, and also the vitality of the poem." (On Rhythm) Guo Moruo also said that he "paid high attention to rhymes and always read the poems for many times after making them." (Guo Moruo's Opinions on Making Poems) Therefore, Zhu Ziqing pointed out, "Mr. Guo Moruo should be especially mentioned, because his poems mostly boast good rhyming and well-organized lines." (Forms of Poems) Many contemporary poets, including He Qifang, Ai Qing and Zang Kejia, generally agreed with that. He Qifang said, "Poetry is the type of literature best depicting the social life. It is full of imagination and emotions and, usually, directly expresses emotions. In addition, it is extremely concise and has distinct rhythm. This makes it quite different from proses."[3]

Ai Qing said, "A poem should be as precise and concise as possible. It should be like a bomb with tremendously solid shell wrapping the explosive… I have never pieced a poem together to meet the rules on rhyming. I follow my conception and the rhythm in my mind. It is fine as long as the poem reads and sounds smoothly."[4]

Zang Kejia wrote in his Conciseness, Generally Good Organization and Rhyming: "Mao Zedong talked about conciseness. I think it hit the nail on the head and should be greatly helpful for poets like us." Rules on making classic poems and ballads should be based to make new-style poems so that the latters can be concise and generally consistent with the rules on antithesis and rhyming as well as innovative and inclusive. A great number of excellent poets in creation of new-style poems emerged in the 1950s and 1960s, such as Guo Jingzhi, Guo Xiaochuan, Zhang Zhimin, Li Ji, Wen Jie, Yuan Zhangjing, Li Ying and Yan Zhen. Nowadays, the new-style poetry saw a decline because that many poets do the opposite, making poems similar with proses.

Mao did not specify his opinions on reform and innovation of classic poetry. However, he showed agreement with expert Mao Guangsheng's opinions on liberation of Ci poems and said, "The classic rules on making poems are so strict that they lead to ideological restraints. I think that young people should not spend too much time learning to make classic poems. However,

---

3   See About Poem Making and Reading.
4   See Ai Qing's Opinions on Literature Creation.

the earlier generations who have devoted themselves to make ancient-style poems should try to be proficient." He did not mention how proficient they should be. However, he asked, "Can a metrical poem be called a metrical poem when it doesn't keep consistent with the rules on rhyme and tune?" Clearly, he meant that the new-style metrical poems should be metrical. Guo Moruo had the same opinions. His article titled About Nationalization and Popularization of Poems said, "In my opinion, some types of ancient-style poems will exist for a long time, such as wujue (a four-line poem with five characters to a line), wulyu (an eight-line poem with five characters to a line), qijue (a four-line poem with seven characters to a line) and Qilyu (eight-line Chinese poem with seven characters to a line), which have experienced the historical test. These poems are similar with ballads, which are easy to understand and depict vivid living scenes. I think the ordinary people like such types of poems." Ma Kai, another Chinese poet, repeatedly emphasized the significance and importance of the reform and development of ancient-style poems. He wrote: "Generally speaking, to inherit and develop metrical poetry means to inherit the tradition to express true feelings through poems at the same time of reflecting the reality and people's thoughts in contemporary times. It also means to follow the classic rules on making poems while allowing changes. Why? That's because the classic rules are golden rules developed by the ancestors through thousands of years' study and practice. We should not abandon them. However, we should allow changes. Even the greatest poets in the history, such as Li Bai and Du Fu, made reform of ways to write poems. It is not an exception in contemporary times."[5]

Ma's opinions kept in line with Mao's opinions. The reform and development of metrical poetry focus on innovation of content, language and rhyme as well as allowing changes while following the traditional rules. Many famous scholars and poets, such as Yu Youren, Huo Songlin, Liu Zheng and Ding Mang, agreed with that, though it will take time to practice. To sum up, Mao's theories on making poems are practical and have great guiding significance for the development and innovation of Chinese poetry.

The content above is based on the author's speeches at the workshop held by Beijing Poetry Association and the 13th Annual Meeting of the Mao Zedong's Poems Research Society. The author, with an autonym of Zhou Xingjun, is vice chairman of Chinese Poetry Society, vice chairman of Mao Zedong's Poems Research Society, and first vice president of Academy of Chinese Traditional Poetry.

---

5   See Ma Kai, On Traditions and Changes.

8

Land Reform was a Great Revolution in the Sphere of Production Relations

Wang Ruifang

Regarding the land reform movement led by the CPC, recently some people think it was a "historical failure". They have argued that land reform movement tried to overturn the landlord class, and established predatory property relations, undermined rural productive forces, thus underline the conclusion that land reform and rural poverty has a direct relationship and so on. However, can the facts prove these arguments?

From the overall macro perspective, Land reform has not only completed the great transformation of the ownership of the land ownership to the peasants' land ownership, but also brought about the historic changes in the rural society. It has not only changed the social structure, organizational form and social political structure of China's rural areas, but also made small farmers' mode of production, way of life, customs and spirit of life have also changed significantly. Through the land reform movement, a new Chinese rural society, which is quite different from the old society has appeared which also has world-wide significance.

I. The aim of land reform was to liberate and develop the productive forces

Land, means of production (including farm animals etc.) and workers (farmers) are the basic elements in the agricultural productive forces, and the binding mode among labor, land and production tools determines the mode of agricultural production is reasonable or not. The fundamental reason of land reform was the original unreasonable landlord land system: farmers had little or no land, while only the people who owned the land could utilize their land plots. The separation of land ownership and use rights seriously had affected farmers' investment in land and the accumulation of agricultural capital, so it was difficult to make a major breakthrough in the development of the agricultural productive forces. This land system has not only restricted the development of agricultural productive forces, but also hindered the democratization and prosperity in the development of rural areas. In order to liberate the rural productive forces and develop agricultural production, unreasonable landlord land ownership was abolished, which was the basic reason and the basic purpose of land reform. The reason and purpose shows that land reform decision given by the leadership of the Communist Party of China was aimed at liberating and developing of the agricultural productive forces, not only for the relief of the poor and elimination poverty. In this land reform movement, the major means of production and land were distributed to landless peasants and farmers, the reason was the rational allocation of the production means, the adjustment of rural production relations, and changing the mode of the agricultural production, realization of the unity between the means of production and the farmers' land, farm etc., rational distribution of production factors once again, so as to liberate and develop the productive forces of agriculture. The improvement of agricultural productive forces after the accomplishment of the land reform movement were mainly manifested in: firstly, farmers with unprecedented enthusiasm and raised the upsurge of the construction of water conservancy; secondly, the increase in the labor force and land investment; grain production was improved with the increase of purchasing power of means of production and the agricultural production has recovered quickly.

The movement to complete the great change from landlord land ownership to the farmers' land ownership, it had realized Chinese farmers' dream of "land to the tiller" which was longed for thousands of years. This was a great change in agricultural productive forces of China since the establishment of private ownership of land, it is one of the largest and most complete distribution of the land ownership and a great revolution in the liberation of agricultural productive forces. It was a fundamental change of China's rural social production, which has laid a solid foundation for the further improvement of agricultural productive forces.

II. After the land reform, material and cultural life of the farmers were greatly improved

Along with the recovery and development of agricultural production, the improvement of the living standard of farmers was the inevitable result. The improvement of living standards of farmers was absolutely due to the land reform movement, the poor peasants and farm laborers got production tools and living materials for free including land, cattle, farm implements, houses and food, and those people had certain production and living ability; but what is more important is that the rise of agricultural production, the increase of purchasing power and the reduction of the burden due to the production enthusiasm of farmers. The general increase in the income of farmers improved the purchasing power of farmers, which laid the economic foundation for the improvement of their cultural life. The improvement of rural medical and health conditions, fertility rate and the reduction of mortality rate has directly led to a substantial increase in the rural population, which is an obvious concentrated expression in improvement of quality of life for the majority of farmers. The farmers who got freedom politically and economically have also began to demand higher needs for their spiritual and cultural lives. The vast rural areas began to popularize education: the establishment of private schools and private schools. Not only the number of students increased significantly with the number of rural primary schools, but also various literacy classes, the newspaper reading groups and the blackboard in many remote rural areas have also appeared; the vast rural areas established different levels of cultural institutions, the majority of farmers also set up thousands of rural art and cultural performance troops. They enriched and developed their own cultural and recreational life in various forms.

III. The land reform has destroyed the feudal patriarchal clan system

Before the land reform, China's rural areas remained as a feudal patriarchal society having a long historical basis. The Kuomintang's Baojia system and the feudal patriarchal clan system constituted the basic organization structure of China before the land reform. In the land reform, the Communist Party of China intervened in the rural areas with strong political backing for deterrence, confiscating a large amount of land owned by clans, destroying the economic base of the feudal family/clan system, holding down the political power of the village chiefs and confiscating the ancestral temple. The dominant clan forces which had lasted in China's Rural Society for thousands of years suffered a fatal blow and thus began to perish.

In the continuous propaganda and inspiration of the CPC and the government, the clan concept began to dissolve, the slogan "kiss families no other people" was replaced by the slogan "the poor is a family of the world". They came to realize that farmers are as a whole, class affection is more important than family affection, clan surnames were divided into classes. The class consciousness had replaced the clan ideology, and gradually became the mainstream ideology of the majority of farmers.

IV. Land reform has changed the political pattern in the rural areas

The process of land reform was actually a political movement that the new regime mobilized the peasants to revolt against the feudal landlord class. And the majority of farmers were mobilized and organized, which inevitably brought changes in rural political power, the replacement of rural grassroots regime and the transfer of rural political authority. The original rural grassroots regime dominated by landlords and rich peasants was replaced by the new political forces that are formed with the new rising farmers. The land property of the landlord class was confiscated, and they lost greatly economically, after the severe political criticism, they also lost their political authority. Rural grassroots organizations after the land reform movement were mastered by the Communist Party and the farmers led by the CPC. The farmers' movement were organized into farmers' representative congresses and farmers' associations, and became the backbone of the newly formed rural grassroots political system. On the basis, village people's representative congresses were established all-across the country. Most of representatives in the village level congresses were directly elected by the village people, with full mass participation. The village people's representative congresses elected the village government, the village government implemented the resolutions issued by the congresses and were put under the control of the people's congresses and accepted their supervision. In this way, the majority of farmers who were liberated economically in the process of land reform realized their dreams regarding politics and the local rural grassroots governments were firmly controlled by the farmers.

Through the land reform movement, the Communist Party of China has realized the comprehensive integration of the rural society. The new-village grassroots governments led and established by the Communist Party of China controlled social resources with the core being land and guided farmers to participate in various mass movements. In this way, the political consciousness of the Chinese Communist Party was effectively implanted into the ideological world of the masses of farmers, the political appeal of the Communist Party of China and its political influence was greatly strengthened. The state power was effectively extended to the most basic level of the rural society, expanding the functioning of the state and administrative areas through the peasant associations led by the Communist Party and enhanced the new rural grassroots political system. This new type of rural political structure and the political authority and political resources received in the land reform movement by the Party and the government became a powerful force for guiding farmers to take the road of cooperation.

V. Land reform has vigorously promoted the rural social customs reform

With the reform of the land system, the old social norms and social customs which were based on the feudal land ownership were shook. Traditional social norms were attacked and transformed, and its binding on farmers was weakened, which gradually formed new social norms, new conducts and new values that adopted to the new land system and to the economic and political situation. The degree of women's liberation is always the measure of the degree of social civilization. The distribution of land between men and women were realized equally, providing economic security for the independence of women; the new marriage law and its implementation abolished the unreasonable feudal marriage system, protecting the legal rights of women and making equality between men and women a solid reality. Rural women gaining higher status in the society not only actively participated in anti-feudal struggle, the political life and rural social life, but also participated in agricultural production and could not be ignored as a labor force.

Along with the anti-feudal struggle in the rural reform movement, the new people's political power in the villages have quelled the social evils of the old rural society, feudal superstition was criticized, the witch and God cult were banned, many bad habits like early marriage and infanticide were dismissed, freedom of marriage began to prevail, rural new customs and customs began to form, the farmers' political consciousness and social values begin to change, a new countryside different from the old society gradually took roots among the people.

The majority of emancipated peasants sincerely hailed: "Don't forget the Communist Party and Chairman Mao". This has been the most vivid description of the mental world of peasants after the land reform. The Communist Party and its leader Chairman Mao enjoyed a high prestige in farmers' mind, this shows that after the land reform in rural areas a new folk custom to revere and respect the CPC and Chairman Mao had spontaneously formed. This new folk custom became a new spiritual resource, which laid a deep psychological foundation for the Chinese Communist Party to mobilize the masses of farmers to participate in the reform of the rural society.

The author Wang Ruifang is a researcher at the Institute of Contemporary China Studies attached to CASS; the article was first published in *Social Sciences in China* on December 16, 2013

9

Is Guo Moruo A Controversial Literary Giant?

He Gang

Recently, an article was published titled as *A Controversial Literary Giant Guo Moruo*[1] in the Internet, arguing that Guo Moruo was very smart and his achievements in some academic circles could be said to be "unique" but these cannot cover up his defects as a scholar, "deleting the historical data and his tendency of plagiarism" were the apparent aspects" of his academic misconduct.

The writer of this unlucky article has finally declared that "pointing out to such defects of him" is to present an intact historical literary figure Guo Moruo instead of expecting things to be perfect. But as we examine the whole article we see subjective opinions and lack of objective arguments as well as author's personal evaluations instead of historical facts. Essentially, it shares the same texture as the article titled as *Shameless Scholar Guo Moruo* which was spread in the Internet and still is the representative "work" that has caught our attention for its distorting the truth. From the current standpoint, how should we evaluate Guo Moruo on earth? It not only involves Guo Moruo, the specific figure being judged and discussed, but involves more about the conception of history and also the correct perspective we should use to treat the people who have great contributions to the development of historiography in the New China. Nowadays, some people have collected their personal defects in terms of morality, styles of work and study and what they may conceal would be the real, integral and

---

1 Guo Moruo, November 16, 1892 - June 12, 1978), courtesy name Ding Tang was a renown Chinese author, poet, historian, archaeologist, and government official from Sichuan, China.

objective history, which is not only helpless to enrich the historical data but rather helpless to deepen people's perception of history. Below, I will argue that from the perspective of the overall history, it will be valid to make comments on Guo Moruo's works in the following six aspects.

First, as Guo Moruo really realized scientification of Chinese historiography, by which he developed a way for Chinese Marxist historiography, laid the pattern and started the way with guideline, he is the pioneer and founder of Chinese Marxist historiography. Guo Moruo represented a new age, namely the academic age of Marxism. In the 20th century, Chinese historiography has encountered a fundamental change, which was marked by historical materialism surpassing modern evolutionism in the conception of history, so as to really develop scientific orientation. In 1920s, Guo Moruo, as an exile in Japan, has overcome all sorts of difficulties to apply the systematic ideas of historical materialism to the specific study of Chinese history for the first time. Taking *The Origin of the Family, Private Property, and the State* as his "guiding inspiration", his work titled as "Study on the Ancient Society of China" published in 1930 has systematically expounded on Chinese history especially the development course of ancient Chinese history and has demonstrated the scientific nature and strong vitality of Marxist historiography, paved the way for the bright orientation for the study of Chinese history and marked the establishment of Chinese Marxist historiography. Succeeding him, with the emergence of works by Lv Zhenyu, Jian Bozan, Fan Wenlan and Hou Wailu Marxist historiography appeared as a new force which rapidly developed among China's history circles and showed thriving vitality. In his 60-year historical study career, Guo Moruo wrote abundant extensive works and left great works to the later generations in the fields such as Chinese ancient history and staging study, study on history of ancient Chinese thought, study on historical figures and collation of ancient books just because he has embraced historical materialism as a "critical weapon".

Secondly, in respect of his works on oracles, bronze inscriptions and ancient writings, Guo Moruo had made remarkable contributions. He paid attention to the "creative use" of historical materials and such "creativity" was intensively reflected in interpretation of the archaeological materials – oracle and bronze inscriptions unearthed in of the late modern times. Dong Zuobin commented, "He has established an ancient Chinese cultural system study and discipline imbued with historical materialism by combining the written materials in the Book of Poetry, The Book of History and Book of Changes and the significant materials in the oracle inscriptions and in the Chinese bronze inscriptions of Zhou Dynasty." In the book titled as "Science of Oracle", Guo Moruo "published his oracle inscription examples" and ranked "four people whose names including 'Tang' in oracle", with his master works of Study on Oracle-bone Inscriptions, General Compilation of Oracle Inscriptions and so on.

In respect of phases analysis and dating, oracle inscriptions, fragment conjugation, proofreading the repeating parts and with the complete editing of the incomplete inscriptions, he set up a scientific system for the compilation and settlement of the science of oracle; the comprehensive document assembly of oracle mainly edited by him – Oracle Compilations adopted the arrangement of classification by phase and included the examination of 41,956 pieces of oracle bones, which has been a milestone and monumental work in the field of "historical oracle" studies. In his studies on bronze ware which included inscriptions from the Yin and Zhou Dynasties, Guo Moruo made a breakthrough analysis of "the chaos period of 800 years in the two Zhou Dynasties", which was an epochal contributions as well, with the main works of Study on the Bronze Ware Inscriptions of the Yin and Zhou Dynasties, Comprehensive Study on the Chinese Bronze Inscriptions and so on. The standard historical division method established by him has utilized a classification based on the time and country, which has established a systematic complete system for the handed-down bronze wares of the "chaos period", which can still be regarded as the building block in the studies of the bronze ware.

Thirdly, more importantly, in respect of historical data collecting and sorting, especially the in the collection work of the ancient writings, Guo Moruo "explored the reason in the practical work" instead of only remaining in the traditional exegesis approach and textual analysis and criticism. He wrote: "I study the oracle inscriptions because I want to reveal the origins of the Chinese society, but I haven't rigidly adhered to the origins of characteristics, history and geography". The goal sought by him when making textual criticism and his pursuit for the exegesis of characters has achieved a rational textual research of the Chinese history, which has greatly enriched and developed Marxist science of historiography.

Fourthly, Guo Moruo's achievements in historiography are important components of the "Chinese style": with distinct historical sense and strong time awareness. Guo Moruo inherited and carried forward the historical research tradition of facing the reality and the approach of humanistic pragmatism which closely combined academic research with social reality. He wrote: "Our expectation for the future society forces us to come up with the requirement of clearing the past society", therefore, I have written the "Study of the Ancient Chinese Society"; on the 300th Anniversary of the

Jiashen Year he sharply put forward the realistic issue of preventing the ruling power from "being proud is the start of fall" by profoundly summarizing the reason for the fall of the Ming Dynasty and revealed the historical lessons of Li Zicheng Peasant Uprising why and how it successfully won the political power, but had failed soon. In the comprehensive multidisciplinary research of historiography, Guo Moruo "sorted the materials of the ancient history using anthropological findings as the tool" and achieved the initial integration of Chinese historiography with the newly developing social sciences such as archaeology, economics, anthropology and sociology in order to "pave a path in the studies of ancient history" as a contribution to the Chinese historiography, which was also in conformity with the development trend of the world's historiography.

Fifthly, he explored innovatively and dared to criticize and surpass himself. In the question of division between the phases of slavery and feudalism in China, Guo Moruo amended his propositions for many times and included the lower limit of slavery in the boundary time which lied between the Spring and Autumn and the Warring State Periods. He only felt "almost all blank" when he first saw the oracle characters, but he was firmly determined to "solve their codes continuously, utilize them, and disclose their secrets". Till the "historiography revolution" which began in 1958 when others championed to "emphasize the new and de-emphasize the old", "break the system of dynasties" and "overthrow the emperors, generals and ministers", Guo Moruo strived forward against this trend, and he made his utmost efforts to correct the "left-leaning" error by reversing the verdict for Cao Cao, and fought hard to promote free academic discussions and enabled the occurrence of the situation wherein "hundred schools of thought freely contended".

Sixthly, by integrating literature and history, he pursued the popularization of historiography and promoted its mass character. Guo Moruo guided the readers to history starting from literature, and his ebullient style of writing made readers hardly feel bored when reading his academic writings, besides his writing style enabled readers to feel strong aesthetic sense and made them eager to seek the wisdom in his works, which provided valuable referential source for the later generations that strove for the popularization and promoting the mass nature of Chinese historiography. To speak frankly, since he was restricted by the circumstances of the historical age and also by his own subjective conditions, certain flaws and mistakes, inevitably co-existed within Guo Moruo's lifetime academic achievements, such as cursoriness and "formulation" trace in his initial works, and "excessive praise" for or being "prejudiced" towards certain historical figures.

However, as the old saying stipulates: "we should not cover the great virtue with a single mistake", we must point out that Guo Moruo made great and major creative and valuable contributions to the development of the academic discipline of Chinese Marxist historiography. Guo Moruo is not a controversial literary giant, instead, we think those who slander Guo Moruo are actually the true shameless literates.

The author He Gang is the deputy director of Sichuan Guo Moruo Research Center in the Leshan Normal University; originally published in *Social Sciences in China*, December 9, 2013

10

Mao Zedong Did Not Support the View of Secluding China from the Outside World

Xue Guangzhou

China's reform achievements after the revolution were impressive, on the pretext of praising these achievements, some people regard the government policies before the reform and opening-up period as aiming to "seclude the country from the outside world", consequently those arguments that place Mao Zedong in an opposite position regarding reform and opening-up, deserves our consideration. For example, some people have argued: "Mao Zedong has advocated the traditional culture of our country, and adopted an attitude of indifference towards the bourgoise culture, pursued the seclusion of Utopia", some people also said: "After the founding of the PRC, due to various reasons, basically China was put in a long-term closed situation." There are many similar arguments, which are popular in the Internet, which cause a harmful impression and especially mislead the young generations. After the founding of the New China for a long period of time, our country was in a state of being blocked and attacked by the Western hostile forces. In November 1949, the United States and other 14 countries set up the "Paris-based Coordinating Committee" in Paris, which was an organization to impose embargos against the socialist countries, in particular, its main target was China. Especially, on February 1, 1951 the General Assembly of the UN adopted a resolution with respect to the intervention of the Central People's Government of the People's Republic of China in Korea, which was proposed by the US, which meant to carry out an economic "embargo" and political isolation. This was an obvious attempt to stifle, suppress and surrender the new People's Republic of China.[1]

---

1 Under the Export Control Act of 1949, exports from the United States to the Soviet Union and other socialist countries were controlled based on their military significance. In addition, the Act established a "short supply" export control program to deal with the post-war worldwide shortage of many goods. The Export Control Act of 1949 continued to be in effect for 20 years.

The blockade and embargo had not ended until the United States and China signed a joint communique in Shanghai in February 1972, which had lasted for 22 years. As some scholars have pointed out, western countries did not let us enter the western markets in over 20 years, so there was no natural sense of opening-up.

Although faced with the blockade and embargo of the Western hostile forces, Mao Zedong and the Chinese communists did not give up the opening-up policy. In "On the Ten Major Relationships", Mao Zedong analyzed "the relationship between China and foreign countries' as a major relationship, and pointed out: "I think it is right for us to put forward the slogan of learning from foreign countries. Now some of our state leaders do not want to mention, and even dare not mention this slogan. It's going to need a little bit of courage". And specifically said: "Our policy is that we should learn from the strong points of all nations and all countries and all things are really good in politics and the economy, science, technology, literature and art". Historical facts show that Mao Zedong conducted a fruitful struggle to break the foreign blockade and isolation against the United States and other western countries, in order to expand economic and trade exchanges with foreign countries. Therefore, the argument that Mao Zedong adopted a policy of seclusion is indeed unfounded, which is contrary to the historical facts. Of course, as one scholars said: what Mao Zedong learned all national strengths and the guiding ideology and practice for development of foreign trade and economic relations did not rise to be a basic national policy, and had not reached a standard of a full liberalization. As a witness, Deng Xiaoping had a very accurate evaluation of this, he said: "When Comrade Mao Zedong was alive, we also wanted to expand economic and technological exchanges, including developing economic and trade relations with some capitalist countries, and even attracting foreign capital, carrying out equity joint ventures etc. But at that time the conditions were not right and people blockaded us…. therefore we cannot ignore the achievements of Comrade Mao Zedong under today's international environment when we are dealing with the construction of four modernizations."

The author Xue Guangzhou is a professor of the Department of Marxist theory and a researcher in the Research Department of the Central Party School of the CPC; the article was first published in the journal *Chinese Social Sciences* on November 18, 2013

11

A Historical Evaluation of New China's Foreign Aid Policies

Zhang Jun

China's foreign aid has a history of more than 60 years. When talking about China's foreign aid, we can hear different voices, there are both words of praise and critique. It is normal to have different opinions and views when discussing on such a long history and when evaluating such complex issues. However, both criticism and praise should be based on historical facts. One sided conclusions drawn by castrating the history will not be conducive to our understanding of what happened in the past, nor will it help us to advance our current practice.

The first important fact is that after the founding of New China, it was faced with an extremely difficult international environment. The United States not only adopted a hostile attitude, but also carried out a policy of containment and subversion against China's foreign diplomatic activities, in other words, the struggle between China and the United States was not a spat, but a real fight at touted outrance. The Korean War was an example for this. In addition to such struggle, there was also covert actions against China, for example, when Prime Minister Zhou Enlai led a delegation to attend the Asian-African Conference in Bandung, a bomb was placed in the plane of our delegation that landed in the Hongkong airport, the plane had crashed shortly after the take-off. At that time, the Chinese leaders' visits to some open activities embodied the risk of attacks or assassinations. In this context, against China's own will, it was forced to an isolated situation in the international community. In order to break this isolated situation and create space for the sustainable development of the new China, China needed to make friends in the international community, and its foreign aid was aimed to serve this purpose, thus it was a necessary strategic expenditure. Therefore, until the mid-1970s, China's aid policy has two natures which reflect the historical facts above: firstly, we stressed that foreign aid was mutual, and it has been an important content of "Eight Principles" put forward by Zhou Enlai about our foreign aid, that is to say, the aid recipients should be those countries who oppose imperialism and hegemonism together with China, who are our allies against colonialism. We supported them in order to enhance our strength and weaken the strength of imperialism and hegemonism; secondly, we repeatedly stressed that the aid to the Third World countries is our international obligation, when only the Third World countries would become truly independent, can China be eventually and truly liberated. Although when we were poor, we still afforded assistance to other developing countries, this was neither an ideology dictated policy, nor a hot-headed leader's arbitrary decision, but a foreign policy based on the realistic internal and external environment and conditions of the New China.

The second basic fact is that China's aid has been widely welcomed by the recipient countries of Africa, it was responded by "a warm welcome", because China's aid didn't aim self-interest, but reflected the sincere desire that these countries and regions can win national independence and national development, which could be a real "timely assistance". If we only take Guinea, an African country, as an example: in the history, Guinea was a colony of France, after declaring its independence, Guinea was imposed comprehensive economic sanctions from France including withdrawal of technical personnel and building materials. France had also greatly destructed the infrastructure in Guinea which it could not take to France. France was the main food supplier of Guinea but it stopped delivery of rice to this country. Furthermore, in order to achieve a comprehensive and quick collapse of the Guinean economy, France smuggled counterfeit banknotes into Guinea, to create a hipper-inflation, which was very similar with new China's situation at the beginning days. Chinese delivered the much-needed food aid to Guinea, since then, in the framework of Guinea's own economic development plans, China continued to provide economic and technical assistance to help it achieve economic independence. This behavior sharply contrasts with the attitude of "attaching strings when aiding the needy" and control seeking attitudes adopted by the United States and some other western countries. China's aid has caused a "Chinese cyclone" in the new Guinea Republic, which was envied and hated by the United States and other Western countries, later this "Chinese cyclone" swept the whole African continent. Since the foreign aid by China reflected its sincere desire to help "poorer brothers" in the Third World, China has always received sincere and complete support from them. China's resumption of its legal seat in the United Nations was just one example, those African countries did not only help China politically, but have also provided the necessary resources and technology for China's economic development. Recently, China's rapid economic development in the Africa countries is not only caused by the practical needs of economic development in the African countries, but also the fruit of China's aid to Africa in 1960s and 1970s, and laid a solid political and historical foundation for the further development of Sino-Africa relations.

The third basic fact is that the rapid development of China was not a simple copy foreign development models, but one that suited to China's conditions, which selectively absorbed foreign experience, and which blazed a path of its own. The world is diverse, the development roads are also diverse. For developing countries, a path of development which suits their national conditions is one important necessary condition for their economic development. China has developed an idea that in order to ensure an international environment for its sustainable development, it should respect the diversified development paths chosen by the countries of the world. This is natural due to national differences. This idea is a strategic choice by China when its advocates the concept of harmonious world in the era of deepening globalization. However, since the end of the cold war, the western countries have increased intervention into the affairs of the third-world. They interfere with the economic development and political reform process of the aid recipient countries, and aim to export their political and economic rules and values, and limit their ability to independently choose the path of development suitable for them. Under these conditions, we support the independent development of aid recipient countries, with the aid view as "a necessary strategic expenditure" which is still valid. China is still faced with the heavy tasks of eliminating domestic poverty and at the same time aims to increase aid to those needy countries, which provides us with offspring development space in the international stage. We think this international moral responsibility is worthy of recognition.

In short, the historical significance of foreign aid cannot be measured by the financial figures of our aid, the success or failure of them cannot be simply calculated by the calculator. Let us, just make an assumption: if China could not resume its lawful seat in the United Nations in 1971, would China enjoy today's development and friendly international environment? It is not persuasive and cannot hold water with the test of history to evaluate China's aid policy according to some controversial aid practices regarding aid to few countries, instead we should make our evaluation by realistically considering China's overall aid policy, when judging its success or failure.

The author is an Associate Researcher in the Institute of European Studies, attached to CASS; the article was originally published in the journal *Social Sciences in China* on November 8th, 2013

12

Immortal Mao Zedong

Fang Wei

On December 26th, 120 years ago, a baby boy was born in a small village in Hunan Province, China. At that time, people did not think that this boy would so deeply change the fate of China and affect the development of the world for a long time in the future. The boy was Mao Zedong. In human history, only few people can give so deep and shocking impact to the fate of people like Mao Zedong has. A person, as long as without political bias, as long as reading Mao Zedong's articles in an objective manner, knowing his career, understanding his thoughts, will be deeply affected by his personality. In human history, very few people have such grand passion like him, his life pursuit has been full of twists and full of fascinating events, which make people excited; very few people like him can be so familiar with the trends of history, and has developed a strong insight to make rational and penetrative predictions, consequently he could accurately predict the direction of social change and development trend, and make timely judgments; very few people like him can devise strategies within a command tent, winning thousands of miles away at the same time, writing magnificent poems. We can say that every field he involved, even inadvertently, has left the unattainable, thick, heavy and bright chapters. However, what is the most powerful, not only his thought, gifts and bold strategy are rare in the history, but also his career, his pursuit, his sincere feelings and infinite love to hundreds of millions of people.

His thinking had a strong sense of practical concern. He is committed to solve the problem of China, and he put his ideas on national historical experience and realistic foundation so that it can be closely linked with the development and the fate of the country and the sufferings of the people and the times. He never hidebound, never really put the international authority of superstition and carry out the practice of revolution and construction in China with the International Song. He has combined the basic principles of Marxism with China's revolutionary practice and designed a victorious path for the Chinese revolution. He was the real forerunner of Sinicization Marxism in China. Mao Zedong Thought is the first historic leap, in combining the theories of Marxism-Leninism with China's realities, Mao Zedong Thought is the crystallization of the collective wisdom of the members of the Communist Party of China with Mao Zedong as its main representative. His thinking efforts have never stopped. Although in his later years, his body was gradually aging, but his mind was still young and he was still making an unremitting exploration for the cause of Chinese socialism and became a great initiator and founder of socialism with Chinese characteristics, and has made initial pioneering exploration for it.

The pursuit of his revolutionary political career always aimed to achieve the equality and happiness for the overwhelming majority of people. The noble ideal and belief of "serve the people" has run through his whole hard life. Under the leadership of Mao and his comrades, Chinese people won the national independence and people were liberated, created a new China through long-term revolutionary struggle. As one of the founders of the party, Mao Zedong led the construction of an advanced Party; and as one of the founders of the Chinese People's Liberation Army, he created the people's army. As Comrade Deng Xiaoping said, Mao Zedong made immortal feats for the Chinese nation, "without Mao Zedong, the Chinese people would, at the very least, have spent much more time groping in the dark". After the complete victory of the new democratic revolution and creation of the new China, and after restoring the national economy, Mao Zedong promptly launched the socialist transformation of the private ownership and led the establishment of the basic system of socialism. He was the first leader who proposed that the Chinese revolution should develop in a unique way of its own and has begun the great exploration of combining the basic principles of Marxism with the realities of Chinese society, and in 1956 he has proposed this important idea for the second time.

His pursuit didn't aim personal or a familial happiness, but national independence and the liberation of the people, which is the human's stateless world. In order to achieve this pursuit, he joined the army, joined the revolution with his comrades to create a great new China in 28 years period of time after the foundation of the PRC, wining the victory of the new democratic revolution. After the birth of the new People's Republic of China, he launched the socialist revolution and construction, and continued to struggle for the independence and prosperity of the development of the socialist movement in the world and the Third World countries. In this process, his six close relatives sacrificed their precious lives for Chinese people's revolutionary cause and the world's permanent peace, even for his eternal pursuit and career.

Due to the emergence of Mao Zedong as a leader, the 20th century has indeed encountered a radical change in its development route. When we put Mao Zedong in the river of human history, standing at the historical point to observe and comment his thought, his career and his pursuit, we could not help sighing that he has used the limited life of more than 80 years to create a new peak in human history!

Mao Zedong was the son of people, he was the people's explorer and the people's ascetic. In his mind, in his pen, in his words, the people are God, the masses are the real heroes; the people's interests are above all, it is the power to create history. He cannot tolerate any abuse of power and activities that would harm people's interests, he said, "Corruption must be cleared, or the Soviet flag would not be hit down and the Communist Party would lose prestige and morale! Fighting against corruption and degeneration is the bounden duty of our party, no one can stop!" He always advocated maintaining high morale for the people, and could say heroic utterance at the age of 70. He was always sincere, consequently even if he has made mistakes in his old age, the people can forgive him; even he has made mistakes in work, people can understand him; even if he has left, the people will remember him for a long time. In this sense, the link that has created the true soul of contemporary Chinese communists is the strong affinity between Mao Zedong and the People!

As an ancient saying goes, the ultimate ideal is to prove one's self through his virtues, and the next best through his accomplishments, and the next best through his words. Mao Zedong has gone far beyond. On the occasion of the 120th anniversary of Mao Zedong's birth, let us once again review his life-long struggle, learn from his ideas and his pursuit, we are fully confident that Mao Zedong Thought will be shinning forever even though he has left, it will be echoed in the sky, will continue to affect our future. Mao Zedong, will be forever immortal!

The article was first published in the journal *Social Sciences in China* on December 27, 2013

13

Mao Zedong's Contributions to the Exploration of Path of Socialism with Chinese Characteristics Should Not Be Belittled

Li Jie

Since the death of Mao Zedong, a thought trend of negating Mao has surged up. This trend is mainly reflected in three aspects: First, errors made by Mao during his exploration of socialist construction are intentionally deemed as "crimes". For example, the serious difficulties and even the starvation caused by the decision-making misplay of the Great Leap Forward and the People's Communes Movement are described as deliberate cold-blooded acts disregarding human life. Second, the history of the Party is blemished and distorted by the theory of power struggles which is borrowed from the west. The Yan'an Rectification Campaign, Gao-Rao Event, as well as the improper critique of Peng Dehuai at the Lushan Conference and the Injustice done to Liu Shaoqi during "the Period of 1966-1976", are all considered as inner-party struggles manipulated by Mao to strengthen his individual power. Third, the achievement in socialist revolution and construction under the leadership of Mao is purposely belittled and the New China led by Mao is assessed with the full ignorance of its merits and light.

Behind this thought trend, is the historical nihilism which became prevalent in the recent years. Under the false flag of reflecting on history, the ideological trend of historical nihilism has made a big fuss about the errors once made by our Party. As written by these people, the theme and the main thread of the development of Chinese modern history has been cursed as a bloody history which is darker than the European Middle Age; the historic change achieved in the New China is depicted as a backward history which is much worse than the past, even worse than the period when China was colonized by western powers. And the image of Mao Zedong as a great national hero and the leader of Chinese people in building the New China is degraded to a feudal despot who was even more tyrant than the First Qin Emperor. All these show that what these people intend to make nil is the great national spirit of Chinese people, as well as its honor and hope. Gong Zizhen, a thinker of Qing Dynasty (1792-1841), once said, "One should learn history before he understands the great truth," and "one could not annihilate a hostile country unless he first erases its history." This proves that the negation against Mao Zedong is not just a historical issue, but closely related with the view of history. The view of history is concentrated reflection of the values of a nation, era and the state, which involves the fundamental issue of establishing China's mainstream ideology and the system of socialist core values. The view of history determines the values. Assessment of any historical figure, a phenomenon or an event in history will directly affect the value judgements of outstanding figures, phenomena and events of the present. From the significant perspective of the construction of socialist core values system, we must fully recognize the significant role of establishing the Marxist historical view, and educate the citizens, accordingly. In order to deny Mao's achievements, some people have even distorted the history based on superficial arguments and data and concocted such a conclusion that Mao Zedong had made no contributions to the building of socialism with Chinese characteristics. This obviously contrasts the real facts. China's exploration of its own socialist construction path was started by the Chinese communists represented by Mao Zedong. People generally agree that such exploration has begun by 1956. Actually, this exploration was launched before that time in 1954, the fruit of which was China's first Constitution issued in 1954, as well as the socialist system which was established through the Three Major Socialist Transformations.

For example, in respect of political system, the People's Congress system was the most important accomplishment. The 1954 Constitution clearly stated: "the People's Republic of China is a people's democratic state led by the working class and based on the alliance of workers and peasants," and that "all power in the PRC belongs to the people. The organs for people to exercise such powers includes the National People's Congress and local people's congresses at all levels." This article has not only defined the nature of the state, but also established the political system of People's Congresses as the main leading power organ, which were different from the Soviets (councils) in the Soviet Union. In addition, the system of multi-party cooperation and political consultations under the leadership of the CPC has been another unique achievement of the PRC. As stated in the Common Program (first constitution) which was enacted in 1949, "The Chinese People's Political Consultative Conference is the organizational form of the people's democratic united front. It shall be composed of the representatives of the working class, the peasantry, and members of the revolutionary armed forces, intellectuals, the petty bourgeoisie, the national bourgeoisie, national minorities, the overseas Chinese and other patriotic democratic elements."

Thus, the New China was born accompanied with the system of multi-party cooperation and political consultation system under the leadership of the CPC, which was kept and maintained after China stepped into the socialist society. This unique system has been one of the long-tern basic political system of the state. Thirdly, the system of regional autonomy of ethnic minorities was another unique achievement of the PRC. The 1954 Constitution specified that "the People's Republic of China is a unified multi-ethnic country," and "regional autonomy system shall be implemented in each minority nationalities region." Each ethnic autonomous region is an integral part of the PRC. This article has established an ethnic regional autonomy system which is different from the federal system of nationalities in the Soviet Union. Compared with the Soviet Union and other socialist countries, all the above political systems are innovative and unique, which were the institutional products and crystallization of the China's new-democratic revolution and socialist revolution. The exploration of the path of building socialism with Chinese characteristics by Chinese communists represented by Mao Zedong has been an integral and major part of the scientific system of Maoism, which was the realization and development of the first historic leap in the localization of Marxism in China after the establishment of the New China. Such exploration has played as the thought motive and source of wisdom for Chinese communists to constantly carry out theoretical innovations during the new period of Reform and Opening-Up and socialist modernization drive. As indicated by Hu Jintao in the Report to the 17th National Congress of the CPC, "We must never forget that the great cause of reform and opening up was conducted on a foundation laid by the Party's first generation of central collective leadership with Comrade Mao Zedong at its core, which founded Mao Zedong Thought, led the whole Party and the people of all ethnic groups in establishing the People's Republic and scoring great achievements in our socialist revolution and construction, and gained invaluable experience in its painstaking exploration for laws governing socialist construction. The victory in the new democratic revolution and the establishment of the basic system of socialism provided the fundamental political prerequisite and institutional basis for every inch of development and progress in contemporary China." At the same time, we should also acknowledge that, as we observe with many great thinkers, Mao's exploration of the path of building socialism with Chinese characteristics was historically limited by his era and possessed historical limitations. This was mainly reflected as two aspects: firstly, although he initiated and nurtured the historical task of exploring China's own socialist development path, which embodied a high level of consciousness and theoretical innovation and although a unique path with Chinese characteristics had begun to take shape in many respects, he failed to break up the restrictions of the concepts of traditional socialism as to the aspect of the economic system. Those new systems with Chinese characteristics were impacted by left-leaning forces or failed to be improved or could not be carried forward, amply. Secondly, since the second half of 1957, the wrong ideological tendency of magnifying class struggle had become stronger, which meant that the correct judgment on the domestic principal contradiction of the Chinese society agreed during the 8th National Congress of the CPC was fundamentally shaken and neglected. In the meanwhile after various struggles, the idea of taking class struggle as the major link finally ascended to a dominant position in the guiding ideology of the CPC after the 10th Plenary Session of the 8th Central Committee of the CPC in 1962, which later led to the launching of the Cultural Revolution, which turned into an obvious civil strife initiated by the leadership, exploited by counterrevolutionary groups and which brought serious disaster to the Party, nation and people. In the process of China's socialist development, the grand historical transition from the highly centralized planned economic system to the vigorous market economic system and the shift from the guiding principle of taking class struggle as the main link to the policy of taking economic construction as the central task was achieved by the second generation of Chinese communists represented by Deng Xiaoping. This has not only opened up the new period of Reform and Opening-up and socialist modernization drive, but also achieved the second historic leap in the sinization of Marxism.

The author Li Jie is vice president of Chinese Academy of Social Sciences, and the Director of Institute of Contemporary China Studies; originally published in *Social Sciences in China* on September 16, 2013

14

Mao Zedong Has Made At Least Five Major Contributions to the Chinese Nation

Li Jie

The historical image of Mao Zedong has for some time suffered considerable damage and smears, due to the prevailing criticism of Mao and to the deliberate disregard, distortion and negation of history. Long devoted to studying Mao Zedong, I would say that Mao has made, to say the least, five major contributions to the Chinese nation, to the New China and to the Communist Party of China.

Firstly, it was Mao Zedong who led the Chinese people to weather the long revolutionary struggle, and finally gain national independence, liberate the people and found the New China. This is the most historically significant contribution he made. It is well known that after 1840, when western powers like Britain and France came to invade, take advantage of and plunder China, the country was reduced to a semi-colony and its state sovereignty was severely trampled upon. Feudalism, which had lasted for thousands of years, lingered on in an already rotten Chinese society characterized by insuperable social contradictions and extreme poverty. In the midst of domestic strife and foreign aggression, the Chinese people were oppressed both by domestic feudal forces and western powers. Given the grim situation, countless people with lofty ideals rose up, making unremitting efforts for the sake of national independence and the people's liberation. These people's names range from Lin Zexu, Wei Yuan and Gong Zizhen in the early period, to Hong Xiuquan who staged the Taiping Rebellion, Kang Youwei, Liang Qichao, and finally to Sun Yat-sen who led the great Xinhai Revolution of 1911.

Nonetheless, it was Mao Zedong and his comrades-in-arms who pointed to a way out and defined its direction. Sticking together, the Chinese communists fought dauntlessly for 28 years to salvage China from subjugation, at the cost of tens of millions of fighters' lives, including six family members of Chairman Mao. Of these six martyrs, five lost their lives during the period of the democratic revolution, and the other one was Mao Anying, who sacrificed himself in the war to resist US aggression and aid Korea after the founding of the New China. Comrade Mao Zedong and the great men of that generation achieved notable merits for the Chinese Nation. To quote Deng Xiaoping, had it not been for Mao Zedong, the Chinese people would have had to grope in the dark for a really long time.

Secondly, it was Mao Zedong who set the Chinese people on the path to socialist modernization after the People's Republic of China was founded. For ages, China was an agrarian country developed under a self-sufficient smallholder economy. In modern times, whereas the western world vigorously carried out industrial revolutions and thus modernized its societies, China failed to keep up with the global wave and was consequently left far behind. This is an important reason why the miserable Chinese nation was left poor and weak and in a passive position for over a hundred years. Therefore, since the founding of the PRC, Mao Zedong and his comrades-in-arms never forgot the need to establish an industrialized China, because nothing was more important than industrialization at the time. Thus in 1953, when the national economy was at the beginning of its recovery and the war to resist US aggression and aid Korea was drawing to a close, China started its first Five Year Plan. With the help of the Soviet Union, it undertook 156 projects and preliminarily solved the fundamental problems of industrialization. From Mao's time onwards, the core of the following generations of leaders, from Comrade Deng Xiaoping to Comrade Jiang Zemin, Comrade Hu Jintao and finally to the CPC Central Committee with Xi Jinping as General Secretary, have been carrying forward this tradition, and now China is smoothly implementing the Twelfth Five-year Plan. While enjoying the achievements of industrialization, we cannot forget the great contributions made by the revolutionary elders.

China's industrialization never stopped. Even over the ten tough years of "the Period of 1966-1976", China strived to eliminate all sorts of barriers and move on with its industrial development. Most remarkably, China successfully launched the first self-developed man-made satellite in 1970, and the first recoverable satellite in 1975. The Gezhou Dam Key Water-control Project was also started in the 1970s. At about that time, China also began to import western chemical equipment in batches and sets after the

Sino-U.S. relationship was normalized. In the mid-1970s, therefore, China had already taken the first step towards modernization, in other words it had built relatively complete and independent industrial and national economic systems, addressed the basic problems of industry and introduced manufacturing. It is noteworthy that the conception and strategic planning of the four modernizations were initially presided over by Mao Zedong himself. In 1964, the 3rd National People's Congress formally proclaimed the four modernizations of industry, agriculture, national defense and science and technology. Although they were not achieved as scheduled, the foundation for the first step had been laid. It is often said in academia that China completed its initial industrialization in the 1970s, and this was the precondition for overall modernization. We are now approaching the goal of overall modernization step by step. It can be said that we will basically achieve modernization in the mid-21st century and approach the levels of moderately developed countries. This will be a great historical step forward.

Thirdly, it was Mao who significantly beefed up China's national defenses. It is well known that for a long time after 1840, many people with high ideals deplored that China had borders but no defense, as it had not set up defenses in spite of its long borders and vast sea. With or without defenses, it would have been unable to resist the invasion of foreign ships and armament. Consequently China even suffered defeated by Japan during the Sino-Japanese war's sea battles, something which shocked the country's intelligentsia a great deal. After the PRC was established, Mao Zedong had to start from scratch in an extremely difficult situation, without financial resources or an industrial base, and empowered the Chinese national defense industry to make noticeable progress. It was he who proposed building powerful naval forces to consolidate sea defenses and building powerful air forces to consolidate the air defense. In the latter half of the 1950s, he again proposed to strengthen national defense and enhance the three-line construction (of national defense, industry and communication). At that time major industries, including the defense industry, were developed in the coastal areas rather than in the hinterland. In the mid-1960s and the whole of the 1970s, China's national defense industry, especially the three-line construction, was laid out more reasonably. From the coastal areas to the hinterland, and further on to the western regions, industrial bases were built in all regions, including atomic and nuclear test bases, an impressive achievement. Due to this, although wars periodically broke out around the world from during the 1950s and the 1960s, China's border defenses and national defenses remained stable, because no country dared to harass it.

This can be counted as another of Mao's great contributions.

Fourthly, it was Mao Zedong who set up an advanced Marxist party–the Communist Party of China (CPC). Mao first laid the ideological foundation of the CPC, which is the ideological line of seeking truth from facts. Meanwhile, he also built a sound mass base and fostered a fine tradition of going deep among the masses, namely, the mass line. Most importantly, since the CPC had shouldered since its birth the sacred mission of winning national independence, liberating the people, achieving national prosperity and enriching the people, it must be equipped with a scientific world outlook and methodology which allows it to understand and change the world and thus rejuvenate China. This world outlook and methodology was the adaptation of Marxism for China, for which Mao paved the way and which has endured to date. When Mao was alive, however, nobody successfully summed up the core of Mao Zedong Thought until Deng Xiaoping took up the task. He boiled down Mao Zedong Thought to three key aspects: seeking truth from facts, pursuing the mass line, and sticking to the principle of independence. These three key aspects constitute not only the philosophical foundation of Mao Zedong Thought, but also that of the theoretical system of socialism with Chinese characteristics.

Last but not least, it was Mao who greatly improved China's international status. After the Opium War, China had little standing in the international community. This situation was not turned around until the anti-Japanese War, and particularly until China won the war, since it was the first outright victory against aggression in modern Chinese history. For a long time after that, however, the country was embroiled in internal battles. With unrelenting efforts, Mao Zedong and the CPC finally founded the PRC, won ultimate peace for the nation and established it as a great power in the world.

After the founding of the New China, the US-dominated West didn't recognize the newly-born regime, and the US proclaimed that "things have come to a close". By this phrase, it was meant that the New China founded by the CPC would not last long, so it would not be considered to establish diplomatic relations with China until the CPC stepped down. In other words, the ruling position of the CPC and the status of China in the world were denied. The CPC disregarded this and was fearless in the face of tremendous pressure. Sticking to the principle of independence, it finally withstood the test and triumphed in the war to resist US aggression and aid Korea. Not until then did Americans feel the need to have dealings with us. In 1954, when the international conference to tackle the issues of the Korean Peninsula and Indochina was to take place in Geneva, the US had no choice but to invite China to take part even though it was unwilling to admit it, because without its participation the two issues could not be solved.

In 1972, the then US President Nixon paid a visit to China at a time when the U.S. had no diplomatic relations with China and didn't recognize the international status of the New China. Nevertheless, Nixon came to China to seek the normalization of Sino-US relations and signed the famous "Shanghai Communiqué". This remarkable diplomatic achievement gave a huge boost to China's international status and opened the door for China to normalize its relations with western countries, which also laid a foundation for the opening-up. In the meantime, the PRC also restored its lawful seat as a permanent member state in the United Nations and drove out the representative of the Kuomintang. This was greatly contributed to by many developing countries, China's "poor friends". As Mao Zedong and Zhou Enlai said repeatedly, "we should never forget our 'poor friends', because it was they who carried China in a sedan chair into the United Nations".

On account of the aforementioned five historical achievements, it is fair to say that Comrade Mao Zedong is an immortal national hero. He devoted his whole life selflessly for the independence of the Chinese nation, the liberation of the Chinese people, the prosperity of the New China and the well-being of the commoners. Chinese people remember him well because had it not been for Mao Zedong, we could never have had such a happy living environment. Therefore, every time the CPC reviews history, it will stress that it was Chairman Mao's establishment of the New China and him leading us down the socialist road that paved the way for all the development and progress the country achieved later. Surely we have to add that we would never have taken the road of the reform and opening up if the CPC had not boldly led us to break away from the shackles of traditional socialist views and of "leftism" after the Third Plenary Session of the 11th CPC Central Committee. In this regard Comrade Deng Xiaoping should take the credit, and so should Comrade Jiang Zemin, Comrade Hu Jintao and President Xi Jinping, and the sustained efforts of generations of CPC members.

The author is the vice president of the CASS, director of the Institute of contemporary Chinese Studies; the article was first published in the journal *Social Sciences in China* on September 23, 2013

15

Resolving the Theoretical Paradox of Historical Nihilism

Han Jiong

Historical nihilism has originated on Western soil at the turn of the 19th and 20th century. At the time, capitalism had turned from the "age of capital" with increasingly global expansion into the "age of empire" which emerged risks (Eric Hobsbawm).

In those days, some western scholars who had keenly been aware of that point, have then started questioning the belief of rational optimism, historical progressivism and rational structure to nature, which the Western culture had advocated since the Enlightenment, and they have praised that non-rationality played an important role of blessing and protection on human survival and development. Nietzsche has summed those phenomena of denying historical tradition and ethical principle as nihilism, which was the origin of historical nihilism. In the 1970s, the Western radical left wing has stepped into political failure in their anti-government activities, which led the left turn its attention to the culture field, expecting to deconstruct the existing system through sporadic and lasting anti-government activities whose political complexion reduced gradually.

Originally, historical nihilism hasn't emerged independently in the Chinese academic soil, but due to several challenges China has suffered during the process of modernization. In addition to some realistic reasons, from the perspective of history and philosophy, the rise of current historical nihilism in China is mainly influenced by western post-modern historiography which was introduced in the 1990s. Post-modern historiography introduces the concept of "culture" and the perspective of "reader", and tries to show that history has its openness whether in the past or in the future, and everyone has every reason to "combine" or "interpret" history freely. This theoretical opinion is helpful for breaking historical determinism, such as western European centricism and doctrinarism. Besides, this opinion advocates to stand more closely to read historical texts, thus it can be seen that some parts of this theory are reasonable, and some constitute its "Achilles' heel", which can cause serious social harm by applying the irrationalism view, which leads to deny the inner causal relations among the historical phenomenon, thus leading to deny the historical law and truth.

There are two methods used by historical nihilism to deal with historical facts: one is ignoring historical development, and assuming and deducing abstractly, even denying or distorting the facts; the other is resorting to ironic and joking interpretation to spoof, derogate or defame positive historical figures or events, or propagating negative characters to reverse a verdict. Those two methods relatively in a more direct manner display the ideological character of historical nihilism which we can call as "explicit" historical nihilism, hence it's easier to distinguish.

Whereas "implicit" historical nihilism tends to carefully select or "find" some fragmented historical facts or deconstruct or reconstruct major problems in the national history or world history by sub-dividing the entire history, which results in presenting a forged "history". In general, the basic reason is that past history consists of numerous "events" occurring in historical time and space. The so-called historical fact is accidentally made of isolated "events", and how to connect those "splashes" or how to measure those "weight" in historical interpretation totally depends on history scholars' individual subjective trade-off and judgement. Hence, in terms of the same historical event, there can occur disparate even opposite meanings or judgements. These second kind of ideological trends deal with historical facts "skillfully", and their ideological color is relatively veiled but they also contain elements of historical nihilism, which has its perplexity in practice, so that we should be more vigilant against them.

The internal connections among historical phenomena are quite different, but as a whole there are two kinds, that is, causal association which connects historical facts consisting of historical phenomenon, and non-causal association. If a person wants to draw a relatively accurate composition of history, or clarify the true situation of historical phenomenon, it implacably requires to seek the causal association among historical facts. The non-causal association also influences the emergence and change of historical phenomena to some extent, but it doesn't play a decisive role. The historical nihilist either ignores or denies objective internal causal association among historical facts, or regards the correlativity among historical facts with the same degree of attention and neglects their "dispersion" degree, which results in that all relevant figures and events are took as historical elements and connected with each other in accordance with some story lines, besides are known as "historical memory" or "historical representation". Consequently, historical truth is naturally and totally covered by those various "historical narration" activities written by writers, and also is misunderstood by readers in the interpretation of historical texts. Therefore, history as a whole and its inherent law are thoroughly deconstructed and denied, let alone the historical justice.

In order to avoid falling into the theoretical paradox of "something being nihility and something not being nihility" when criticizing historical nihilism, we must stand firm to safeguard the important role of causal judgment in the historical cognition, and make great efforts to reveal complicated causal chains among the historical phenomena. The judgment of historical facts is the foundation of historical value judgment, but this is not enough. It should be understood that in the face of the same judgment of historical facts, how to make an objective and impartial evaluation and then form a certain value judgment is more important. The key of that is to clarify causal chains among a series of influential factors involved in historical facts and then aim to conclude a convictive causal judgment. If ignoring the quest and retrospect of cause of fact judgment, it is easy to directly give a value judgment which lacks evidence and lacks logical support, which can mistake one's value judgment in "well-founded" way, and consequently, leads to falling into value nihilism.

Thus, how to seek the causal association among historical phenomena or how to guarantee that a certain link among the historical phenomena is the essential link? Seeking the judgment of historical cause can't be separated from practical experience accumulation on historical research, and scientific research procedure and rules, both are very important. What's more, it also depends on the guidance of scientific historical perspective. Scientific historical perspective is helpful for avoiding detours, and enables revealing the historical truth with less price, while the one-sided historical perspective often leads to a wrong research path. Some thinkers, as Nietzsche and Martin Heidegger, have begun with criticism on historical nihilism, but finally they have become the "completers" of historical nihilism. The reason why they were unable to think outside the box was that their conception of society and history was mistaken. Historical materialism emphasizes to reveal positive internal relations among historical phenomena, whose ontology is the most scientific, and its epistemology is the most convincing, and its methodology is the most systematic so far among all historical conceptions, including global view of history (universal view) and post-modern historical view.

Now, as China's reform and opening-up further develops under the background of globalization, it's worth noting that there are two trends in the evaluation of the history of the People's Republic of China: one "weakens" the legitimacy of the Chinese New Democratic Revolution, and exaggerates the historical function and role of reform, which uses the historical period after the Reform and Opening-up in order to deny the historical period before the Reform and Opening-up; the other trend "weakens" the great achievement brought by China's Reform and Opening-up, and overstates those emerging social and economic problems during the process of reform, which uses the historical period before the Reform and Opening-up to deny the historical period after the Reform and Opening-up. The above-mentioned two trends separate historical periods before and after the reform and opening-up, even set the two historical periods against each other, which belongs to typical historical nihilism and is extremely wrong. Actually, the two periods have internal continuation and coherence. The period before the Reform and Opening-up has laid the solid foundations of institutions and ideological guarantees, as well as provided financial support for the Reform and Opening-up which had further developed the existing institutional advantages and further enhanced the power of ideas. The mistakes made during China's construction before the Reform and Opening-up have promoted socialist construction to move towards reform; the deep economic and social problems exposed during the reform have showed that we must unswervingly adhere to the economic and political system of socialism of Chinese characteristics. The thing throughout those two historical periods is that the Chinese people led by Chinese Communist Party have conducted practical activities for socialist revolution and construction in the specific time and specific social environment, and with the promotion of those activities, the Chinese's practical ability for building socialism with Chinese characteristics has increasingly enhanced and improved. At present, "China Dream" is the proof and indication of this theoretical improvement of that practical ability and focuses on the reality. The common essential value of two historical periods is the liberation and happiness of the majority of laboring people, the main part of the Chinese nation.

The author is from the School of Marxism of Shanghai University of Finance and Economics; the article was first published in the journal *Chinese Social Sciences Today* on June 5, 2013.

16

China's Historical Course Can Not Be Denied

Yang Jun

Looking deep into history, each country and nation have its unique ways of development and the "history" interwoven with various contacts and interactions is in essence a natural historical course dominated by immanent general laws of development. Therefore, the historical inevitability behind all the contingencies cannot be denied and or opposed.

China was a self-contained country with glorious ancient civilizations who had made great contributions to the development of human society. However, in modern times, the ancient China was constrained, bullied and slaughtered by the Western powers due to its conservative, closed, and backward tendency. In semi-colonial and semi-feudal China, the fundamental role of economic inevitability, the national crisis of subjugation, the decadent dominance and heavy oppression of feudal forces and bureaucratic capitalism as well as the people's deep sufferings had inherently determined the historical themes and basic tasks of modern China as follows: to fight for freeing China from subjugation and revitalize the Chinese nation. Looking back into history, the salvation movements and modernization movements fought by the Chinese were extremely difficult and have encountered great twists and turns. Although, the "Self-strengthening" Movement, the Peasant Revolution, the Reform Movement, and even the great bourgeois revolutionary movements such as the Revolution of 1911 have contributed to the social progress of China, but they did not achieve the fundamental historical tasks of rescuing the nation and save the people leading them to liberation.

In the historical course within the capitalist path, the national conflicts have entered in repetitive dilemmas. Besides, the objective material system was being prepared for the emergence of China's new advanced theories and social forces. With the roar of guns, the October Revolution brought us Marxism and its theories. The combination of Marxism and the Chinese workers' movements had produced the Chinese Communist Party. Since then, the Chinese people's revolutionary struggles were guided and supported by scientific theories. After the New-Democratic Revolution, the Socialist Revolution and Construction, as well as the great revolution of Reform and Opening-up, the Chinese people had not only achieved two fundamental historical goals of national independence and the liberation of the people, but also achieved great success in realizing the great prosperity of the country and the great rejuvenation of the nation. Though China's modern history was full of numerous difficulties and obstacles as well as mistakes and twists and turns, but the essence and mainstream of the history profoundly revealed that the history and people choose Marxism, choose the Chinese Communist Party, choose socialism, choose the inevitability of the Reform and Opening-up and choose legitimacy and progress.

However, when the Chinese people had achieved earth-shaking changes and were striving to realize great prosperity on the path of socialism with Chinese characteristics, historical nihilism thought of trend has surged in the dark. Those "public opinion elites" or "opinion leaders" who are from different subjective backgrounds and even not familiar with history or who didn't seriously study history became coincidentally "interested" in the modern history of China and often uttered "amazing speech" openly to deny this history completely. One thing they had in common is to denigrate the revolutionary struggle of the Chinese people for national independence and the liberation of the people, to deny the socialist development direction and its great achievements, to distort the socialist essence of Reform and Opening- up and to vilify the revolutionary leaders who promoted social progress, especially laying their focus on attacking on Mao Zedong. These speeches or comments, by using the network, illegal publications and other media channels continued to spread the wrong claims, which have a very negative impact on the public opinion and on the political identity of the masses.

In a sense, history is a human-centered science and people are always out of their understanding of the reality and planning about the future to review their own past and study history. The reason why China's modern history is of special significance is because this history is directly related to the historical choices and development direction of its contemporary guiding ideology, leadership core, basic system and the chosen fundamental path. Historical nihilism messed into this field, fundamentally speaking, its starting point was based on facing the past society and its ending was to serve the present era. Because China's revolutionary path and its results do not meet their favorite reformist road and the bourgeois republic goals, they are eager to change the flag, to take the Western capitalist road and in an attempt to deny contemporary China's guiding ideology, fundamental system and the way forward from the historical basis and logical premise, thus they can "find another way" to make reasons and basis, create public opinions and interfere with the decisions of the ruling party.

In the western countries, it is more common that the historical nihilists confuse facts with fiction and history with literature or narration. But in China, the historical nihilists on the issue of modern history do not deny the objectivity of historical facts and laws, but the crux is that they completely distort and deny the historical facts and laws guided by historical materialism. Besides, they try to use their so called "reason" (that is, the Anglo-American civilization model and development path are the only "right path") to outline the relations of historical events and the central axis of historical evolution. In order to achieve the "reason" of transcendental idealism and realize the ultimate value goals, the historical nihilists have made complete distortion and thorough denial of the history and carried on subjective construction of "My Six Notation to Classics". Naturally, historical nihilists do not pay attention to the authenticity of historical data, but they follow up clues to pick and choose, imagine, weave and put together historic data to illustrate their own viewpoints, sometimes they even impose violence upon the historical facts, abandon or distort some most important historical facts. In the same way, in order to make history coincide with the "reason" that they have imagined, they treat the history in a sense of anti-historicism which are full of thoughts like either this or that, binary opposition, cutting off history, western superiority, discarding traditions and etc.

The already existing and past history cannot be changed, but we can deepen our understanding of it. The statements and claims of historical nihilists violate the development laws of history and oppose the fundamental interests of the Chinese people and the requirements of China's development and progress, so we have to remind them: China's historical course cannot be denied!

The author is a professor in the Faculty of Finance and Public Administration, at the Zhejiang University of Finance and Economics; the article was originally published in the journal *Social Sciences in China*, July 15, 2013.

17

Historical Philosophy on How to Appraise Historical Events and Figures

Ma Rong

Different historical figures[1] are always nurtured by different historical periods and social environment. In his book *On the Role of the Individuals in History*, Plekhanov has argued that the role of an individual cannot transcend the limitations of history. On the one hand, plenty of people have opportunities to step into the same social stage, however, those who play leading roles will depend on their endeavors and character; on the other hand, although this leading role cannot easily determine the trend of history, he will put his stamp on the development of history, which will be decided by his characteristics and his weight in the power structure.

I. Controversial historical events and figures can be seen within the development era of every country

There are some historical and controversial events within the development era of a country, especially in an era when the country encounters a critical historical transformation. As a decision-making role, one or several important historical figures who could be judged and criticized by the society as a result of their every single specific decision. Each society has different interest groups whose interests will be influenced directly or indirectly by every historical events and radical changes of social policies. Therefore, the result of certain historical or social impacts of some crucial

---

1 This article was first published in the journal *Leaders* (Hong Kong), 40th Issue, 2011/6, and the journal *Newsletter of National Sociology Research*, 90th Issue, June 30, 2011.

policies will possibly satisfy the expectations of some people in the society while disapproved by others. After the event, the powers that be certainly try to possess the right for final explanation of this event, and the opposition of others have to be held back under temporary high pressure temporarily, which will be expressed again, waiting for a next favorable turn in the history. Once under sound political circumstances, the controversies over judging historical events and figures will emerge again on the political stage of a country.

Different comments of later generations on historical figures often result from their familiar social setting, knowledge structure, value and thoughts which they will consider as basic standards to simply affirm or deny those historical figures who had played a key role in the development of the history. Then here comes two questions: Whether these views on historical figures are divorced from the social background at that time, for example, to evaluate historical figures on one hundred years ago and their accomplishments on the basis of current political ideology and social rules; and if we have become a stern commentator on what predecessors have done and how they did it.

People always have totally different views on how to draw a conclusion regarding the social consequences of some historical events and how to assess some historical figures. Not only are their opinions entirely contrary, but also have strong emotional feelings which make people become aggressive when talking about it. Sometimes the authorities will choose to avoid discussing these sensitive issues which may cause the differentiation in society or the mass social conflicts between the populace and the elites, for instance, to take administrative means to prohibit the news media to talk about it in public or to ban the relative publications of books and articles. Though these measures could control the development of the event for a little while, they cannot solve the problem fundamentally. And the result is that the problem is just laid aside and the conflict is concealed temporarily.

In order to resolve the social conflict led by these different ideas regarding historical events, truly understand people's struggle in their mind and reach an accommodation finally among different voices, these issues will sooner or later need to discuss on the table so that dissidents can reach an agreement and turn to a new page in history together. However careful consideration should be given by the authorities and academia before discussing theses sensitive issues in public and lead populace and elites to look at history historically so that the open discussions on these issues could have positive affection which will promote the social cohesion instead of social split or differentiation.

II. How to achieve "viewing history in a historical way?"

Firstly, to remind people to use rational thinking instead of emotional thinking to determine the macrocosmic trend of history and the social role of historical figures in it as possible as they can and avoid to be lost in the micro textual research separately. More scientific analysis than emotional resentment should be used when it comes to evaluate historical events and figures; more calmness and objectiveness from the perspective of academy than personal feelings should be considered when it comes to appraise historical events and figures. Catharsis can only intensify the conflict rather than promoting general understanding of historical events and reaching an agreement between dissidents. Certainly, it is definitely difficult for those people who were seriously harmed or whose relatives were severely hurt in these historical events. But they would convince themselves if they were able to start from the overall interests of the country, society and the long-term development of the Chinese nation.

Secondly, to understand the restraint of historical conditions to human activities which is called historical limitation at that time objectively and try not to judge our predecessors by today's political ideology and knowledge structure. Except for having a meeting in Moscow's building, he had never seen capitalist society himself, hence it would be hard for him to have a deep understanding of market economy and to tell the essential difference between the steel produced in modern chemical factories and in traditional factories.

Thirdly, to analyze any historical event and historical figure from the perspective of calmness, objectiveness and multiple aspects, and to assess the measures they have taken on the basis of objective influence on the development of the social afterwards. It is suitable here to apply the doctrine that practice is the only test of truth. As every historical figures were humans with blood and bones but not gods, their growth and improvement would definitely be affected and limited by the social cultural environment, and it was impossible for them to understand and deal with their surroundings rationally and considerately. People make mistakes, big or small, meaningless or vital. Thus, it is necessary to analyze the historical events and figures objectively.

Fourthly, the most important thing of evaluating and discussing historical events and figures is to learn lessons and experiences from them and to warn those who come after. We should turn these experiences and lessons to the treasure of knowledge so that all experiences from successes and failures that we have gone through can be fully utilized in the development of society in

China. I certainly disagree with the vindictive attitude which convicts historical figures. It should be left in the past after an objective and profound historical evaluation. Holding a grudge or trying to stigmatize the individuals who were in charge back then and to punish people who were related to them so as to vent people's resentment may cause a new round of unfairness and plant the seeds of enmity, which is definitely not good for the whole society.

III. What needs to be done for guiding people to evaluate history in a historical way?

Scholars need to make positive guidance work to guide people to learn to view history in a historical way. First of all, they need to introduce the scientific way to people to evaluate the history and guide them to learn the history from a macroscopic aspect instead of a microscopic aspect, and to teach people to gradually master the rules of how the historical events and figures that occurred under certain conditions should be appraised objectively. Meanwhile, scholars might as well introduce successful solutions from foreign countries regarding solving historical confrontations, for example they can examine the methods of the US government in healing the injury felt by the two confronting parties and bring about a reconciliation that will embrace the whole country. These cases will be beneficial to helping people have a wide field of vision and develop their national thoughts. Second, the discussion and evaluation can be started from those less sensitive historical events and figures that happened a long time ago so that there is enough time to guide people to the right direction of discussion and ponder. When more and more people in society begin to accept this objective and rational way of analyzing and evaluating historical events and historical figures, and when ethos of rational thinking take up the main trend of media and publishers, then it is possible to turn the discussion to historical events and figures of modern times without causing aggressive, emotional and irrational thoughts and assessment.

In one country and society that has once been buffeted by sever social revolutions and upheavals, it is crucial to lead the masses to discuss the controversial historical events objectively and rationally and reach a consensus of opening a new chapter in history by healing over the differentiation among the public, which can be regarded as the only way to throw away the burden of history, move on with light packs and build a harmonious society. Otherwise, the government will have to face the great pressure of making an open evaluation of these historical events and figures asked by some people. Only in these discussions can the basic constitutional rights, such as the freedom of speech and freedom of thought be truly achieved.

It is necessary to have historical perspective and objective attitude for normal people and social elites so as to create an atmosphere of peace and calmness in the society and people's mind. And I think the discussion should be qualified with the following three characteristics:

Firstly, insisting on academic thinking by looking on historical events and figures with scientific and objective attitude and systematic and developmental vision. Since the consequences of these historical events and figures usually come out under a certain historical circumstance and social environment, which is restricted to the objective conditions and marked on the historical features at that time, it would be more objective and calm only by having an academic attitude to the discussion and research.

Secondly, persisting with rationalism by evaluating historical events and figures with systematically rational analysis and weighing them carefully, in other words, it is essential to detach ourselves from personal emotion and researchers' values. A general, conclusive and simple moral judgement on a certain historical event or historical figure should not be made only on the basis of some facts and rare results.

Thirdly, a positive 'move-on' attitude is recommended. We really do not need to struggle with the results after a new chapter in history or conduct trials on responsibility for certain historical events or historical figures. Normally, people possibly have two different attitudes towards what happened in the past, even those events that left painful memories: one is to get to the bottom of things by requiring everyone to check those historical events in detail and confirming the specific responsible person in order to judge them morally or initiate judicial process. It will be inevitably a long and disputable process in this way of recognizing historical truths and the effects of historical figures, which makes all participants more aggressive and sensitive. Emotional discussion will undoubtedly poison the social atmosphere and destroy social reconciliation and people harmony. The other one is to have forward-looking views, which means to analyze the historical events and figures in the perspective of systematic and interactive evolution and on a macro-level basis. The purpose of reviewing contributions and mistakes is to learn lessons and experiences for later generations so that they can achieve more success in the future. Discussions with emotional and radical feelings undoubtedly will debase social morality and will severely destroy the harmony of society and community. And the other attitude is to look forward, which to analyze historical events and figures from a systematic, interactive and evolving perspective and macro level, and give an overlook at the panorama of history. And the purpose of discussion is to learn lessons and experiences for descendants so that they can continue to achieve success in the future.

IV. To protect and defend the heroes of the people

People in a society can be divided into two categories, elites and the ordinary people, such as workers, farmers, soldiers, students and businessmen. Elites have deeper thoughts regarding the social structure, institutional construction and democratic principles, and are keener to sum up historical experience and social development trend. They usually hold a more active and rational attitude when evaluating historical events and figures. Normal people do care about state affairs, but they are so occupied with daily life and work that they do not have plenty of time to read classics and books on social science. Under the influence of perceptual knowledge, it is too difficult for them to establish an understanding on the basis of systematical analysis and rational thinking which makes them easily influenced by public opinion, and their viewpoints could go to excess from one to another. The society can be stable in a long term only if a reliable hero and a truly faithful value system exist in people's mind.

Every country has its own hero. No matter if they are traditional or modern democratic society, people still aspire such a charismatic heroes emotionally as US President George Washington, President Lincoln and Martin Luther King; Britain's Arthur Wellesley and Premier Churchill; France's Charles de Gaulle; German Chancellor Otto von Bismarck; Russia's Peter the Great and Golenishchev-Kutuzov; India's Mahatma Gandhi and Cuba's Jose Martí and so on. In spite of mistakes made by them, they after all liberated their countries and earned honors for their nations and makes their citizens feel proud and honorable to be born and serve this country. In this case, people are willing to neglect or forgive flaws on these historical figures.

Compared with the ordinary people, intellectuals are more rational and fastidious, or they are used to appraising every historical figure thoroughly and even hoping this kind of appraisal to be comprehensive and objective. In order to draw lessons from history, they would rather pay much more attention on mistakes made by historical figures and criticize these mistakes merciless.

There is no doubt that it is obviously necessary for a nation or a country to review experiences and lessons and lead a healthier development in the future. However, the intellectuals and the elites have to take ordinary people's national proud and psychological demands into consideration in case of destroying the image of their hero easily and rudely. For a nation which has experienced colonial and semi-colonial rule and had fought against invasions in the past, it will undoubtedly lead to a crisis of faith and confidence losing. Those leaders have turned into a historical sign for their countries and nations after they have already become the symbols of a party or the victory and success of the country. The negative criticisms on these leaders would make the general public feel confused about their past and lose confidence in the future, which is not a good thing for cohesion, stability and development of this country.

V. The aim of appraising history is to create a better future

The influences that may have been imposed on future development of society and social integration must be taken into consideration when we appraise the historical events and figures. This is a responsible attitude on future, on nowadays and future. Some important historical figures had both merits and demerits in their lives, but when they have become some symbol of social development or of an era, keeping focus on finding their mistakes would be harmful to development and integration of the whole society. For example, George Washington, one of the greatest men in American history, was the leader of the Continental Army in the American Revolution and the first U.S. president. As the hero for the United States, he was known as "the father of his country". But some facts that were revealed by history researchers show that this great person was insistent on implementing slavery on black people, and not only did he imprison several black slaves in his own home, but he refused to give them freedom. However, if Americans use nowadays doctrines and opinions of human rights of opposing slavery to judge George Washington, and ignore the real social environment back then, they could have reached very negative conclusions. And if they insist on doing so, are there upsides or downsides for their own culture?

The US president Nixon broke the ice between China and the U.S. with his superior judgement and insight but ruined his own reputation for Watergate during the presidential election. So should we deny all his political work despite this blot? It has been controversial for what influence the Japanese imperial Hirohito has exerted during the war of aggression against China and World War II. Since he has ascended the throne in the year of 1928, the wars that were launched under his name killed tens of millions of people in 14 years, which committed heinous crimes to the Chinese people, the Asian people and people from the world. Many countries in the world have ranked Hirohito as the number one war criminal, but he evaded his trail of Tokyo International Military Tribunal under the aegis of the US. Later, the attitude of Hirohito towards the war had changed a little, and in 1978, after all the tablets of class a war criminals being transferred to Yasukuni shrine, he specifically demonstrated that he would not visit there. If we insist on ascertaining his criminal responsibility (which we have reasons to do) in the war and ignore his changing attitude and behavior after the war, will it bring the positive or negative influence on the relationship between China and Japan?

Some have doubted that after February Revolution of overthrowing the Tsarist regime in Russia in 1917, whether Lenin, who faced a travel ban in Switzerland during the World War I, had reached a secret agreement with the German government so that he could return to Russia? Lenin did negotiate with the German government back then through the Swiss communist party, and the German government agreed and helped Lenin take an airtight travel cabin to return to Russia. The German government was deeply involved in the mire of the world war in Europe back then and considered that Lenin's return to Russia would probably exacerbate Russia's domestic turmoil, thus be an opportunity to relieve the tension between itself and Russia. Consequently, German army could get out of the predicament. On the other hand, Lenin was eager to go back to Russia to promote the revolution and seize the power, so the fact that he signed with the German government a secret agreement which would harm Russia's interests and beneficial for Germany interests could be possible. But even if this is true, would it change Lenin's role in the Russian revolution? If Russians once again start to debate how to correctly evaluate the events related to Lenin's return to Russia, will it have a positive or negative impact on the cohesion in the Russian society?

According to some scholars, Sun Yat-sen who had launched the revolution to overthrow the Manchurian government, in which he signed with the Japanese government some secret agreement to gain their support that it was as prejudicial to the interests of Chinese people and the country as it is seen today. If these were true, would it totally change the role of leadership in this revolution and the role of "father of his nation"? In spite of taking consideration of China's circumstance and diplomatic situation in 20th century, nor the wrong definition or poor understanding of nationality from the elites of Han nationality, what influence will it bring to China's social development and cross-strait dialogue between China and Taiwan if we smudge Sun Yat-sen on the basis of these events?

Chiang Kai-shek made contributions in social stability and economic development and also mistakes which were caused by suppressing opposition faction after he fled to Taiwan, and the following Chiang Ching-kuo also made contributions by taking Taiwan's economy off the ground and launching political reform. For these events, people hold mixed comments.

People who are able to objectively analyze social development history of Taiwan have arrived at a common understanding which is that their behaviors include both merits and demerits. The democratic progressive party had overdone the activities of "De-Chiang Kai-shek" after they ruled the Taiwan government, which aroused disgust of Taiwan people and lost their votes.

Liang Qichao was fiercely opposing Li Hongzhang at first and accusing him of endangering and betraying his country. But after Li Hongzhang was dead, Liang Qichao wrote biography himself for Li Hongzhang and endeavored to keep fairness in this book, in which he showed great understanding about what Li Hongzhang had done under that historical circumstance. In the preface of Li Hongzhang, he wrote that "Li Hongzhang has been blamed by the Chinese people. We are neither the same party in politics nor good friends in life though, I am not intend to do him wrong. So most of this book is taking defend for Li Hongzhang. Though there are some dissents, we must evaluate the history in a fair way." The words of taking defend for Li Hongzhang are to evaluate the history historically. What he said is "Li Hongzhang was cursing by a large number of people back then, but he was dead already and no longer can affect the politics, so we should show more mercy and try to understand his behavior in his time." "We must evaluate the history in a fair way" is the warning left by Liang Qichao[2] telling us how to appraise historical figures.

It is helpful for us to draw experiences and lessons and become more mature on politics if we could appraise important historical figures in our own country rationally and objectively, but it will be on the contrary, that is to lead a country and its people to an abyss of division and civil war, if we let emotional and aggressive feelings drift. Not only do we need to be responsible for the past history, but also need to be responsible for the future and descendants when we guide the general public to appraise the historical events, because a dark social circumstance which is broken and leaves everyone in pain shouldn't be the world that we leave for them.

---

2   Liang Qichao, Li Hongzhang, Baihua Literature and Art Publishing House, 2000, pp. 1-2.

VI. The lessons to be drawn from the historical event that the Soviet Union has simply criticized and denied Lenin and Stalin

In 1950s, Khrushchev had a confidential report in which he gave a sharp criticism on mistakes that Stalin had made when he was alive. Whether from the rule of value or the consequences of society, there is no doubt that Stalin did make plenty of serious mistakes. He hurt farmers' interests in rural collectivization; he persecuted thousands and thousands of comrades-in-arms, intellectuals and the public in the counter-revolutionary purges in 1930s; he forced plenty of minorities to emigrate from their homeland during the Soviet Union's great patriotic war against Nazi Germany; he also supported chauvinism towards the communist parties of other countries. These are all undoubtedly true.

But people also should not forget that Lenin and Stalin were the leaders and founders of the October Revolution and the Soviet Union. Under the guidance of their leaderships, Czarist autocracy had been overthrown, and landlords, aristocracies and foreign invaders were beaten. The Soviet Union has completed industrialization in a very short period after Stalin has adopted an autocratic and centralized approach, and kept economy growth at a two-digits rate in 1930s when economy in western Europe and the United States were in depression, which turned the Soviet Union, an agricultural country that feed on slavery, into a powerful industrial country in 20 years. It established a great foundation for heavy industry and armament industry, and by taking advantage of these industries, the Soviet Union had defeated the strong fascist Germany in European continent and protected the very first communist country in the world, and kept a high levels of living conditions, education, accommodation, medical insurance, and old-age security for the Russians, which earned wide respect from the world. Lenin and Stalin have been portrayed as heroes and the sign of victory representing the whole nation and the Soviet Union and honored by the peoples all over the world.

However, the confidential report of Khrushchev to 20th CPSU Congress, has completely denied Stalin. The criticisms might have an element of truth or rational basis, but for the masses, they dishonored communist activities to an abyss. Meanwhile, these criticisms caused questions by the vast populations and many cadres about the history of the Soviet Union and the legitimacy of the Communist Party of the Soviet Union: does a party that produced a monster leader and which covered the truth for a long time still have the right to rule the government? After this confidential report, prestige of the Communist Party and the government of the Soviet Union has been hit hard. After 1960s, economic development in the Soviet Union has become much slower than before, which may have some relation with the low mental status of cadres and the general public.

Later in 1980s, in order to promote the Reform and New Thinking, Gorbachev chose to re-evaluate the Soviet Union's history, in which he brought up that for launching a democratic and open reform, definiteness and thoroughness[3] should be fully demonstrated to reflect the pain and suffering of history. Under his leadership, irrational ideological trend went mad. Russian scholars sighed in retrospect that "you would feel like falling into an irrational world when you read various publications that were published in 1980s to 1990s, a sorrow world that spoke sarcastically about our history, mocked the fallen from the war, desecrated the glory of Russia and teased Russia.[4] It is not difficult to imagine how hard the confidence must has been crashed to the general public for their founder and history has been simply denied to a monster and a hell."

Thus, for many people, the ideological trend of Stalin turning from a great leader to a autocratic monster started to grow, and the Communist Party of the Soviet Union naturally became accomplice in these historical events, which caused millions of communist party members to withdraw. After Yelstin announced the Communist Party of the Soviet Union as an illegal organization, there wasn't any communist party member who stepped out to defend the party. Then the Soviet Union was disintegrated under this macro political environment.

In the two decades since the collapse of the Soviet Union, politicians and intellectuals from Russia have been reconsidering about their denial of Stalin and the history. Russia hasn't turned into a prosperous country as people expected after the denial of Stalin, dismissing the communist party and building a democratic power, but brought power failure, declining economy and social chaos. Even those dissidents felt deeply grieved about Russia's decline. At the same time, people began to reevaluate Lenin and Stalin. The writer Zinoviev, who had hated Stalin in his youth and been a political activist who had tried to assassinate Stalin, described in his novel Temptations in 1990s a story about an anti-Stalin youth group, calling a heated debate and after the discussion, declaring that Stalin was innocent, calling Stalin "one of the greatest figures in human history". In the novel To Reach the Turning Point which was published in 1996, Solzhenitsyn wrote about the death of Stalin and said that people are all aware that they have lost a great person, but what they haven't understand is how great Stalin is.[5] In 2003, there were 40% respondents who were in favour of Stalin; in

---

3   Liu Shuang, *On the Disintegration of The Soviet Union from a Historical Perspective*, China Social Sciences Publishing House, 2009, p. 112.
4   V. A. Lisichkin, *The Third World War—Information Psychological Warfare*, Social Sciences Academic Press, 2003, p. 227.
5   Zhang Jie, Russia Re-evaluates Stalin, *Historical Trend: Chinese Scholars on The*

the ranking of the ten most prominent social activists and Russian century figures in 2000, Lenin was ranked the top and Stalin was following him.[6]

In less than 20 years, Russians first fiercely criticized Lenin and Stalin, but in the end they gave a high affirmation to both Lenin and Stalin. Why the same people would have the different attitudes and views toward Lenin and Stalin? I think these questions should lead the Chinese people to ponder? We could say that after experiencing all the consequences, the Russians have finally learned the cause and won rationality over perception and senses. This is an example to tell us to keep a clear mind and never take such a route.

VII. To use rationality to appraise the historical figures and freeing the masses from confusion and controversies

We must take into consideration that whether the society and the masses have been well prepared emotionally before we start to discuss the important and controversial historical events and figures. An intensified opposition must be caused inside the people, or between the masses and the government, and social turmoil and division if we don't liberate the masses from the absolute and emotional state of mind in advance, or if we don't have the ability or condition to guide the masses to discuss in an objective and historical way of thinking, or cannot view history in a historical way. These will cause people unwilling to give a full and complete historical analyze for historical events and figures and give a conclusion according to the simple moral judgment. Discussions like these will not achieve positive consequences. The reason why we don't evaluate the historical events and figures for now is possibly for fear of this negative result.

Since the general public have controversy about historical events and figures, and ask to discuss about these questions, then the longer we stall, the more problem we may have. On one hand, the new generation lacks emotions and experiences about our historical environment and atmosphere, and they may not understand these events and figures objectively and historically for a generation gap may increase the difficulty of reaching consensus. On the other hand, a new generation may also have indifferent sensations about the historical events and figures that happened long ago, so the emotional entanglement may fade after many years. If these two conditions are both possible, when do we pick to start the discussion and make a closure on these sensitive

---

Disintegration of The Soviet Union and the Evaluation of Soviet Union, Li Shenming, editor in chief, People's Publishing House, 2007, pp. 180-181.

6   Roy Medvedev, *Putin's Four Years in The Kremlin*, Social Sciences Academic Press, 2005, p. 414.

historical issues? What social conditions do we need to start a positive and rational discussion? The answers could only be found in a comprehensive investigation among the masses and intellectuals.

VIII. Beware of foreign powers intervening and taking advantage of our discussions on historical events

Every country in this world has its own strategy opponents and hostile external forces who are willing to see this country going to division or being weakened by domestic turmoil. These external forces could be our neighbor countries, or rival countries which have different ideologies with us, or the political elements that have been exiled to other countries, or elements of terrorism, secessionism and extremism. These external forces will try hard to find and raise "the fifth column" to split and weaken our country, so we could never ignore the interference of the external forces when we want to start a discussion of historical events and figures. Before we are fully prepared for the thought, we should not start discussion blindly by following the internal demands and external pressures, which will lead us into the trap of our enemies.

Full preparations and positive guidance on concluding some historical events and figures may lead this country and nation to the right direction and drop off the burdens of the history and move forward more easily. However, if the masses lack necessary preparations, and do not have explanations and analysis logic on basic values and emotions, then they possibly cannot use any initiative to affect the trend of discussion. And the influence bringing by external forces on discussion may exceed our predictions.

Lisichkin, a Russian scholar, once analyzed the western influences that has been imposed on encouraging the Soviet Union to reevaluate its history, and pointed out that "a series of methods need to be taken when the weapon of history was used in psychological war, including to eulogize some historical figures and talking good about the history in this period, or to demonize them and talking bad about the history in this period. One usual way to do is re-write the history.[7]

During this process, the article that commended Denikin, the military officer of the counter-revolutionary white forces, was published, the article that portrayed the last tzar Nicholas II as a noble and generous monarch was published, in which it was said that his family being cruelly executed reflected how cruel the Soviet Union government was. And Lenin was described as a spiritual incarnation of evil empire, and the October Revolution was a coup

---

7   V. A. Lisichkin, *The Third World War—Information Psychological Warfare*, Social Sciences Academic Press, 2003, p. 39.

launched by a few thugs, which was the most tragic event in Russian history in the past 1000 years[8]. Encouraged by some western countries, some people tried their best to debase on the historical events, memorial dates and even the victory day of the Great Patriotic war,which was one of the most sacred memories for the general public.[9] When separatists from Georgia launched their slogans of "long live the great Georgia" and "exile all nations who are not Georgian" in public, numerous secret envoys from western democratic countries came to Tbilisi.[10] It was these western "supporters of democracy" who came to the capital of Georgia to further boost the flames, making the momentum of national division irreversible and playing a key role in the "Color Revolution" of Ukraine and other countries.

Examining the Western research publications which are supposed to do researches on China, we can see that Western countries have been in preparation for pushing China to re-evaluate our history. These works can be either oral history studies of some historical events in an academic way, or the whole new explanation of Chinese history (such as a new research view on the Qing Dynasty that is to view the Qing Dynasty as the regime of a different nation, or to legitimize the division activities in Tibet, Xinjiang and Inner Mongolia), or they could be the new form of government documents, which are re-arranged purposely, or the clarification by some parties that were engaged in historical events. In conclusion, foreign countries use various methods to re-write and re-establish Chinese history to satisfy their political purposes so that they will push Chinese to reconsider their own history. Some of these preparation work are cultural exchange project of the government, and some of them are cooperated researches organized by academic groups (such as universities), and the left are projects of protecting human rights launched by non-government organizations. These activities usually will be attracting plenty of people from all walks of life, intellectuals and scholars, some of these people are with strong political purpose while the others are not. Many scholars do not have the drive to purposely affect Chinese political progress, but this is not important. What is important is that in western media and publications, these historical events and figures have already been "posed" or "concluded", and some "facts" will be used to together prove these conclusions. These preparation work look loose in format but have separate aims in foundation, which are perfectly matched. If we can review what methods have the western powers used to add the fuel on the process of re-consideration of the Soviet Union

<hr>

8   Liu Shuang, *On the Disintegration of the Soviet Union from a Historical Perspective*, China Social Sciences Press, 2009, p. 90.

9   N. I. Ryzhkov, *The Tragedy of the Great Power: The Nationality Issue and the Disintigration of the Soviet Union*, Xinhua Publishing House, 2008, p. 18.

10   Ibid., p. 48.

history that was launched under the guidance of "new thinking of reform" of Gorbachev, we will be learning experiences form it. Therefore, while we are thinking about how to evaluate Chinese historical events, we must take warning from retrospection the path that the Russians have gone before.

Gong Zizhen has written in his book that "to destroy a country one must destroy its history first; to ruin the rule one must destroy the history first; to bury talent or to abolish value one must destroy their history first."[11] These are the edification that we must remember when we read history of Chinese revolution, ponder over 60 years of history of China's foundation and appraise Chinese historical figures. At last, I think that China is not the only country that needs to be freed from prejudiced and irrational thought pattern. In order to build a peaceful world, Americans also need to be freed. For the past one century, Americans were deeply influenced by the ideology of opposing communism. Occurrence of the McCarthy era in the 1950s was not an accidental phenomenon but with public foundation. The thought of "cold war" and the ideology of "fight against communism" are still taking strong root. It is good to win at zero cost, but the US would use any methods to gain victory for liberal countries in this world. It is even feasible for them to send troops, start a war, kill people and set fire to win the victory of democratic regulation. Maybe on one day in the future that American people would start to learn that ideal of communism is not so much different as the ideal of Christianity, which also has intentions of universal value that humans are long for and pursuits of human rights, equality and freedom that people are looking for, and only on that day could the US have the chance to know China in an objective way, accept the concept of harmony in diversity, and stop promoting the so-called "Jihad activities", such as "color revolution", in China and other countries, and only in this way could the US abandon the ideological pursuit of using democracy to liberate the world. And only after the US can recognize the ideology of harmony in diversity can they stay away making the same mistakes the way they make in North Korea, Vietnam, Afghanistan and Iraq, and have the chance to live with other civilizations in peace. Of course, this is should be the concern of the US, not ours.

The author Ma Rong is a professor in the department of sociology and researcher at the Institute of Social Anthropology attached to Peking University; he was the former director of the said department and the institute.

---

11   Liu Shuang, *On the Disintegration of the Soviet Union from a Historical Perspective*, China Social Sciences Press, 2009, Preface on p. 2.

Postscript

The articles in the book were selected, arranged and edited under the guidance of Li Shenming and Li Jie. There are also some other people who have taken part in this work, including Yin Yungong, Wu Li, Fan Jianxin, Song Yuehong, Jin Minqin, Gong Yun, Wang Yiqiu, Peng Caidong, Xu Yanguang.

The book was proofread and compiled by a group of people led by Li Jie. The first section of the manuscript has been proofread preliminarily by Qin Yicheng, Gong Yun and Xu Huaqin. On that basis, Li Jie has proofread, modified and complied the whole manuscript, besides, he has added the second section and given the book its title.

During the process of edition, the book has also enjoyed authors' great support, including Gao Xiang, Zhou Qun, as well as from the editors of the journal *Chinese Social Sciences Today*. Zhao Jianying and Wang Yin from China Social Sciences Press have showed their generous support for publishing the book. In addition, Li Jianbin from the Institute of Contemporary China Studies has contributed to the selection of photos. We are thankful for their contribution to the creation of this book.

Leading Group of the Research and
Disciplinary Construction of
the Marxist Theory, in the Chinese Academy of Social Sciences.

January, 2014